ADVANCE PRAISE

"James Morrison has written an important book that we need in our more cynical and angry times...Morrison brings great empathy and discernment to the sociopolitical context of those years. Hopefully, James Morrison is not done bringing his deep historical experience and understanding to good causes that we may have forgotten."

—ERNEST J. DICK, CONSULTING ARCHIVIST AND ORAL HISTORIAN

"When I was a boy, my father used to regale me with accounts of the Great Depression and how he learned to read and write. He left home to obtain work on the railway in Northern Ontario. In addition to obtaining regular meals and meeting new Canadians, he learned to read and write in the classes held for workers in boxcars. Years later when I was Ontario's lieutenant governor and launched literacy reading camps for First Nations adults and children alike, I turned to the Frontier College of today. I derived a particular pleasure reading such a well researched book on this subject by author James Morrison."

—THE HONOURABLE JAMES BARTLEMAN, TWENTY-SEVENTH LIEUTENANT GOVERNOR OF ONTARIO

"Through Fitzpatrick's life and work, Morrison's *The Right to Read* affords us a fascinating perspective on class, labour, religion, education, immigration, and citizenship in Canada in the late nineteenth and early twentieth centuries."

—STEVEN SCHWINGHAMER, HISTORIAN, CANADIAN MUSEUM OF IMMIGRATION

T0278979

JAMES H. MORRISON

THE RIGHT TO READ

SOCIAL JUSTICE, LITERACY, AND THE CREATION OF FRONTIER COLLEGE

THE ALFRED FITZPATRICK STORY

NIMBUS
PUBLISHING

Nimbus Publishing Limited
3660 Strawberry Hill Street, Halifax, NS, B3K 5A9
(902) 455-4286 nimbus.ca

Printed and bound in Canada

NB1488

Editor: Marianne Ward
Editors for the press: Emily MacKinnon and Claire Bennet
Cover design: George Kirkpatrick Book Design
Interior design: Jenn Embree

Library and Archives Canada Cataloguing in Publication

Title: The right to read : social justice, literacy, and the creation of Frontier
    College, the Alfred Fitzpatrick story / James H. Morrison.
Names: Morrison, James H., author.
Description: Includes bibliographical references.
Identifiers: Canadiana (print) 2022023910X | Canadiana (ebook) 20220239193
    | ISBN 9781774711309 (softcover) | ISBN 9781774711828 (EPUB)
Subjects: LCSH: Fitzpatrick, Alfred, 1862-1936. | LCSH: Frontier College—
    History. | LCSH: Educators—Canada—Biography. | LCSH: Literacy—
    Canada. | LCSH: Education—Canada. | LCSH: Social justice—Canada.
    | LCGFT: Biographies.
Classification: LCC LA2325.F57 M67 2022 | DDC 370.92—dc23

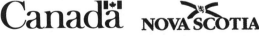 

Nimbus Publishing acknowledges the financial support for its publishing activities from the Government of Canada, the Canada Council for the Arts, and from the Province of Nova Scotia. We are pleased to work in partnership with the Province of Nova Scotia to develop and promote our creative industries for the benefit of all Nova Scotians.

To Jessie Lucas (1894–1996)

*Secretary, treasurer, bursar, registrar, and archivist of Frontier College,
1920–1963, without whom this story could not have been told.*

TABLE OF CONTENTS

Foreword ——————————————————————————— 1

Introduction ——————————————————————————— 3

CHAPTER 1 *Beginnings: Family, Church, and Community 1862–1884* — 6

CHAPTER 2 *Itinerant Minister: Answering the Call 1884–1899* ———— 33

CHAPTER 3 *Activist: Finding a Cause 1899–1906* ————————— 55

CHAPTER 4 *Revival: Enablers of Alfred's Passion 1906–1914* ———— 92

CHAPTER 5 *New Initiatives and the Great War 1914–1918* ———— 126

CHAPTER 6 *Establishing a National College 1918–1922* ———— 166

CHAPTER 7 *"Fight of My Life" for Survival 1922–1931* ————— 208

CHAPTER 8 *Final Years of Advocacy 1931–1936* ——————— 237

Epilogue ——————————————————————————— 258

Acknowledgements ——————————————————— 266

Published Writings by Alfred Fitzpatrick ——————— 268

Bibliography ——————————————————————— 271

Index ——————————————————————————— 276

FOREWORD

BY JACK PEARPOINT, PRESIDENT OF FRONTIER COLLEGE FROM
1975-1990 AND CO-DIRECTOR OF INCLUSION PRESS

LITERACY AND SOCIAL JUSTICE INITIATIVES IN CANADA OWE AN
enormous debt of gratitude to Alfred Fitzpatrick. Consistent with
the Canadian practice of understatement, there is no Fitzpatrick
memorabilia, no photos or accomplishments listed in school text-
books. That is why this is an important book.

Fitzpatrick was a social justice reformer from Nova Scotia who
was decades ahead of his time. His humanitarian instincts drove
him to the margins of our booming economy where immigrant
labourers sweated in brutal conditions with no hope of advance-
ment. These emergent citizens were out of sight and out of mind to
Canadians—but not to Fitzpatrick. In his bones he knew that with
access to education, they could break the poverty cycle. He created
and proselytized an impossible dream to bring education to these
new Canadians. It was his personal mission. It was absurd, but he did
it anyway—and relentlessly created opportunities for these neglected
workers on our geographic frontiers.

He began with Reading Tents, backpacks of books, and volunteers
who would teach their fellow labourers after working a shift beside
them on the rails, in the lumber camps, and in the mines—wherever
Fitzpatrick could recruit volunteers. The term "labourer-teacher"
evolved to crystalize this educational innovation.

Decades later, Frontier College continues to exist, still with unstable and inadequate funding. But the tradition and values that Fitzpatrick established remain unaltered. In the twenty-first century, the college has made literacy a national issue by implementing children's reading clubs, homework clubs, and book distribution with the help of hundreds of volunteer tutors. Similar volunteer networks provide support to adults whose education has been limited. Thus this little voluntary leader of a college continues to innovate, challenging Canadians to respond to the unmet educational needs of new immigrants, unhoused kids, Indigenous Peoples, prisoners, and more.

We live in challenging times. Identifying key questions before acting is vital, and that translates into understanding our own history. Alfred Fitzpatrick was a remarkable innovator, who mobilized privileged citizens to learn with and from other Canadians. As we struggle to acknowledge the hidden stories of residential schools and exploitive immigrant labour policies, we can learn from Fitzpatrick's creative wisdom and adapt it for our future. That journey to our better future begins by appreciating our own amazing history, like that told in this book. It is not about making Fitzpatrick a hero, rather gleaning his vision and injecting that catalytic force into our new vision for all Canadians. Let this book be the start of your journey to a better future.

Fitzpatrick's mission was clear and it remains steadfast. How and where the college operates has changed since Fitzpatrick's time, but the ethic of service and the courage to reach out to support people who have been missed by mainstream institutions remain secure.

"Whenever and wherever people shall meet,
there should be the time, place, and means of their education."

That was Fitzpatrick's brilliant summation of the college creed—and it is still the creed today.

INTRODUCTION

IN 1977, THE UNESCO LITERACY PRIZE WAS AWARDED TO THE Canadian literacy organization Frontier College in recognition of its "meritorious work in the field of adult education." The idea that led to Frontier College was conceived in 1899 by Alfred Fitzpatrick of Pictou County, Nova Scotia, to address the mistreatment of workers on the Canadian frontier. As it nears its 125th year of existence, Frontier College continues to serve the disadvantaged and marginalized in Canadian society.

Alfred Fitzpatrick's most striking early contribution to adult literacy was the labourer-teacher concept—that a teacher would labour side by side with a worker at their job then teach them at night. This would remain the standard pedagogy for Frontier College well into the twenty-first century, with labourer-teachers working and teaching in lumber camps, on the railroad, in the mines and the farm fields. But Canada was changing through the last century in terms of how work was done and how education was being delivered and to whom. Thus Frontier College changed as well.

Over the last half of the twentieth century, it became clear that technology, communication, and employment were now firmly linked. There were no hiding places any longer for those who could not read or write. To be illiterate was more than to be marginalized —it was to be ignored. In response, the college looked to its early twentieth-century roots—to take education to those who did not have it wherever they might be. By the 1970s and 1980s the college had initiated programs with the disadvantaged, people with a disability, English-as-an-additional-language learners, and new immigrants to Canada. In the 1980s, innovative programs like Beat the Street (basic literacy for unhoused people tutored by trained street people) were established. Tutoring penitentiary inmates and organizing a job placement program for ex-offenders were also being offered. By the early twenty-first century, "reading tents" were being raised at various urban and rural locations across Canada to promote reading among young people.

Beginning in the 1990s the college also involved itself in technological projects in isolated Canadian communities and Inuit education programs in northern Canada. Frontier College continues to partner with Indigenous communities, and in the spirit of Truth and Reconciliation organizes summer camps with First Nations, Métis, and Inuit communities to provide youth living both on and off reserve with literacy and numeracy skills.

There have been many changes in Canadian society since Alfred Fitzpatrick's death eighty-six years ago—an economic depression, a world war, continuing social and political tensions, and today a wired world of computer technology and global communication systems. Still the challenge Fitzpatrick made to all Canadians throughout his lifetime remains. That challenge is to take education and literacy to all those who do not have it, whoever and wherever they may be. The original frontier of manual labour camps in Canada's wooded wilderness is no more, but illiteracy is still prevalent in many parts of Canada with its attendant problems of unemployment and poverty. These are new frontiers.

Ralph Waldo Emerson, one of Fitzpatrick's favourite writers, once wrote, "An institution is the lengthened shadow of one man." Certainly, the various programs Frontier College has initiated over the past century have not all been successes. Every Frontier College initiative, however, has always had its genesis in the life opportunities that education could provide to learners. Its philosophy has been grounded in the belief that education, be it beginner's literacy or secondary or higher education, is a basic human right. With this in mind, over the years since the death in 1936 of its founder, Alfred Fitzpatrick, Frontier College has lengthened his shadow over a wide span of projects that reflect many of the founder's values and ideals, including his struggles for pluralism and equality in the face of elitism and orthodoxy. As Canada's oldest adult literacy organization, Frontier College continues to protest and serve on today's new frontiers, wherever they may be.

This is Alfred Fitzpatrick's story.

CHAPTER 1

BEGINNINGS: FAMILY, CHURCH, AND COMMUNITY 1862–1884

JAMES FITZPATRICK

WITH A STEADY RHYTHMIC SWISH, HE GRADUALLY HARVESTED *the hay crop. The brown-beige timothy in the intervale stretched before him. He paused, tilted his straw hat, mopped his brow, then leaned on the curved handle of his scythe and rested. He gazed at Fitzpatrick Mountain. It was summer 1817. He had arrived in the settlement of Pictou, a two- to three-hour walk away, twenty years before from "Amerikay." Pictou had been called a township, but he found that it was hardly even a settlement. There were barely a dozen buildings, which included a blacksmith shop, several barns, a windmill for the gristmill, and a jail—a settlement encircled by dense forests. In addition to a few houses, there was also McGeorge's tavern for those who desired spirituous liquors, usually the timber men. In the winter, due to its size, the tavern would host the "spirituous services" of the Presbyterian Church—a rather different congregation, and a different kind of spirit.*

James had not stayed in "town" long. By 1806, he had acquired a 125-acre grant of land south of Pictou, married, begun a family with Janet Murray of Scotsburn, and started to reclaim his grant of land from the forest. Now seventy-three years old, he was still reclaiming.

The previous two years had been disastrous. In 1815, as potatoes were being planted, thousands of mice poured over the countryside like locusts, devouring grain, seed potatoes, and all in their way. That was known locally as "the year of the mice." Food had been scarce that winter. Unfortunately, 1816 was no better. This time it was the "year without a summer," when the crops were frozen in the ground by June and farmers wore greatcoats while plowing. He shivered to think of it.

He had considered heading back into the timber woods to stay and work in a woods camp as he had done some two decades before when he first arrived in Pictou. However, with the Napoleonic Wars at an end, the Royal Navy's demand for lumber from "His Majesty's woodlot" had all but disappeared and buyers were scarce. In addition, he had a family to take care of, with the hope that one of his sons, perhaps Alexander, who was now seven years old, would work with him and eventually take over the Fitzpatrick farm.

Still in thought, James heard the rustle of the cut hay behind him. He glanced over his shoulder and saw the Reverend Duncan Ross of the Presbyterian Church striding purposefully toward him. He shivered again, quickly turned his head to his work, and stepped, swung, stepped, swung, clocklike with the whisper of the cutting blade. He knew what was coming.

"Seamus, I've not seen you in church lately."

"No, Father. I've been busy with the haying."

"What about before then?"

"Well, I'm quite taken up with the planting."

"And before that?"

"Reverend, a man has to cut pine timber for the English ships in the winter."

"Still, I feel that, as you are a man of different faith, Mr. Fitzpatrick, you should come round so we could talk these things over sometime."

"Aye, Father, as soon as haying is done, I'll come and talk with you all day."

Reverend Ross turned and bustled away. James paused and once more wiped his brow as he watched him depart, then gripped the scythe and resumed his work. As far as he was concerned, the haying would never be done.

Alfred Fitzpatrick was born in Pictou County, Nova Scotia—a highland outlier of Scotland. Pictou's history is somewhat similar to what historian John Prebble, in *The Lion in the North*, called "the long bloody brawl that is Scottish history." The town of Pictou was founded in the last half of the eighteenth century by Highland Scots who sought to escape political, religious, and clan rivalries that were so integral to Scotland's past. Some were survivors of the 1746 Battle of Culloden between Scotland and England and the repression that followed. They were all part of a larger migration of Scots who arrived in tens of thousands in northeastern North America throughout the eighteenth century. The settlers in Pictou County came from the Highlands and Lowlands of Scotland, from parts of Northern Ireland, especially Protestant Ulster, and by a more indirect route from New England. Most came as impoverished, landless settlers seeking peace and a piece of land in a community they could call their own. A number dealt with entrepreneurial land agents, but others simply squatted as far from anyone else that the land would allow. The North Shore of Nova Scotia bordering the Northumberland Strait was not an ideal location for them, with dense forests to be cleared and exposure to the rigours of harsh winters, but there were not many choices, so it became somewhere the new arrivals would call home. There were already others settled there who also called it home. What was to become Pictou already had a name—Pictook—given to the area by the original inhabitants, the Mi'kmaq. "Took" is a shortened form of "nebooktook" or "in the forests," and "Pict" may refer to the explosive sound that would not be unusual for an area rich in coal and, therefore, highly pressurized coal gas beneath the surface.

The Mi'kmaq had demanded that there be no white settlements when the Treaty of Paris was signed in 1763. Nevertheless, when the settlers arrived in the early 1770s, many of them took shelter in Mi'kmaq wigwams during their first difficult winter. The Mi'kmaq also shared their woodland skills with the newcomers. One of the early Pictou settlers, John Robinson, described the local Mi'kmaq as "a friendly, harmless, well-behaved people, ready to do any little service for you they can." However, with the arrival of more and more whites who settled their land and the corresponding exposure of the Mi'kmaq to smallpox, tuberculosis, and alcohol, the nine hundred Mi'kmaq who lived near Pictou in 1775 had, within a century, shrunk to two hundred and fifty. They had been replaced by European settlers who now considered themselves "the natives."

Pictou, with its trim sheltered harbour, sits at the termination of the Cobequid Mountain range, which stretches along north central Nova Scotia. Its location, barely twenty kilometres from Prince Edward Island, provides immediate access to the rich fisheries of the Northumberland Strait. Pictou is also the egress point for three rivers that spread like a three-pronged talon into the interior. These are in turn fed by brooks and streams whose fluid energy would be harnessed a few years after Scottish settlement by water wheels that would power gristmills, sawmills, and lumber mills. It should not be surprising then that a community called Millsville was established in the first half of the nineteenth century. It was the community in which the story of the Fitzpatricks begins.

Alfred Fitzpatrick was of third generation Scots-Irish descent on both his father's and mother's side. Much of his ancestry was from the Highland Scots who had arrived in 1773, some 190 of them crammed into the ship *Hector*. The Philadelphia Company had acquired this large parcel of land in Nova Scotia, some 80,000 hectares (200,000 acres), during the period of land speculation that followed the signing of the Treaty of Paris in 1763 that had ended the Seven Years War between Britain and France. The Philadelphia Company advertised the territory widely and touted it as being located on a secluded harbour surrounded by marine life, wildlife, and vast timber lots of pine, hemlock, and oak. The negatives of the severe climate and prolonged isolation were not publicized.

The new settlers had been transferred from the spare, wet, and treeless crofts of Highland Scotland to the thick forests, rich soil, and diverse seasons of the land bordering the Northumberland Strait—a land where winter seemed endless. This required a new agrarian wisdom that meant men and women had to figure out things on their own or with the help of neighbours rather than depend on the many generations of experience in their ancestral land of Scotland. In addition, they would be 60 kilometres of virgin forest and rugged hilltops (the highest being 400 metres) from Truro, the nearest European settlement, and over 320 kilometres by sea from Halifax, the colony's capital. Their task then was to clear, settle, plant, and survive by making a home in this new land. Such an undertaking would require physical strength, stamina, and firm cultural values. The most important of these cultural values would be their religion.

"One Dutchman, a theologian; two Dutchmen, a church; three Dutchmen, a schism." So goes a wry Dutch truism that likely arose during the religious wars in Europe in the sixteenth and seventeenth centuries. This proverb could very easily have applied to the situation in Scotland as well. With the founding of the Church of Scotland in 1690, there followed a series of fractured relationships within the church. In 1733, the First Secession movement took place, and a decade later, in 1747, the Secession in Scotland split into two more groups: the Burghers and the Anti-Burghers. The tension that existed among these three was carried to Nova Scotia by the new immigrants. By the end of the eighteenth century, the Church of Scotland predominated in Halifax, the Burghers in Truro, and the Anti-Burghers in Pictou. An examination of what distinguished each of the sects will not be undertaken here, but an acknowledgement of how serious these differences were must be recognized. It is important to appreciate this fractious relationship, as it shaped the social and political lives of these communities and their interaction with each other. Each brought clergymen from Scotland that reflected their theological stance, and even when the Burghers and Anti-Burghers came together as the Presbyterian Church of Nova Scotia in the first half of the nineteenth century, religious and political loyalties were already deeply embedded such that the Burghers always supported the "Tories" (Conservatives) and the Anti-Burghers the Reformers in Nova Scotia.

The Scots settlers of Nova Scotia were a formidable, theologically minded people, and their beliefs were firmly attached to the Gaelic language. As there was no complete Bible in Gaelic until 1801, all Presbyterian ministers translated from the English Bible into whatever local dialect was present in their congregation. The sermons were often punctuated with shouts and exclamations of their faith. This was indeed an oral culture. In addition to valuing the oral nature of "the Gaelic," the community also placed a heavy emphasis on a good education for all; thus literacy was a vital component of their culture and their character.

In this way, the rivalries and the rituals of the home country were reflected and refracted by the Scottish settlers of nineteenth-century Nova Scotia. They had migrated to the New World to escape and to settle—to begin again in the rugged coastline of northwestern

Nova Scotia in an Atlantic maritime region marked by fierce climatic changes and, at times, an unforgiving physical environment. This would surely be a test of their cultural values as well.

The town of Pictou was the economic, religious, and social centre of the district. In addition to its agricultural potential, natural resources, and advantageous position on the Northumberland Strait, Pictou was also a vibrant and at times rowdy political forum. As noted, the political tensions would also include religious and intra-ethnic tensions: the Conservative Church of Scotland Highlanders on one side and the Reformer, Free Church Lowlanders on the other. The election of 1830, for example, was notable for its violence, with feet, fists, and clubs in evidence on both sides.

The violence and the possibility of more of the same was such that the sheriff of Pictou had a fence constructed down the centre of town to control the lineup in front of the polling station—a fence that separated the warring political supporters of Conservatives and Reformers in the struggle for responsible government in Nova Scotia. Education was frequently a major campaign issue. For example, one of the candidates, Reformer Jotham Blanchard, was a tenacious and vociferous advocate for government financial support for all public schools in the province, support that would reach fruition in the adoption of the Free School Act in 1864. Blanchard was also ahead of his time when he urged support for circulating libraries in Nova Scotia, an idea that Alfred Fitzpatrick would pioneer successfully in Northern Ontario by the early twentieth century, as is shown in chapter 3.

Political and religious newspapers became common in the 1830s. The first of the county's political papers was the *Colonial Patriot*. In 1827, it was the first newspaper published outside of Halifax.

A Reformer paper, it was succeeded by *The Bee* in 1835. Conservative party interests were expressed by the *Colonial Standard* beginning in the 1850s. Religious perspectives were represented by the *Guardian* (1838), the *Presbyterian Banner* (1842), and the *Presbyterian Witness* (1848), all of which were Presbyterian and Reform minded.

Putting aside the strife-torn political passions, Pictou also saw itself as a cultural oasis. In 1834, the Pictou Literary and Scientific Society was formed, with the goal to promote the mutual improvement of its membership with lectures, essays, and discussions about literature and science. This led to the formation of debating and literary societies in surrounding rural villages as well. The Pictou Philharmonic Society, which provided an annual series of concerts, was formed in the 1850s. By 1871, the Dominion of Canada census recorded Pictou, a community of less than five thousand residents, as having the second highest number of booksellers (five) in the province after Halifax. This represents a telling reminder of the importance of literacy, literature, and religion in the politics and culture of mid nineteenth-century Pictou. These three were tightly intertwined with the necessity of education for all.

For centuries, education had come from Bible readings in the Scottish household, which instilled the values of both faith and literacy, albeit with a strict and narrow focus. The new immigrants to Nova Scotia soon came to terms with the fact that beyond "book knowledge," other basic skills were necessary to survive in this difficult terrain. Thus early Presbyterian ministers like Rev. James MacGregor, who had arrived in Pictou in 1786, barely thirteen years after Pictou was founded, had to be both "a man of the cloth" as well as "a man of the soil." A graduate of the University of Glasgow, MacGregor firmly believed that secular and sectarian education needed to be harnessed together. He advocated for scientific education as well as the construction of a Presbyterian divinity hall to train locals in the ministry. In his view, this link between education and religion was the best means for people to manage their lives. Another Presbyterian minister, Thomas McCulloch, would assist MacGregor greatly in translating these words into action.

Young Reverend Thomas McCulloch, age twenty-seven, and his wife, Isabella, arrived in Pictou in November 1803 on their way to Prince Edward Island. Trapped by the ice-clogged Northumberland Strait, they stayed for their first winter in Pictou and then for another thirty. McCulloch, also a graduate of the University of Glasgow, had studied both divinity and medicine. He was also conversant with literature, languages, and the law. These subjects would prove useful, as he soon began teaching in his Pictou home after he realized his minister's salary would be insufficient to sustain him and his family. Unlike MacGregor, who trod the evangelist trail throughout the county, McCulloch was a "town man" who had taken up teaching. With the encouragement of MacGregor and others in the church, his teaching became an obsession.

Upon his arrival in Pictou, McCulloch was appalled by the lack of morality in his new charge. Pictou in the early eighteen hundreds was a rough-and-tumble, rum-soaked settlement that due to the Napoleonic Wars was undergoing a timber boom. With its extensive virgin hardwood in the interior, the natural port of Pictou was growing wealthy by exporting a commodity that the British Royal Navy was desperate to acquire—white pine. In this time period, over forty thousand tons of pine was shipped to Great Britain each year, much of it from Pictou, making it a thriving community. However, McCulloch believed that such prosperity would destroy the community unless a stronger presence of morality and learning was developed. He strove to instill a sense of virtue not only from the pulpit, but also in his classroom. Education and morality through religious knowledge was his goal. McCulloch wrote, and no doubt Rev. MacGregor would have agreed, that education was the greatest barrier against barbarism and the best rational system to improve oneself. They were echoing what many in that period were saying, including Scottish poet Robert Burns in his poem "Here's a Health to Them That's Awa" where he connects freedom with literacy.

"Here's freedom to him that wad read,

Here's freedom to them that wad write."

Within a decade, McCulloch had founded the Pictou Grammar School. It would be a precursor to the more famous, non-sectarian Pictou Academy, a secondary school established in 1816. In Nova Scotia at that time, there was only one other secondary school in the province, King's College in Windsor, but it was limited to Anglicans. Consequently some 80 percent of the province— Presbyterians, Baptists, and Methodists, as well as Catholics—were not permitted to enrol. Although King's College received support from the Provincial Assembly in Halifax, an education at Pictou Academy on the fringe of the forests was dismissed by most of the political elite of the capital. It was called derisively the "Athens in the wilderness."

By 1818, this "Athens" had twenty-three students. In order to gain recognition for the academy, McCulloch sent three of the seven students of the 1824 graduating class to be examined in their studies by his alma mater—the University of Glasgow, Scotland. The examiners were so impressed that they granted degrees to all three—an academic tribute to the persistent pedagogy of Thomas McCulloch. "Athens in the wilderness," indeed! Over the next century, Pictou Academy would provide a foundational education for a multitude of doctors, lawyers, university professors, and university presidents, as well, of course, as a substantial number of Presbyterian ministers, including Alfred Fitzpatrick.

Millsville today is little more than a name on a map nestled between Dalhousie Mountain and Fitzpatrick Mountain. Slightly over 175 years ago, it was a thriving farming community of second- and third-generation Highlanders who had settled much of the area. The names on the land grants, like Young, Mackenzie, and Grant, reflect the Scottish heritage of the community.

At the height of Fitzpatrick Mountain, after a gradual ascent of three hundred metres, is a view of the Northumberland Strait to the north, and on a clear day one can see Prince Edward Island some twenty-five kilometres away. Before it was known as Fitzpatrick Mountain, oral tradition accounts tell of a major battle there in the late seventeenth century, before the Scots arrived, between the Mi'kmaq of Pictook and the invading Mohawks. This struggle was part of a longstanding conflict between these two First Nations that didn't end until the early eighteenth century.

Fitzpatrick Mountain was initially known to the Scottish settlers as Rogers Hill. It received its present name when a land deed of 125 acres was awarded in 1806 by the Duke of Cornwall to one James Fitzpatrick of Carrick Macross, County Carrick, Northern Ireland (Ulster)—Alfred Fitzpatrick's grandfather.

James Fitzpatrick had come ashore in Pictou in the early eighteen hundreds at the end of a rather peripatetic journey. He was born in Ulster to a Roman Catholic family in 1744. In the 1790s, perhaps due to the Irish "troubles," he migrated to the newly independent United States of America, where he settled in New Jersey. Here he married, but his new wife and their only child, Grace, died during childbirth.

Fitzpatrick, perhaps from grief or a desire for a new beginning, migrated once more, this time to Pictou. He was now in his mid-fifties—not an auspicious age to begin farming as a single man in the forest-strewn North Shore of Nova Scotia. In addition to his advancing age, Fitzpatrick faced two other major challenges in this Highlander controlled part of the province—he spoke Irish Gaelic in a Scots Gaelic settlement, and he had been raised a Roman Catholic and was now in a part of Nova Scotia that was fervently Presbyterian. In the early 1800s, there were only three others in this area who had such "disabilities"—the two McCara brothers, who were Lowland Scots and spoke no Gaelic, and another Catholic settler, Peter Condon. All found a solution to their problems by marrying Presbyterian women who spoke Scottish Gaelic.

Pictou, a Presbyterian Highland Scots town, did not have a plethora of spousal choices for a Catholic Irishman like Fitzpatrick, who no doubt did not advertise his religion. Nevertheless, in 1804 James married Janet Murray, daughter of one of the early Scots founders of Pictou. The Murrays were of Highland origin. Janet was Presbyterian, thirty-one years younger than Fitzpatrick, and spoke only Scottish Gaelic. Family lore has it that when they were married they could scarcely understand each other. Nevertheless, they did understand each other well enough to have six children, three boys and three girls, in quick succession.

In 1806, two years after the marriage, Fitzpatrick received his land charter of 125 acres just south of Pictou town on Rogers Hill, which then became known as Fitzpatrick Mountain. Janet made sure that all six of the children were raised as Protestants and were all well educated at home. Due to her influence, three of her grandsons would become Presbyterian ministers. Her husband, James, was another matter. The written records are somewhat ambiguous, but the Fitzpatrick family oral tradition suggests that James did not convert to Presbyterianism despite the best efforts of ministers like Reverend Duncan Ross, who badgered him in the hayfields.

Family lore also states that James, like Janet, had a passion for education and made every effort to home-school their six children. Thus, despite the differences of religion, languages, age, and culture, both James and Janet shared a commitment to a well-educated family.

James died in 1847 at the age of 103, and the largest monument in the Scotsburn Cemetery of the St. John's Church, which reads "In peace with all men," stands over his grave. Fitzpatrick family lore states that despite the burial taking place in a Presbyterian cemetery, a priest was also present at the service. Janet died in 1861 and was buried beside him.

Alfred Fitzpatrick's father, Alexander, the third son of James and Janet, was born on Fitzpatrick Mountain in 1810. He took a great interest in farming and as a young man in the late 1820s went with his older brother James to examine a 125-acre stretch of farmland in nearby Millsville, some four kilometres from Fitzpatrick Mountain. James took one look at the uncleared tract of land with its impenetrable forest of hemlock, hardwood, and spruce trees and exclaimed, "Alex, you might as well come home. You can never do anything here." Alex, due to Fitzpatrick stubbornness or the challenge of being finally on his own, responded, "No, I am staying here." And he did.

He chose well, for Millsville was a growing community. It was so named for having four water-powered sawmills and gristmills in the vicinity. Each farmer had his own woodlot. Cutting timber was a substantial supplementary source of income and had been for decades. Surrounded by farms, the gristmills would be used to grind oats and wheat for family consumption and trade. Indeed, a growing, thriving community.

Directly opposite Alexander Fitzpatrick's farm was the Rae family farm. Settler John Rae, a Lowland Scot and son of a tenant farmer, left Dumfries, Scotland, with his family in early summer 1817 and

Alexander and Mary Fitzpatrick, Alfred's parents, circa 1880. (**PRIVATE COL-
LECTION OF GORDON YOUNG**)

made the thirty- to forty-day voyage to Pictou, which was then
considered a major disembarkation harbour in Nova Scotia. Once
settled, he sent for his parents and his two brothers in the early 1820s.

The Raes established themselves on the eastern edge of Dalhousie
Mountain near Fitzpatrick Mountain where they were soon joined
by a number of Lowland Scots. By 1828, the population had spread
into the surrounding area, including Millsville. Some of the hardwood forests were cleared and the timber shipped out, sod and log
cabins were built, potatoes were planted between the tree stumps,
and these new Nova Scotians joined the growing communities of
Scots, both Highlanders and Lowlanders, in Pictou County.

John Rae and his wife, Jane (née Garthet), had nine children, losing one, an infant girl in 1831, likely to tuberculosis or diphtheria, both common childhood ailments for these nineteenth-century settlers. Their first daughter, Mary, was born in 1822. By the early 1830s, the Raes had a young neighbour, Alexander Fitzpatrick, who had cleared some of his land, built a log cabin, and planted an apple orchard. Obviously an industrious young man.

In 1839, at the age of twenty-nine, Alexander Fitzpatrick married his neighbour's daughter, Mary Rae, age seventeen. They moved into the log house Alexander had built on his farmland. Their children began to arrive, and in the 1850s the log house was replaced with a frame house, which would stand for a century. Alexander and Mary lived in Millsville for the rest of their lives. Alexander, who had inherited his parents' love of education, was fond of history and together with Mary taught his children at home, just as his parents had taught him. Another common practice was having a large number of children, as there was much work to be done on a sprawling farm of 125 acres. In quick succession, Mary gave birth to twelve children over the next two decades, losing one child to consumption. With seven boys and four girls, it should not be surprising that some in the community said they witnessed Alexander, who was a faithful Presbyterian, frequently in the barn on his knees. It was not clear if he was cursing or thanking the Almighty for their "abundance."

From 1830 to 1860, Millsville continued to grow with the arrival of Scottish migrants with names like Graham, Murray, and Carson, just to name a few. They took up land and farmed where large land grants were available around Millsville, south of Pictou. By 1840, the population had grown from a few dozen to almost a thousand settlers. The 1851 census provides some insight as to crops raised: potatoes, wheat, oats, barley, buckwheat, and livestock such as cattle, swine, sheep, and horses. These were usually farms of over one

Young's carriage shop in Millsville. (PRIVATE COLLECTION OF GORDON YOUNG)

hundred acres—enough to support the needs of a family and kin, provided the crops did not fail.

As noted, Millsville consisted of four water-powered mills on Four Mile Brook and McCully's Brook for cutting timber and grinding grain. Lumber cut by the "up and down" saw was taken by road to Pictou and then on to the British market. In addition to the water mills were stores operated by brothers Thomas and Robert Young, which dealt in farm produce as well as raw furs— raccoon, red fox, mink, and wildcat—which hung from the walls. A blacksmith/carriage shop, a shoemaker, and a cheese producer had also been established by the 1860s. As the community grew, a place of worship was needed. In 1865, James Rae, Mary's brother, donated part of the original Rae grant on the east side of Dalhousie Mountain to the Millsville community, and a Presbyterian church was completed the same year next to the stores and the blacksmith shop, at the junction of the road leading south from Pictou and between the two properties of the two conjoined families—the Raes and the Fitzpatricks. This was the first church in the community, and ministers came from nearby churches in Durham and Scotsburn to conduct services every second Sunday.

Alfred Fitzpatrick was born in Millsville, Pictou County, on April 22, 1862. He was the eleventh of twelve children and the youngest boy. The eldest boy had died of consumption. Alfred was no doubt schooled at home as were his older siblings, but he would also have benefited from the Nova Scotia provincial Free School Act of 1864, which stated that all schools would be free to all children in the immediate area of a school. The Millsville school that year (1864) had seventy-five pupils between the ages of six and twenty-five. Given the age spread and the small size of the school, it would have been both regimented and chaotic at times. This depended greatly on the teacher's ability to discipline and manage a large class of students of such disparate ages. The teachers, both men and women, would board with the parents of their students for two weeks at a time if they were not from the community. Some served as moral examples for many of the students. In his later years, Alfred often spoke of one teacher, Anderson Rogers, who "was eagerly welcomed by the Fitzpatrick boys, because his very presence was an elevation to all who lived where he was." Books were scarce and students were required to study the Nova Scotia Series, which contained language, literature, and history, the latter two mostly British. Also, liberal use of the "tawse," a heavy, three-foot leather strap used for punishing any misbehaviour or misdemeanour, could always be anticipated. Small wonder that when the students reached their teens, they dropped out of school to work full-time on the farm or leave the community entirely for work elsewhere.

Alfred was fortunate. According to a family member, the family supported Alfred in both financial as well as work considerations—as the youngest son, it was the six boys his senior who did many of the daily chores. Nevertheless, Alfred respected and appreciated what they were doing and how they did it. In his book *The University in Overalls* (1920), he described how to handle a peavey and the best way to fell a tree. In all of his later writings, he would espouse the belief that all physical labour was of value, be it skilled or unskilled, and that work done well defined who a person was. These were, indeed, lessons from his community.

The Fitzpatrick family in tiny Millsville could not escape the political and economic realities of the region and the province in which they lived—realities that would contribute to the dispersal of the Fitzpatrick family and Alfred himself in the years to come. By the 1870s, the once prosperous province of Nova Scotia was in a steep recession. Many in Pictou blamed the economic downturn on the confederation in 1867 of Upper Canada (Ontario), Lower Canada (Quebec), New Brunswick, and Nova Scotia—all British colonies that became a federation called Canada. Pictou town and county, together with most of the rest of Nova Scotia, had opposed this political union from the beginning. In Nova Scotia, many were members of the Joseph Howe–led Reform party, who were quite prepared to voice their dissatisfaction with this "confounded confederation," as they feared that this political change would also bring about a severe economic downturn for the region. As if to prove them right, Canada did have an economic recession in the 1870s, but this was due to a worldwide economic depression that affected Britain and its many colonies, as well as the United States. Imports and exports, the lifeblood of a shipping community like Pictou, were down everywhere as the economic crisis went from bad to worse in 1873 and after.

For farming families like the Fitzpatricks and all of their neighbours, the outcome of this economic downturn was disastrous. Prices for their crops and lumber plummeted. In a family with eleven children, there was enough to eat but money was scarce, only being spent on the essentials of the household. Local paid work outside the home was non-existent. Thus many of the community left the province to "go west, young man," as the adage of the age put it, and earn enough to support themselves and hopefully have enough ready cash to send home. But they would also see and experience new adventures very different from their upbringing in rural Nova Scotia. This would be a familiar refrain for many Nova Scotians in the century to come.

Six of the seven Fitzpatrick boys left home. John (b. 1848) went to Boston, returned to Pictou for a number of years, then moved to Saskatchewan and finally Northern Ontario, where he died in 1934. James William (b. 1850) studied law at Dalhousie University for two years, taught school in Cape Breton, Nova Scotia, then moved to Maine, where he was a success in the insurance business. He would later, after 1900, be a successful businessman in Northern Ontario, where he supported younger brother Alfred's literacy work. Isaac (b. 1854) travelled west to California at the age of twenty-three to work in the redwood forests, and the family lost touch with him for many years. He stayed there for two decades before eventually returning to Pictou. As will be shown, he would play an integral role in Alfred's future. Walter (b. 1857) settled in Massachusetts and returned to manage the family farm after his father, Alexander, died at the age of eighty-seven. Leander (b. 1859) followed his brother Isaac to California in 1880 and also worked in the redwood forests. He drowned there a year later in a river drive at the age of twenty-one. This incident would have a tremendous impact on Alfred.

The one Fitzpatrick son who might have been prepared to carry on the family farm tradition was Thomas (b. 1852); however, he sustained a severe head injury at a young age when he fell from a haymow. He would be cared for by the family his entire life. After the deaths of his parents, in the late 1890s Alfred assumed this responsibility in Ontario until Thomas's death in 1924. It was left to the four daughters—Jane (b. 1840), Jennie (b. 1843), Mary Annie (b. 1846), and Margaret (b. 1864)—to marry, stay in Millsville, and look after the farm and their aging parents, Alexander and Mary, as daughters were expected to do.

Thus, Alfred was raised in an agrarian family that was settled but not dormant. Given the out-migration of his brothers, he would eventually follow the same pattern but for very different reasons.

As noted, Alfred was born just before the Nova Scotia Free School Act was passed in 1864. Sheltered from the daily drudgery of farm labour, he spent much of his time on his studies both at home and at school. He read widely and in various subjects—history, science, and religion. He would often read to his brother Thomas. Another brother, Leander (called Lee), just three years older than Alfred, was Alfred's closest friend. They worked together, swam in the local pool beneath the falls near their home, and took long hikes in the forest around Fitzpatrick Mountain. Leander's death in California in 1881 would change Alfred's life.

In addition to family and school, the Presbyterian Church was the other important part of Alfred's life. Most of the Scottish settlers arriving in the district in the first few years of the nineteenth century were from Church of Scotland parishes. By 1835, St. John's Presbyterian Church in Scotsburn, five kilometres from Millsville, was completed. In 1865, Millsville erected its own Presbyterian church. It is likely that the Fitzpatrick family attended this church, as it was geographically convenient. At the same time, due to sectarian disagreements, some church-going families from this district would often walk or ride to Pictou to attend services. Regardless of where they attended, they would follow the same service format.

Sunday was a day of complete rest for all Presbyterians; even recreation was unthinkable, with only the necessary farm chores being completed. The Scottish Sunday was for some a grim interminable day with the church service, meditation, prayer, and religious instruction. The service would usually be a three- to four-hour affair, with the first service in Gaelic at eleven o'clock followed by a service in English. If bilingual (English and Gaelic), one was expected to attend both, and often even the Gaelic-only speakers remained for the religious uplift that a minister might provide. The Presbyterian ministers were under considerable pressure to deliver inspirational sermons. To read a sermon was unpardonable and not tolerated. If a minister did not know his Bible and its message well enough not to read it, he was scoffed at. A rousing sermon punctuated by loud "amens" or "hallelujahs" was the expected norm. Not surprisingly, as schools, businesses, and commerce continued to promote English, the last bastion for the functional use of Gaelic for these Scottish immigrants was the church, with services in their own language. In addition, religious music was considered a distraction from spiritual contemplation, and ornamentation like stained glass windows was viewed in the same way. Choirs became more common only in the 1850s, and church organs were introduced only after long and at times acrimonious arguments.

Aside from the Sunday service, weekdays also included a daily worship and instruction in catechism in the home. For many in the community, there was a family altar in the home and morning and evening family worship. It would be no exaggeration to state that the children in the community of Millsville were raised on oatmeal porridge and catechism. Financial support for the church came in the form of money, materials, and labour. In the mid-nineteenth century, in the absence of any government support, the church in every community was the social security structure in terms of health, employment, literacy, and support for the less fortunate and the aged—all needs that each congregation had. The Presbyterian Church and all it represented would be another integral and influential part of Alfred's upbringing and later life.

In the mid-1870s, Alfred completed his common school studies in Millsville and was accepted at Pictou Academy in the town of Pictou, a school that attracted many young boys and some girls from not just Pictou County but from the whole Maritime region. As has been noted, the academy was one of the very few educational institutions in the province that served as a secondary and preparatory school for university. Although from its founding it was non-sectarian, in a county that was 85 percent Presbyterian, the majority of its students were of that faith. Other Nova Scotian educational institutions had a sectarian foundation, as the province's various religious communities—Baptist, Methodist, Anglican, Roman Catholic, and Presbyterian—jockeyed for support from the public purse for funding. They would eventually establish a plethora of post-secondary institutions grounded in faith: Acadia University (Baptist); King's College (Anglican); and Saint Mary's and St. Francis Xavier Universities (Catholic). Dalhousie was founded in 1818 as the only non-sectarian institution in the province.

Alfred entered Pictou Academy in 1876 at the age of fourteen. He boarded in town for the duration of his education. Pictou Academy stood on an incline at the northern edge of town on the corner of High and Wellington Streets. A five-minute walk away was St. Andrew's Presbyterian Church, also called the "Scotch" church. A rock-solid construction of sandstone, as were many of the nineteenth-century buildings in Pictou, it was established in 1822 on the corner of Church and Coleraine Streets not far from Pictou Harbour.

From Pictou Academy, Alfred would have seen Pictou town laid out before him. In the distance he could view a very busy harbour full of sailing ships and some small steamers. He would have

Pictou Academy was established in 1816, and Alfred Fitzpatrick joined the school in 1876. (PICTOU HISTORICAL PHOTOGRAPH SOCIETY)

also heard the sharp steam whistle of the Intercolonial Railway train as it puffed into Pictou. The Pictou Branch Railroad line from Truro to Pictou had been completed in the Confederation year of 1867, and it gave the town access to the capital, Halifax. This Pictou Branch was the only rail line available from Halifax to the Northumberland Strait. Goods from Halifax shipped to Pictou could then be sent on by boat to New Brunswick, Prince Edward Island, and up the St. Lawrence River to Quebec City and Montreal. With the rail line and its port, the town of Pictou then was a major commercial link between Nova Scotia and the other Canadian provinces.

By 1876, the year Alfred started at Pictou Academy, the line between Truro and Rivière-du-Loup, Quebec, was completed with the Pictou Branch Railroad subsumed into the Intercolonial Railway. Once the line was completed, there were two major impacts on Pictou: the commercial rail travel from Halifax could bypass Pictou on its way west to other parts of Canada; and the Intercolonial Railway connection from Pictou to New Brunswick, Ontario, Quebec, and elsewhere in North America made extensive, rather comfortable travel quite feasible. Consequently, young women and men like Alfred's brothers began to migrate out of Pictou and the Maritime region for jobs, adventure, and settlement; Alfred would do the same. In the 1881 census, Pictou County had reached its peak in terms of population with 35,535. Over the next two decades, the population went into gradual decline, decreasing by over two thousand.

The town of Pictou would have been a very different experience for young Alfred coming from a small farming hamlet like Millsville. Although only a few kilometres away, a trip to Pictou town by horse and wagon would have been undertaken only occasionally to sell produce, to vote, or for other business dealings. Given the workload of the Fitzpatrick farm, there was little time or energy to make frequent trips. The town itself was a thriving seaport and crossroads for road, rail, and sail. The Ambrose Church map of 1864, in addition to a grid map of streets, houses, and businesses, also contained a directory noting a dozen hotels, a hairdresser, McPherson and Co. booksellers, a "House of Entertainment," and the "What Cheer House." Such cosmopolitan trappings were hardly comparable to "downtown" Millsville.

Alfred began his studies at the Pictou Academy under Principal A. H. MacKay. MacKay had graduated from Dalhousie University in 1873 with a degree in physics and mathematics and became principal

A. H. MacKay (centre front) pictured with his class in 1881. (**PICTOU HISTORICAL PHOTOGRAPH SOCIETY**)

of the academy the same year. He would return to Dalhousie for a biology degree in 1880 and remain as principal of Pictou Academy until 1889.

MacKay followed the same principles that Thomas McCulloch had formulated decades before: that knowledge should be made available well beyond the walls of the classroom and that literacy was paramount in every society's social and economic development. He embodied the inextricably linked elements of nineteenth-century Presbyterianism: the importance of the socialization efforts of both family and school, which would, it was hoped, instill the attributes of self-control and co-operation.

Perhaps MacKay was not the ideal model for this kind of leadership in a preparatory school. He was a sergeant in the Pictou Battery of the Garrison Artillery and carried his militaristic form of discipline into the classroom. One of his students explained that MacKay was known as "Little Goosey" because of his authoritarian form of control. He would badger and belittle his students as they wrote on his classroom blackboards, which they regarded as instruments of torture. Physical discipline was not unusual in the Nova Scotian schools of the nineteenth century, and MacKay used the leather tawse liberally for punishment. Whether Alfred was on the receiving end of any such bullying is not known, but he certainly would have been aware of it.

Perhaps the sheer size of Pictou Academy led to MacKay's controlling demeanour. With increasing enrollment, local financiers as well as some elsewhere in the province contributed funds to replace the original building with a three-storey structure, completed in 1880, two years before Alfred graduated. Pictou Academy was to be an educational model for other provincial academies and now consisted of a laboratory, a well-stocked library, and ornithology and entomology collections—some amassed decades before by Thomas McCulloch and displayed so they could be viewed by the general public. In addition, there were four well qualified teachers to provide instruction on the various subjects of the humanities, sciences, and languages.

In the years that followed the construction of the new school, Pictou Academy became the largest secondary school in the province with an enrollment of 290 students in 1885. The school's sterling reputation was such that one-third of the students were not from Pictou County. Like Alfred, three-quarters of the students were fourteen years of age or older, and in this environment the competition for academic grades was fierce. Top-of-the-class marks at Pictou Academy qualified students for automatic entry into any university in the Maritime provinces, and Dalhousie was usually the school of choice. It was, after all, the institution of which Thomas McCulloch had become president in 1838, serving as such until his death in 1843. Years later, in 1916, Pictou Academy alumnus Stanley MacKenzie, president of Dalhousie and a contemporary of Alfred at the academy in the 1870s, described any graduate of the academy as a "lad of parts" who worked hard, a scholar, a thinker, and a doer. It is doubtful if all graduates measured up to this description of the virtuous role they were expected to play. Nevertheless, this esprit de corps certainly pushed some of them to considerable achievements. Alfred would be one of them.

Fitzpatrick family lore remembers Alfred as a studious young man, and he rewarded his family's support with academic success. In 1881, he was one of two Pictou Academy students to win a $400 matriculation prize, which he won again in 1882. It is not clear why Alfred did not utilize this funding to enter Dalhousie. It may well have been due to the financially constrained circumstances of the family. Shortly after graduation, Alfred became an accredited teacher and was able to support himself financially and contribute to the family coffers to some extent. But his teaching career was short-lived, interrupted by a "higher calling." In 1884, Alfred applied to and was accepted by Queen's University in Kingston, Ontario, where yet another Pictou Academy graduate, George Monro Grant, was principal. When Alfred left Millsville in summer 1884 on a path to the ministry, he took with him the values, traditions, and history of family, community, and church as well as the solid education that the academy had given him.

CHAPTER 2

ITINERANT MINISTER: ANSWERING THE CALL 1884–1899

GEORDIE GRANT

AMONG THE IMMIGRANTS FROM THE "HIGHLANDS AND ISLANDS" *of Scotland was twenty-six-year-old James Grant. A man said to be of simple Christian piety, he acquired a land grant in Albion Mines, Pictou County, in 1826, some sixteen kilometres from Pictou town. He farmed and served as a schoolmaster in the district. He and his wife, Mary Monro, had five children. The third child, George Monro Grant, was born in 1835. Raised on the small farm, George (or Geordie as he was called) loved nature and exhibited an innate curiosity about everything mechanical. In 1843, at the nearby coal mines, a crank driven hay-cutter was set up at the pit head. Geordie and his playmates decided to try it out. The boys took turns cranking the machine while Geordie fed it hay. When a bundle of hay clogged the slashing blades, Geordie impulsively thrust his hand in to untangle it. The crank revolved and the twirling knives severed his right hand at the wrist. As he was rushed home, his comrades ran beside him and one consolingly shouted, "Dinna greet, Geordie. I hae the fingers."*

In mid-nineteenth-century Nova Scotia, doctors could not reattach Geordie Grant's fingers and hand to his arm. His father thus determined that since he would no longer be a farmer, being unable to do manual work, he would be a scholar. With home-schooling from his parents until he was twelve, Geordie would indeed become a lifelong student, scholar, and leader of civic and religious discourse unimpaired by the black glove that he wore on the stump of his right arm.

Alfred Fitzpatrick stepped down onto the platform of the train station in Kingston, Ontario, at the end of his long rail journey from Pictou Landing. It was September 1884. Carrying his carpet bag he walked to 61 Arch Street, his lodging for the school term. Arch Street ran past the entrance to Queen's University, where Alfred would spend the next eight years.

He was one of ninety-two students admitted to Queen's in 1884, and one of twenty-two who were "ministry bound," some of whom were from Pictou County and more than likely graduates of Pictou Academy and known to Alfred. There were also ten women, most of whom entered Queen's to study medicine. In the late 1870s, Queen's had been among the first universities in Canada to admit women to a degree-granting program. A number of these male and female students would become Queen's University alumni with whom Alfred would maintain contact long after his graduation and who would assist him with his life's work. But it was Queen's, its history, its professors, and its curriculum, that would inspire him the most.

Queen's University was a welcoming place for aspiring young Presbyterian ministers. Queen's was a religious-based institution, as were many of the other post-secondary denominational universities across the country. The University of Queen's College, based on a Presbyterian foundation, obtained its university charter in 1841. In subsequent years, it would become one of the foremost non-denominational schools in Canada, turning out graduates, including

Presbyterian theologians, who would have a significant impact on Canadian culture.

In March 1842, Queen's College opened its door with two professors in a small rented house on Colborne Street. The classes being offered in arts and theology attracted some fifteen students, with seven studying for the ministry. Born in penury, the college sought financial support from both the Church of Scotland and the Government of Canada West (Ontario). Both provided meagre funding. The years to follow were not easy. Fredrick W. Gibson, in his *Queen's University Volume II*, described it as "three decades of profound instability," especially when in 1868 the Government of Ontario ended its annual grant to denominational colleges. Within two years, in 1870, the number of students at the college was twenty-nine, only fourteen more than when it had opened some thirty years before. Yet it did not close. The 1870s saw women being admitted for the first time in Ontario, an expanded curriculum of subjects, and the inclusion of Queen's alumni in the decision-making processes of the university. This decade also saw the appointment in 1877 of the Reverend George Monro Grant as principal.

George Grant, pictured here in the 1880s, was Principal at Queen's University from 1877 until his death in 1902. (**QUEEN'S UNIVERSITY ARCHIVES**/V28 P-94.1)

If one were looking for a model of the stereotypical "muscular Christian" of nineteenth-century Canada, George Monro Grant would be a leading contender. Author, educator, Presbyterian minister, and Canadian nationalist, George Grant was born in 1835 on a farm in Albion Mines (now Stellarton) in Pictou County, some ten kilometres from Millsville, Nova Scotia. Growing up there, he would have experienced the same religious, political, and cultural tensions of Presbyterian life in Pictou County as Alfred did three decades later. Grant also attended the renowned Pictou Academy before going on to the University of Glasgow in 1853 where he remained until 1860, exhibiting leadership in academics as well as athletics. He returned to Nova Scotia in 1861, a Presbyterian minister with decided views about the role of the Presbyterian Church in a rapidly modernizing Canadian society; the most important to him being the Church's need for a closer relationship between reason and revelation, as well as a closer connection between the secular and the sectarian. Furthermore, Grant had a passion for evangelizing. Given this multitude of interests, it is not surprising that one member of his congregation found him to be "far too much taken up with concerns of this world ever to have become a minister."

After a brief stint in River John, Pictou County, in 1863 Grant was "called" to Saint Matthew's Church in Halifax, the largest and wealthiest congregation in the province. In his usual energetic fashion, Grant soon immersed himself in a number of social institutions in Halifax, including Child Immigration Schemes, Halifax Industrial School, and Dalhousie College. He would sit on the Dalhousie Board of Governors until 1885.

In 1872, he was invited to travel across Canada by a member of his Halifax congregation. Sandford Fleming was a surveyor and engineer who had carried out the first systematic study of a Canadian coast-to-coast railway line. He was a personal friend of Prime Minister John A. Macdonald and now chief engineer for the promised national railroad to Victoria, a fundamental condition of British Columbia's entry into Confederation. Fleming had already surveyed routes in New Brunswick and Nova Scotia a decade before when the Intercolonial Railway from Quebec City to Halifax was

being built. His trip across Canada with George Grant as his secretary would, Fleming hoped, confirm his calculations of a Nova
Scotia to British Columbia railway line.

Grant's account in diary form of this journey, entitled *Ocean to
Ocean, Sandford Fleming's Expedition Through Canada in 1872*, began in
Halifax on July 1 of that year. By early October, this small expedition of seven men and a number of different guides recruited along
the way had reached the Pacific Ocean. The journey certainly had
its impact on Grant. It confirmed his Canadian nationalism, and
he joined a cluster of Canadian intellectuals who are called by one
historian, Carl Berger, the "New Imperialists." Grant was convinced
of the contribution of "our North-West" to a greater Canada within
the British Empire.

If Grant sewed his Canadian nationalism on one sleeve, on the
other he attached the evangelizing passion he had learned at the
University of Glasgow. Grant believed that the First Nations and
Métis communities, as well as the new settlers he met on the trek,
would be suitable converts. Grant noted that the Fleming expedition
was always welcomed by First Nations people. Grant's son William,
in a biography of his father written in 1905, wrote that George Grant
also believed in the need for a generous fulfillment in letter and in
spirit alike of every promise made to the First Nations. Grant would
bring these passions of nationalism and justice with him to his new
appointment at Queen's University and to many of the students he
taught, including Alfred Fitzpatrick.

Reverend George Monro Grant became Principal and
Professor of Divinity at Queen's on December 1, 1877. He was
faced with two serious matters upon his arrival. First, what role
would Queen's play in the many factions of the always fractious
Presbyterian Church? Second, contingent on this role, what would
be the future of the university, which seemed to always be peering
over a financial precipice? Religion and funding would be Grant's

two major challenges in the years to come, as they would be for Alfred Fitzpatrick personally and professionally in the twentieth century.

Grant spearheaded a successful fundraising campaign then added a second campaign in his first decade as principal. However, it was clear in the 1880s that the Presbyterian Church could not or would not provide sufficient funding to ensure the survival of Queen's as a modern university. Grant's only other option was to approach the Ontario government for assistance. In order to receive such support, Queen's would have to become a non-denominational college and, at the request of the province, federate with the University of Toronto as a provincial cost-saving measure. Grant rejected the second option outright. This conflict over federation was common knowledge among Queen's students of the time, and Alfred referred to it frequently over forty years later when he had difficulties with the University of Toronto while establishing his own neophyte institution. In a rapidly growing Ontario, Grant believed that a non-denominational college like Queen's would survive with a more ecumenical student population and this would, at the same time, assist the college in its long struggle against sectarianism. In both of these ambitions, Grant was successful; he consequently received the support of the Ontario government.

Free from both church and provincial control, Grant established a School of Theology to serve the Presbyterian community and increased the quality of scientific education in the college, aided in no small measure by the support of his faculty and his "fellow traveller," Sandford Fleming. Fleming was appointed Chancellor of Queen's in 1880. Both Grant and Fleming believed, somewhat unusually for the time, that science and theology did not contradict one another. Referring to the disputation between science and religion arising from Darwin's work, Grant said, "Life is too short to always be discussing the same subject."

The other contradiction Grant contested was the entrenched tradition that higher education could only take place within the walls of the university and thus be available only to those who could afford to be there. Queen's University was already known for its extension studies program, having begun the practice in 1882 with a flexible approach for those who were unable to attend classes for reasons of distance or vocation. By 1894, extramural exams were being administered as far away as Victoria, British Columbia. Queen's faculty would assist any registered students through an exchange of correspondence and assigned textbook readings. Given Alfred's efforts some four decades later to establish a college that would offer degrees solely by extramural studies, Queen's provided an important early model.

Also a part of the university's educational outreach was its support for public libraries. Queen's was frequently approached by alumni in various parts of Canada who were requesting a donation of books to help them start a Mechanics' Institute or a public library in their isolated communities. Queen's University believed that such an institution would assist young people in forming the habit of reading, which would then develop a "noble character." This was a common perception of literacy at the time—providing, of course, the books were appropriate reading material to encourage such "nobility."

George Monro Grant would serve Queen's University until his death on May 13, 1902, in his beloved Kingston. By this time, there were almost nine hundred students at the university, ten times the number upon his arrival in 1877. Ten percent of these students were women. As it entered the twentieth century, Queen's had become a well respected Canadian university. To honour "Geordie's" twenty-five years as principal, the students raised thirty thousand dollars to build Grant Hall in the centre of the campus. Grant would not see its completion, but "his boys," as he called them, had done him proud. Grant Hall still stands.

It was said that George Grant had welcomed Nova Scotian students in particular to the campus, inviting them to Christmas dinner at his home each year and engaging in lifelong correspondence with them, most especially those who went into the mission field. Many of the boys would model their lives and ambitions on his example. Alfred was one of them, and throughout his life he would often refer to Grant with unbridled admiration; in a *Montreal Gazette* feature on the twenty-fifth anniversary of Grant's death in 1927, Alfred described Grant as a "breezy, inspiring, towering man."

Grant's moral suasion was broad and profound. D. B. Mack notes in his entry on Grant in the *Dictionary of Canadian Biography* that "he championed such causes as university education for women in 1879, aboriginal rights in British Columbia in 1886...and he denounced restrictions on Asian immigration to Canada as early as 1881." These were no doubt topics that Grant took up in the classroom as a professor of theology, bringing together religion and secularism. Not all of his students would have accepted his views on social issues and social justice, but it is clear, based on his later life, Alfred Fitzpatrick certainly did.

Preceding his admission to Queen's University, Alfred had already exhibited his scholarly potential. As mentioned, he received a provincial financial award in Nova Scotia in 1881 at the age of nineteen and again in 1882 in recognition of his scholarship while at Pictou Academy. He would continue his academic excellence at Queen's and showed himself, over time, to be a lifelong learner.

Among the holdings of the university archives at Queen's is a handwritten, bound volume of the Register of Students. In it are listed: Alfred's denomination (Presbyterian); his father's occupation (farmer); age at entrance (twenty-two); and his intended profession (ministry).

Alfred Fitzpatrick as an undergraduate student at Queen's University, circa 1889.
(PRIVATE COLLECTION OF JAMES MORRISON)

In his first year, Alfred completed the entrance requirements, English and Latin, and in October of 1885 began courses toward a Bachelor of Arts. Over the next four years, he attended classes in Greek, mathematics, and philosophy, graduating with his degree in 1889.

During his years at Queen's, Alfred was sponsored by a Mr. A. Buntin, who paid for his whole program of studies on a five hundred dollar per year scholarship, a common practice of the Kingston community, which supported some university students. Alfred also received some financial support from Millsville. His younger sister, Margaret, remembered how the Fitzpatrick household was always saving for Alfred's education.

There is very little documentation about this important time in Alfred's life. Fortunately, a handful of letters from his hometown, written before 1900, survived. They provide some perspective on his connections with home and the pressures and expectations his family placed on him. In 1888, his niece Annie Young, who would later serve as a missionary in China, wrote of Presbyterian revival meetings in the Millsville community and noted that "Mother and Father attended the meetings every night." This served as a gentle reminder to Alfred of how important the Presbyterian faith was to his extended family.

There are also three letters from his father. These are printed in a wavering, careful script with some grammatical errors. They were letters of encouragement and of reassurance. The first, written in January 1888, recounted in a positive tone the Fitzpatrick farm news with regard to the number of horses, cattle, and sheep. At the same time, Alexander noted with the typical farmer's trepidation that a bad year like winter 1887 would "wind up the farming" in Pictou. He sent love from "mother," Thomas (Alfred's brother), and himself and added "Pray for us." The second letter arrived three months later. In it Alexander thanked Alfred for the stamps he sent for mailing the letters he wrote. He also included his hope that "God will teach you what work you will do" and ended with the observation that the previous letter was "all i rote for 30 years."

In the third letter, the last in the file, written two months later in June 1888, Alexander reported on family, church, and prayer meetings and again the amount of livestock on the small farm: two horses, ten head of cattle, and thirteen sheep. He closed with love and added that he "is looking forward to hearing Alfred preach." For the decades that followed, Alfred made frequent visits home to Millsville, during which time, no doubt, he was a guest speaker in a number of church services in Pictou County. No doubt Alexander heard his son preach before his death in 1897. None of the letters that Alfred sent home have survived.

Upon graduating with his B.A., Alfred won the Lewis Prize for the best essay in theology. He also received a scholarship to continue his studies in church history. He then began his theology degree program in 1889 with courses in Hebrew, the Old and New Testaments, and church history—all taught by George Grant. Alfred's thinking about his Presbyterian faith as reflected by his family was no doubt challenged. Grant's liberal, evangelical Protestantism, which was a vital part of what became known as the "social gospel," was not a perspective that would have been entertained back home in Pictou County.

Alfred's perspective would have also been challenged by another Queen's faculty member from whom he took courses—John Watson. Watson had graduated from the University of Glasgow with highest honours and became an important part of the Queen's faculty in 1872, when he was twenty-five. John Watson soon established himself as the leading advocate of the philosophy of "constructive idealism," which would greatly influence Canadian Protestant thought and practice. In essence, this approach entailed an equal concern for the secular and the sectarian. Watson would not and could not divorce religion from secular life. By his reasoning, the state existed "for the purpose of providing the external conditions under which all citizens may have an opportunity of developing the best that is in them." This belief in the state's responsibility to its citizens was one that Alfred would adopt in his many approaches to the Ontario government as he sought to establish his reading tents in the wilderness in the early twentieth century.

Watson, or "Wattie" as the students called him, served as a professor of philosophy from 1872 to 1924 and as chair of the philosophy department for much of his tenure. Due to his precise critique of traditional Presbyterian values, his research and teaching contributed greatly to the growing reputation of Queen's University as a centre of original academic scholarship. Watson's influence, like that of Grant, began in the classroom. Both were largely responsible for what became known as the "Queen's spirit," which inspired graduates to engage in social service. There were, of course, a number of students entering the ministry, while others were in academia, business, medicine, and education. For some of these graduates, most especially the theologians, their goal was to achieve a balance between the rock of traditional religion and the swiftly moving currents of social change. One of those affected by this "Queen's spirit" was Alfred Fitzpatrick.

Alfred first took courses from Watson when he started working toward his theology degree in the fall of 1889. Required courses included physics, Hebrew, and Watson's Introductory Philosophy. This was a much sought after course, as Watson—tall, bearded, well-built, and with a magnetic personality—was a dynamic speaker. It is likely that the content of his lectures combined with those of George Grant inspired many of the students to question much of what they had taken for granted in their religious beliefs.

Alfred had entered Queen's University at a time of intense inquiry and turmoil in the Christian world. With the Industrial Revolution, the church had been buffeted throughout the nineteenth century by new challenges to its authority and its place in a changing world. Burgeoning urbanization, the migratory movements of European populations, and the Darwinian questioning of humanity's origins in an increasingly scientific and technological age, served to dislodge the very foundations of the Christian faith in an ever-growing secularization of society. The late Victorian period would witness a landscape strewn with discarded tenets of the Protestant faith.

How much Alfred knew of the social gospel movement at this time is not known. He was, after all, a "country lad" from Millsville who probably had not travelled much beyond Pictou County— perhaps an occasional train trip to Halifax. Due to his rural upbringing and his religious heritage, he was more than likely a very conservative Presbyterian. As noted in chapter 1, Pictou Academy was a prolific producer of the "learned"—doctors, lawyers, teachers, university presidents, and most especially ministers. Alfred was, no doubt, imbued with the traditional values of the faith, and from this background he would see his future as one that served the Church. This was a fine ambition in rural Pictou County, but by attending Queen's University, Alfred was about to be immersed in the social gospel movement.

Queen's University was a prominent advocate for this new theological perspective that swept through the many churches of Canada. Some described it as a movement in search of a theology. John Moir in his *Handbook for Canadian Presbyterians* (c. 1994) is succinct. To him, the social gospel was attempting to apply Christian principles to the problems raised by Canada's rapid shift to an industrialized society. This was a doctrinal shift from saving the individual to a more collective salvation of society by reforming the environment in which the individual lived. It demanded answers to ethical questions that every Christian should consider and act on. Today, such an effort would be called social reform and social justice.

Throughout the nineteenth century, there were a multitude of human rights issues to be addressed: child labour, conditions of labourers in factories, political reform, and the expanding slums of the major urban centres. As Richard Allen writes in his landmark study of the social gospel entitled *The Social Passion*: "One of the social gospel's most important functions was to forge links between proposed reforms and the religious heritage of the nation, in the process endowing reform with an authority it could not otherwise command."

As the nineteenth century ended and the twentieth began, the secular and the sectarian drew closer and closer together to such an extent that many perceived it to be a secularizing of the church rather than the Christianization of secular society. There were a plethora of ideological influences, like social Darwinism, Marxism, progressivism, and German idealism, all of which included criticisms of Biblical scriptures. There was also the proliferation of distractions within the secular world, especially in the urban centres, such as social clubs, music halls, trade unions, competitive sports, and the "cathedrals of consumerism." Finally, as the twentieth century dawned there was the impact of colonialism, immigration, and pluralism.

The result? According to the meticulous record keepers of the largest Protestant congregations—Methodist and Presbyterian—there was a gradual decline in church attendance in the 1890s. The Dominion Census of 1901 verified this, showing a fall in church membership despite an increasing population. Which was the best route to reclaim its adherents? Some believed in increased secularization, which many feared, calling instead for the necessary return to spiritualization. This represented a crisis of faith. It was felt that the church must either adapt to these new conditions or wither away.

But how to adapt?

The response among Protestant churches varied from denomination to denomination. A number of churches took on perceived societal ills at the local and national level. A favourite was the sale of alcohol, which many wished to make a crime. In the late 1890s, however, Grant's response to the prohibition movement was concise and clear. Although favouring temperance, he believed that drinking alcohol was a vice, not a crime, and would be impossible to legislate against. Nevertheless, the prohibition movement was successful. There were also marches opposed to prostitution and to streetcars in Toronto being allowed to operate on Sunday. Finally, there was the Lord's Day Act of 1906, which made Sunday a day of complete rest, forbidding everything from shopping to tobogganing on the Sabbath. In this regard, Reverend J. G. Shearer, a Presbyterian minister in Toronto, was the activist leader of the Sabbatarian movement, which, after an intensive national campaign, succeeded in convincing Parliament to pass the Lord's Day Act. Indeed, "Toronto the Good" was attempting to make it "Canada the Good."

Others, however, took the social gospel to mean improving slum housing, welcoming immigrants, and providing education and literacy for all. There were many in what was the reform wing of the Church that would combine prohibition with social action in order to bring about positive changes in society. Such was the case of Reverend Salem Bland, Methodist minister and one of Canada's leading social gospel thinkers. Bland combined support for the prohibition of alcohol and lobbying for the Lord's Day Act with a socialist strain. He would later argue in his book *The New Christianity* (1920) that capitalism was "rapacious and heartless" and did not follow Christian principles. Although rejecting a Marxist or revolutionary solution, many of these "Christian Socialists" like Salem Bland sought a moral regeneration of Canadian society by the elimination of social problems like poverty and illiteracy.

An essential part of the theology degree was organized by the Missionary Association of Queen's University. Young theology students were expected to proceed to various locations in Canada for mission work during the summer. This was, of course, to expose them to actual contact with a mission posting, inform them of their responsibilities, and deepen their interest in their work. Young men were already being sent to the upper waters of the Ottawa River, where the lumbermen worked and lived in shanties. In the winter of 1891–92, for example, 113 shanties were visited by these itinerant novices. While travelling through these many camps, student ministers were expected to hold religious services for the men and supply them with wholesome literature. As the monthly *Presbyterian Record* stated, "the missionary should accompany the settler, not follow him afar." They were also expected "to care for those who were strangers in a strange land." These were values that Alfred absorbed and would apply to his secular work with workers and immigrants in isolated camps in the century to come.

Students were also sent out to locales far from Ontario. In the summer of 1891, five theology students from Queen's were posted to Canada's North-West; Fitzpatrick was one of them. The transcontinental Canadian Pacific Railway had been completed barely six years before, so Fitzpatrick took the train almost as far as it would take him—to Revelstoke, BC, between the Monashee Mountains and the Selkirk Range, where Revelstoke's first train station had been built just four years earlier, in 1887. Due to the mining and the lumbering industries, Revelstoke would become the largest and most prominent settlement in the interior of British Columbia. Revelstoke had a large Presbyterian population who had yet to build their first church. At least they now had a minister in Fitzpatrick. They would complete their church in 1893.

For Alfred, the Canadian West of the early 1890s was as exotic as any foreign mission could be, for the "heathens," as they were called, were no longer in overseas locations but now were immigrants crowding Canada's seaports and railway stations and settling Canada's West. Many church leaders believed these missions, if successful, would rejuvenate the church. No doubt Fitzpatrick wished to be an important part of this rejuvenation.

This was Alfred's first exposure to the harvesting of gigantic trees like the Douglas fir and the redwood in British Columbia—a logging industry that would strip the Pacific coast from British Columbia to San Francisco of 90 percent of these majestic trees over the next half-century. Logging these huge trees was considered one of the most dangerous jobs in the natural resource industry, with a variety of perilous tasks that would take a man's life in an instant of carelessness. One hundred to two hundred men lived together in isolated camps of ill-constructed shanties in highly difficult and dangerous conditions. Their dawn-to-dusk, six-days-a-week workload meant that there was little or no time for anything else—not that there was anything to do in such circumstances. For Alfred, this was the first time that he understood what his brothers Isaac and Leander had left their Millsville home to do, both having migrated to California to work in forestry. Perhaps by taking up a mission in Revelstoke, Alfred was trying to figure out how he might track down Isaac, who had not been heard from since he headed west in 1876, and find the grave of his other brother and best friend, Leander. But first he must follow his calling.

In 1892, a year after his summer in Revelstoke, Alfred was ordained by the Presbytery of Saint John, New Brunswick, and was expected to address the religious needs of the new settlement of Kincardine, some 150 kilometres north of Fredericton, NB. Kincardine was settled in the early 1870s by over 750 Presbyterians from Scotland; this planned settlement was called the Scotch Colony.

A church was completed in 1878. Alfred should have been content with his new location. With Scots Presbyterians in abundance in a farming community, he was in an environment similar to his childhood in Pictou County, and he was much closer geographically to his home in Millsville, Nova Scotia. In addition, the community of Kincardine had a reputation for paying its ministers in full—not a common occurrence in new rural settlements of the Maritimes. However, in Alfred's restless mind, family responsibilities beckoned. He had plans to track down Isaac and locate Leander's grave.

Alfred served barely three months during the summer of 1892 in Kincardine and then left for mission work in California. He assumed his appointment in Little River, California, about eight kilometres from the busy redwood lumber town of Mendocino and over two hundred kilometres north of San Francisco, armed with his certificate of licensure from his Saint John presbytery with the directive "to preach the gospel of Christ." No doubt he would also have carried a letter of personal reference from Principal George Grant, with whom he maintained contact. In 1894, Grant responded to a card that Alfred had sent him with the hope that he was having a good experience in California. He asked Alfred for details of his work, his location, and his prospects. At the same time, Grant expressed the hope that Alfred would soon come back to Canada. If he did, Grant could guarantee him a "charge" in Ontario. Their close relationship would continue until George Grant's death eight years later.

Little River was a typical west coast mill town. Founded in 1864, it had sawmills, a shipyard, a lumber port, and several chutes for loading lumber into the schooners that would carry it to market up and down the Mendocino Pacific coast and beyond. In these very early days of forest mechanization, the old methods of cutting timber were still prevalent. In every camp, there were several different wood crews, each with a specific task such as cutting off the top of a tree, felling the tree, swamping (clearing trees of branches), and skidding (using teams of oxen to haul trunks to market). The men on the Pacific coast received two dollars a day and were charged sixty cents a night for the "privilege" of living in the crowded conditions of a twelve-foot square, dirt floor shanty. Alfred, as a minister on horseback, soon had first-hand knowledge of these camp conditions and was exposed to the, at times, brutal reality of the lives of these lumbermen. It is here in the redwoods of California that his story takes a particularly personal turn as he finally completes his two-year search in California for brother Isaac.

Jessie Lucas, who was Alfred's personal secretary from 1920 to 1933, recounted a story that Alfred had told her. Apparently, Alfred was on his woods camp circuit in a small carriage through the towering redwoods when he was hailed by a well-built, bearded woodsman by the side of the road looking for a lift. Alfred recognized him immediately as his brother Isaac whom he had not seen or heard from in almost two decades, since Alfred had begun to attend Pictou Academy as a teenager. Without identifying himself as his brother, Alfred stopped and picked him up. Isaac did not recognize him. They travelled on for a mile or two before Alfred revealed that he was Isaac's brother and that he was now a missionary on a religious visitation to the surrounding lumber camps. In the discussion that followed, Isaac convinced Alfred that the men in the camps needed more than "Bible thumping." They needed hope in order to survive in the squalid, unsanitary condition of the camps, and they needed a means by which they could escape their condition. Oral tradition has it that from this meeting in the woods, Alfred began his non-sectarian mission to the camps. At least this was how Alfred told it in the years that followed. This is likely an apocryphal tale with some grains of truth. Certainly, the key elements of Alfred's later life are represented: the prodigal son, the family connection, the rough and rugged environment in which Alfred would pursue his life's work, and the questioning of the value of religion to men in such circumstances. Often myths are more than a description of events. They can also be a persuasive call to action.

Isaac did return home to Millsville in the 1890s, not long after the "road in the woods" meeting with his young brother. Although Alfred doesn't mention it in his later account of the meeting, the two brothers no doubt talked about Leander's accidental death. Isaac did not know where Lee was buried. Alfred tried to find his grave several times, but there is no evidence that he ever did. He continued his mission work in the Mendocino area and postponed his secular activities in labour camps for another seven years. He was, after all, a well-trained "man of the cloth"; his family and community expected him to carry out God's work. Nevertheless, his meeting with Isaac may have planted a seed of doubt in his mind as to whether he was the right man doing the right task.

After three years in California, Alfred returned to Kincardine in 1895 and by September of that year was inducted into the pastorate of the Presbyterian church at Kincardine. With an average Sunday attendance of 110 people, it was a growing church with an admiring congregation and substantial salary of six hundred dollars a year. This, however, was not enough to keep Alfred as pastor for long. In August 1896, he resigned the pastorate in Kincardine.

There were still missionaries needed in Canada's West, and in 1897 Alfred took a posting in Wapella in the southeastern part of what in 1905 became the province of Saskatchewan. Wapella was established as a farm colony with a population of almost four hundred people. After a year in Wapella, Alfred moved on to Fort Qu'Appelle, a Hudson's Bay Company trading post since 1864, some 150 kilometres west of Wapella and 50 kilometres east of Regina. Agricultural development had begun here in the 1880s, and as more European settlers arrived, the Hudson's Bay post was converted to a department store for the new arrivals. Alfred took up his appointment at St. Andrew's Presbyterian Church and began his clerical responsibilities of making his religious circuit to the various farmers and their families.

Fort Qu'Appelle was not far from the thriving community of Qu'Appelle, which was on the CPR rail link to the west and served as a distribution centre for the railroad, bringing both supplies and new settlers to the region. Like Wapella, Fort Qu'Appelle was situated on the transition zone between the Qu'Appelle River valley and the prairies. Again, Alfred lasted only one year in these settled communities, but it is clear that his social gospel training was well-received. He presented his farewell sermon at St. Andrew's Church in Fort Qu'Appelle on April 8, 1899. There was a large congregation present, and they reportedly enjoyed his final address. The text for the sermon was I Corinthians 14:34, in which the Apostle Paul urges men to "Let your women keep silence in the churches: for it is not permitted unto them to speak; but they are commanded to be under obedience." Significantly, Alfred argued against this directive, for he saw no reason why a woman should not exercise her ability and influence for the good of humankind. It is clear from this sermon that Alfred was supportive of and very receptive to the work that women could and would do to assist him in his later goal of promoting learning to labourers in work camps. During his leadership of Frontier College a number of women would work as instructors in hardship posts. But that was to come.

In 1899, Alfred moved east to the woodlands of Algoma, Northern Ontario, to what would prove to be his last religious posting—Nairn Centre, a logging industry town just west of Sudbury. There is little evidence to suggest why Alfred changed parishes so frequently, as there are indications that he was a success in these newly settled farming communities of Kincardine, Wapella, and Fort Qu'Appelle. In 1898, he received a card from a prominent member of the community of Wapella expressing the community's gratitude for all his efforts in initiating the Wapella Gymnasium and Literacy Club. Further, his good work had had "a very positive impact on the young people." When he left Wapella, Alfred was presented with a Bible as a thank-you, a gift he treasured for the rest of his life. But it appears that these agrarian locations were not the constituency that he sought to assist.

Alfred's life was beginning to change. His father had passed away two years before, and his mother was ailing. His brother Thomas could not take care of the Fitzpatrick farm in Millsville on his own. In 1899, with his move to Northern Ontario, Alfred would soon take up the responsibility of looking after Thomas. In addition to this life-changing event, Alfred's faith was changing as well. Although his training in theology at Queen's University had stressed that the first and foremost task of ordained ministers was to evangelize and devote their time to communicating the "good news" of salvation, Alfred's brother Isaac had told him that the missionaries to the woods camps came infrequently and they never addressed the workers' real needs, which were medical, social, and educational. At this stage, it is likely that Alfred began to withdraw his formal commitment to the Presbyterian Church. He was beginning to lose "the call." From 1900 on, he is listed in the Presbyterian records as being W.C., "without charge," meaning he no longer held a ministry in any church. After 1910, he is not listed in the records at all.

Nairn Centre in 1899 appears to be the first major crossroads of Alfred Fitzpatrick's career, from a commitment to the Church to a commitment to the almost half-million "campmen" scattered across Canada that he believed had been left out and would soon be left behind unless something was done. Alfred was now thirty-seven, and he had several more perplexing crossroads ahead of him.

CHAPTER 3

ACTIVIST: FINDING A CAUSE 1899–1906

WEBBWOOD, NORTHERN ONTARIO

IT WAS NOT MUCH OF A COMMUNITY, AS ONLY ONE MAN HAD *lived there—Andrew Webb. He had taken the CPR train out of Toronto in 1883 and swung down in a forested location in Northern Ontario where trees crowded the tracks some eighty kilometres west of Sudbury. Here he built and occupied a shanty for the winter. The CPR line had been completed through the area in 1882, workers cutting, clearing, digging, and laying track, making their way through the "pineries"—the vast forests of white and red pine, cedar, and hemlock. Shortly after he arrived, Andrew Webb was supplying split hardwood to the passing trains for fuel as they sped westward. Soon the CPR set up a woodworking camp here for gathering fuel, and by 1886 it was an important waylay—a stopping place for trains to refuel. It was called, not surprisingly, Webbwood, after its founder.*

With rail transportation in place, the area that bordered the line was soon swamped with thousands of men doing the same thing Webb had done. This time, however, it was not just for CPR firewood and ties, but also for cutting, trimming, and sending building materials to Southern Ontario in a bid to fill its all-consuming maw as it rapidly industrialized. The harvesting of the natural resources of the north would, to a considerable degree, play a major role in the process of making Ontario the richest province in the Dominion.

Here in Canadian Shield country were limitless forests, a rock strewn landscape, swampy muskeg, and isolated pockets of coarse acidic soil that would barely pass as farmland. As one optimistic Ontario Minister of Crown Land predicted in 1899, "The resources of New Ontario in soil, minerals, timber, water power, and other raw materials of civilization are extensive and valuable and quite capable of becoming the home of a hardy, thrifty, and prosperous people, many millions in number."

"New Ontario" offered countless acres of forestry production for the growing pulp and paper industry as well as the more traditional usage of trimmed logs that would be shaped into railway ties, telegraph poles, or construction materials. The forestry industry flourished, with over 125 million cubic feet of pine cut annually between 1896 and 1910.

Alfred Fitzpatrick arrived in the area in 1899 at the beginning of this timber boom in the "New Ontario," but as he put it he was more interested in the harvesters than the harvest. His was to be a different kind of harvest.

Nairn Centre was some thirty kilometres east of Webbwood on the CPR line. The CPR had laid the Algoma branch of its transnational line through here in the mid-1880s. In 1889, a CPR station was built in Nairn Centre as the settlers and woods workers, single or with families, began to arrive. By 1895, there was a one-room log schoolhouse, and a year later the first municipal meeting was held. Neighbour community Webbwood had their two-storey, four-room brick school in 1900 and by 1906 elected their first mayor.

Alfred had arrived at a time many have called the heyday of the logging industry in the area. For him, there was no time to waste to begin the harvesting of his flock. It would not be easy. Nairn

Alfred Fitzpatrick, circa 1900. (PICTOU HISTORICAL PHOTOGRAPH SOCIETY)

Centre was a rough frontier town in those early days. It was said that on Saturday night there would be boot and fist fights among the often drunk lumber labour force in any one or all three of the hotels. After all, in 1900 there were over three thousand men working in the timber woods surrounding Webbwood and Nairn Centre.

There was no Presbyterian church in the vicinity, so once more Alfred began his itinerant mission work. He soon found that the same labour circumstances existed here in Northern Ontario as his brother Isaac had told him about some years before in California. This time Alfred was not going to "wander the woods." He would exchange his hard clerical collar for a soft white high-neck one. Alfred decided to stay in Northern Ontario and begin his life's work of bringing about positive changes in literacy, sanitation, and the health situation of the isolated camps.

Medical assistance was Alfred's initial priority. In summer 1900, within a year of his arrival, he applied for and received medical student admission to Toronto General Hospital, St. Michael's Hospital, as well as Trinity Medical School (which merged with University of Toronto Medicine in 1904). He was scheduled to travel to Toronto and begin his studies in anatomy at Trinity Medical School in September 1900. Whether he attended any classes is not known. Given the need for his work in non-urban settings, Toronto did not appeal. Or perhaps, as was often the case for the easily distracted Alfred, he got caught up in the matters of the moment, as 1900 turned out to be a crucial first step on the path to his future career. In any case, there is no record of him matriculating in medicine. Still, he knew that medical attention was an important part of surviving in the woods; indeed, he later sought reading camp instructors who had some medical training.

For any medical expertise Alfred may have had, he likely had to fall back on the folk remedies of his childhood when ministering to the campmen. For example, he wrote that the cure for a sore throat was to tie a dirty wool sock around the neck. In addition, a few spoonfuls of sulphur and brown sugar might clear it up. One

A worker receives medical attention in a bunkhouse at a railway construction camp in 1910. Alfred Fitzpatrick (with the white collar) sits in the background. **(LIBRARY AND ARCHIVES CANADA/FRONTIER COLLEGE FONDS/C-068794)**

surviving photo shows the administration of the mixture to a somewhat recalcitrant worker with Alfred in the background. While this method would not cure a sore throat, it would certainly prevent possible contagion by keeping others at arm's length. Alfred also wrote in his notebook his cure for typhoid fever: "2 tablespoons of whiskey, 2 tablespoons (heaping) castor oil, 15 drops of turpentine. Take once." His philosophy being, it seems, what doesn't kill, cures!

In addition to medical care, Alfred's other goal for the men working in the camps was literacy. Literacy did not require any further academic training than he already had. However, it did require some systematic research so that he could learn how the issue of literacy was being addressed in similar circumstances. The two pivotal years for Alfred Fitzpatrick's barely formulated life's work were 1900 and 1901—and it all starts with a letter from Webbwood to the Ontario government.

The same summer that he applied to medical school, the summer of 1900, Alfred began what he considered the necessary research to support his literacy cause. In a number of letters dated August 9, 1900, he stated that he was canvassing for support "to embrace the needs of the lumber and mining camps" and that he wanted to collect allotments of small libraries with one hundred to two hundred volumes suitable for lumber and mining camps. He described the dimensions of the book boxes and how they could be shipped and added that the books were not to be of "a sentimental, goody-goody nature" but the most recent books on contemporary topics. Twenty-five percent of the books were to be in French. Daily newspapers and magazines could also be delivered in both English and French. The concept was to start a "camp club" with a minimal membership fee paid by the men, who would then have a vote on adding books in the literature of their choice and full control of the library. Given the low wages of the men, within a year the collection of a membership fee was discontinued.

This letter was sent to a variety of librarians and libraries in Canada and the United States. Responses and advice arrived from McGill, New Hampshire State Library, and Wisconsin Free Library. Mary Spencer, chief librarian at Michigan State Library advised that the concept needed an in-house librarian for "cultivation of literary taste." Amy Wallace, librarian at Carnegie Library of Atlanta stated the women's clubs handled travelling libraries and that Alfred needed a competent administrator and government aid to establish such a venture. Other responses were not so positive. Maine Library Commission thought the idea not practical and felt that the men could not manage a library.

Still, Alfred sent his proposal on to the Ontario government's department of education, which promptly quashed it. The government was not prepared to support such an arrangement, as "the class of people whom you want to assist are unable to read." Undeterred, Alfred turned his attention to the possibility of "travelling libraries," using the established libraries in the vicinity as distributors. To this end, Alfred sent detailed questionnaires regarding the literacy needs of the area to at least fifty lumber company owners, businessmen, and concerned individuals who could best speak with some authority on the subject. In addition to the questionnaires, Alfred also asked them for letters of support for the travelling libraries concept he had outlined as well as advice that would assist him in making his case. These would be sent on to the minister of education.

Within a few weeks, Alfred received several positive responses from supporters like W. A. Charlton, businessman and member of the Ontario legislature; Father P. E. Lefebvre, SJ (Society of Jesus, the Jesuits) of Sault Ste. Marie; and a number of lumber company owners who had camps in the area, like Hale and Bell in Nairn Centre, Saginaw Lumber and Salt Company in Whitefish, and the Hall Lumber Company. Many included handwritten personal comments about the importance and necessity of the work. As far as Alfred's future ambitions were concerned, the die had been cast.

From the beginning, Alfred wanted to maintain a non-sectarian stance with regard to the movement. Being close to the Ontario–Quebec border, there were a substantial number of Roman Catholic French Canadians in the woods camps. Thus, he was especially gratified by the note from Father Lefebvre, whose parish included Camp 8 in Nairn Centre of which 85 percent were Catholics; in his letter, Father Lefebvre commended the movement as non-denominational.

Armed with this supportive documentation, Alfred, in a letter from Webbwood dated September 11, 1900, wrote to the minister of education, Richard Harcourt, about "a movement afoot" for the benefit of the scattered work camps of "New Ontario."

"Dear Sir," he wrote, "There is a movement afoot to induce the Ontario Government to extend the scope of the Public Libraries Act so as to embrace the needs of lumber and mining camps. The Act reads: 'They (Public Library Boards) may establish branch libraries in the municipality.' But as most camps are outside of any organized municipality the consent of the Department of Education is necessary."

He went on to request that the minister allow the Little Current Public Library on Manitoulin Island to "have the privilege" of sending out travelling libraries to the camps in their vicinity to promote public education. He insisted that this request was a humane and reasonable one and that these "isolated masses" ought to be supplied with the best up-to-date literature through a camp library club. He recommended that the province purchase books for travelling libraries; that it allow local libraries to send out small collections to the camps; and that camp library clubs be organized that would help collect books for the camps until such time as the Ontario government could send out prepared libraries. Alfred closed his letter by stressing the importance of the government taking on this extension of literacy to all in the same way that it was responsible for education in the public school system. Education minister Harcourt may not have agreed with Alfred's final point, but from its beginnings he was constantly supportive of the travelling library concept and appreciated what Alfred was trying to accomplish.

Early on, in a trip to Toronto to meet with Harcourt, Alfred established contact with the *Globe*, and the paper ran an editorial entitled "Reading Camp Movement." This was not the first time, nor would it be the last, that Alfred and his work would be mentioned in this prominent national newspaper, which, under publisher J. E. Atkinson, was very progressive for its time. On this occasion the editorial elicited a response from a W. H. Muldrew, first principal of Gravenhurst High School, who had recently published *Sylvan Ontario*, a book about the native trees and shrubs of the province. Muldrew sent along six copies of his book together with fifty volumes from his personal library to help Alfred fulfill his stated objective of showing "the relations between the world of literature and their [the workers'] daily occupations."

Despite such donations of science books, the canvas knapsack that Alfred carried on his shoulders "into the bush" would always contain a preponderance of literature. In this early period, many of the workers had as their first language French or English, and the small libraries Alfred put together reflected that fact. Still, as early as 1904, Alfred was asking his main Ontario government supporter, minister Harcourt, to send out fifteen or twenty books in Italian.

Although 60 percent of the men in Algoma at this time could neither read nor write, many came to the camp library, located in a tent or cabin. These would soon be known as "reading rooms" or "reading tents." Alfred was always on the lookout for books that would be an inspiration to those with little or no literacy skills. In early 1902, he sent two dollars to Booker T. Washington for a copy of his *Up from Slavery* (1901), an account of Washington's rise from slavery into which he was born in 1856 to becoming the founding principal of the Tuskegee Institute in Tuskegee, Alabama, in 1881. The institute was established to provide African-American students with an academic as well as a vocational education. Alfred viewed the Tuskegee Institute very highly due to this combination of academic studies and manual work, as it was similar to what he was trying to accomplish with the working men of Canada. He was disappointed to learn by return mail from Washington that "the supply is exhausted."

Alfred requested specific books in both English and French to be sent by the Ontario government to the early travelling libraries, including Muldrew's *Sylvan Ontario,* the naturalist Ernest Thompson Seton's *Wild Animals I Have Known,* and fiction such as Gilbert Parker's *Seats of the Mighty* and William Kirby's *The Golden Dog.* Contemporary novels, plays, and poetry were the most popular, by authors like Quebec's Louis Frechette, and Maritime poets Charles G. D. Roberts and Bliss Carman.

By far the most widely read contemporary Canadian writer was Reverend Charles Gordon, a Presbyterian missionary who, like Fitzpatrick, had been posted to the Canadian West, Banff specifically, in the 1890s; by 1900 he was a minister in Winnipeg. Under the pseudonym Ralph Connor, Gordon was a prolific writer, and many of his novels, like *Black Rock* (1898) and *The Foreigner* (1909), gave an accurate portrayal of life in the lumber and mining camps of Western Canada. His novels were bestsellers nationally and internationally. Alfred wrote to Gordon and complimented him on being able to describe life in the labour camps better than anyone had. Thus began Alfred's long-lasting correspondence with the novelist, which eventually included a request that he join what would become the Canadian Reading Camp Association board and an effort to recruit Gordon for fundraising. For his part, Gordon contributed substantial financial support to the association in the years to come and joined the board in the 1920s.

The novels collected by Alfred were often too difficult for the illiterate men to read. But not surprisingly, the men did not want to use children's books or primers to learn to read. Consequently, Alfred requested one- or two-syllable versions of a number of classics, like *Kidnapped* by Robert Louis Stevenson and Jonathan Swift's *Gulliver's Travels.* This represents an early effort by Alfred to fit the reading material to suit the adult learner—a pedagogical approach that became more evident in his later publication, *Handbook for New Canadians* (1919).

In late 1900, the Ontario education department sent the first travelling library of fifty volumes to a mining site near Michipicoten Harbour in northeastern Ontario on Lake Superior. Minister Harcourt gave full public credit to Alfred Fitzpatrick for introducing the concept. The travelling library was to be on a short-term loan basis of three months. The Helen Iron Mine Company agreed to "secure comfort and reading material" for the men, no doubt in the hope that this would lessen drinking and reduce the number of men quitting and going to another camp to work.

Also in 1900, with five hundred dollars made up of Alfred's money and a few donations, a sturdy log building, the first of many "reading rooms," was completed in Nairn Centre for the neophyte "Reading Camp Movement," along with two others built that year.

During the winter of 1900 a reading room was built for interested workers at J. J. McFadden's woods camp some thirty-five kilometres from Whitefish in Northern Ontario. It was staffed by Mrs. Alex Scott, wife of the foreman. In addition to a small shelf of books, she offered "music and welfare." This makes Mrs. Scott Frontier College's first instructor. Within a year, there were at least half a dozen other reading tents or rooms at various camps—railway, mining, and lumber—including the Temiskaming and Northern Ontario Railway camp and the Gold Rock mine camp. With the exception of Mrs. Scott, they were all administered by young men. The work attracted mostly university undergraduates, but there were a number of graduates, including two with a master's degree—A. O. Patterson and J. F. McDonald—who looked after the reading camp near Nairn Centre. The second woman to work in a reading camp was Miss B. M. Laverie, who served in a Murdoch Brothers camp of the Temiskaming and Northern Railway near North Bay in 1903. She had a teacher's certificate.

The first "reading room" was built along the Spanish River in Algoma, Ontario. Alfred Fitzpatrick is seen here standing second from the left. **(LIBRARY AND ARCHIVES CANADA/FRONTIER COLLEGE FONDS/C-047545)**

The year 1901 was a flurry of activity for Alfred—correspondence, travel, publicity, and speeches. For the most part, the correspondence he received was supportive. The Mechanics' Institute in Barrie had no books to spare so sent magazines. The president of the Woman's Christian Temperance Union (WCTU) of Ontario stated that their movement already sent religious literature and "comfort bags" to the camps and criticized Alfred for not focusing on the "spiritual well-being of the men in your care," instead distributing novels and non-sectarian papers to them. May Thornley of the WCTU in London, Ontario, wrote, somewhat whimsically, that there was no money to spare, so Alfred's project would have to "live upon love and air and the good wishes of his friends." Hardly helpful!

From the beginning, Alfred was well aware of the kind of criticism he would be subjected to as regards his work. In his personal notes in 1901, he records some of them. "Would the men have any energy left after a day, a week, a month of hard labour?"; "What about the squalid and unsanitary living conditions?"; "There is already an education system in place and these men should have taken advantage of that when they had the chance"; and finally, "They are too old to learn." In the face of these hostile inquiries, Alfred drew upon his Pictou Scottish heritage, using the example of Dr. Norman MacLeod, graduate of Edinburgh University in the early 1800s, who was an enthusiastic proponent of the learning of Gaelic by adults in the Scottish Highlands; Alfred concluded that not a few grey-haired old men in the Highlands gladly availed themselves of the privilege of learning.

Alfred quickly realized that without sufficient government assistance he would be forced to look elsewhere for support. This meant canvassing churches, businessmen, and other individuals for financial contributions. And so he began. At a church in the Georgian Bay district, he told a crowded congregation about the hundreds of men trapped in labour and monotony; they were so desperate for something to read that they treasured the wrappings from patent medicine bottles. He would close with "a man is never too old to learn." He also spoke at a number of churches in Southern Ontario, and a collection was always taken up on his behalf.

In the spring of 1901, Alfred needed a reality check as to his endeavour. He travelled to Kingston to meet with his lifelong mentor, Principal George M. Grant of Queen's University. Grant's encouraging letters, no matter where Alfred was posted, had always reaffirmed Alfred's life decisions, and now he needed reassurance about what he was planning to do.

By his own account in an editorial in the *Montreal Gazette* some twenty-five years later, Alfred intercepted Grant on his way to class.

Alfred greeted him with "Geordie" as his students called him, and Grant responded with "Fitzpatrick, what are you doing now?" followed by a firm handshake with his left hand, having lost his right hand as a youth. Alfred outlined his year in California and his more recent times in the "pineries" of Algoma. Grant invited him to spend the night at his residence, and that evening after dinner, Alfred described the horrendous conditions of the frontier camps where a reasonable day's work, a fair wage, and basic adult education facilities were non-existent. He then outlined his current goal to establish travelling libraries for the camps. He also mentioned that he had withdrawn from an active ministry to focus on the needs of the working man. In response, Grant began to take some of his books off the shelves as a donation to the travelling libraries.

The next morning they discussed how this project might be supported financially. Grant promised to write to his friend Thomas Shaughnessy, president of the CPR, to obtain a railway pass for Alfred. He would also send supportive letters to Queen's alumni, describing Alfred's efforts. Grant was known for his high-profile contacts and his fundraising capabilities. The CPR pass was soon forthcoming as were many invitations from Queen's alumni in church and business for Alfred to present his ideas in a public format. Alfred left Kingston now firm in the merit of what was to become his life's work, as he had the wholehearted and unwavering support for his idea from Principal Grant, a man he described as "the greatest Canadian of the nineteenth century."

A month or so later, in May 1901, Alfred received a letter from Grant who was obviously aware of his straitened financial circumstances. He advised Alfred to use the railway passes for personal as well as business matters, as "your work will suffer if you starve." Again, in November 1901, Grant's letters reinforced "our duty to the lumbermen" and that Alfred's experience had enabled him to "judge what is best." In closing he added, "Do not be discouraged."

Grant would not live to see the results of his support; he died in May 1902. Five months earlier, in January, Grant had written his last letter to Alfred in his elegant longhand script, urging him not to expect any support from the government and exhorting him to look to the "Christian Public" whom he could reach. He then, in his conclusion, added the one recommendation that Alfred would not or perhaps could not ever live by. "My dear Alfred...You must take care not to go beyond your means. Cut your coat according to your cloth and on no account get into debt." Alfred would continue to remember Grant's support and tried to emulate Grant's example, if not follow his financial advice.

Alfred was convinced that an "association" would be necessary for organizational purposes rather than calling his enterprise a "movement." Consequently in 1901 he drew up a constitution for the Reading Camp Association (RCA), soon to be called the Canadian Reading Camp Association (henceforth CRCA). The bylaws clearly stated that the object of the association was "to assist the various Departments of Education to organize reading and recreation rooms in the lumbering, mining, and railway camps of Canada." At this early date, Alfred was already visualizing a national role for the association. It was to be an independent literacy organization with a very specific clientele and an avowed policy of absolute non-sectarianism.

The "object of the Association" then goes on to describe the methods: supply literature, provide instruction and entertainment, and "develop a home-study system of education for isolated manual labourers." Thus, in 1902, the letterhead on letters of correspondence read "Canadian Reading Camp Association: Entertainment and Culture for Manual Labourers: Manual Training for Teachers." This description would be modified on the letterhead from time to time in the years to come but would always focus on the labour and the education of the frontier.

One can already observe the foreshadowing of the "Frontier College" that the CRCA would become twenty years later. The CRCA was an association that any person or organization (church, lodge, or society) could join for an annual fee of one dollar. In essence, it was an association, much like the NGOs (non-governmental organizations) of today, to lobby the provincial governments to provide programs for the neglected of the country and advocate for their welfare. The Ontario Department of Education was wholeheartedly supportive but only half-heartedly forthcoming financially. In response, the CRCA, essentially Alfred, went from being a lobbyist to being an activist.

Log reading rooms had been built. Reading tents had been raised. Library shelves had been stocked with books. Highly educated librarians were in place, ready to provide adult education—but to whom? Few came and even fewer stayed. Maybe the critics were right—the men were indeed too exhausted to learn or too ignorant to even try. The travelling library reading camp concept seemed it might be suffocated at birth.

As the story is told, and there are many such at Frontier College, one teacher/librarian, Angus Gray, who had a teacher's certificate, was posted by Alfred to E. Hall's woods camp fifteen kilometres from Nairn Centre in the winter of 1902–03. After a week or two of sitting and waiting in coat and tie while the exhausted woods men trudged by his reading room after another day of cutting and stacking timber, Gray decided the "passive" library approach was not working. When Alfred arrived in the camp as part of his circuit, Gray outlined to him the method by which better results could be obtained. Work side by side with the men, he suggested. Do the same amount of work during the day as the men. Get to know them.

Share what they were experiencing, and more importantly, find out what, when, and how they wanted to learn. Fitzpatrick thought it could work, and within a few days Gray, the certified teacher, was a "lumberjack" during the day and teacher/librarian for two or three hours at night. Although Alfred called them instructors, the name "labourer-teacher" was more descriptive of what the men and women would do. Edmund Bradwin, who began working as a labourer-teacher in 1903–04 and eventually succeeded Alfred as Principal of Frontier College, always used the term, and it is still used today.

This action would revolutionize Alfred's initial conceptualization of the teaching libraries. Instead of simply living with the men, stacking the shelves, and stocking the books, the new direction was to work with the men and become, as Alfred put it, a friend and a brother.

This account, common at Frontier College in later years, was, like the story of the two Fitzpatrick brothers meeting in the redwoods of California, long considered somewhat apocryphal. However, at the forty-ninth annual meeting of Frontier College in 1949, Principal Bradwin, who had joined the CRCA in 1903, recounted it in a tribute to Fitzpatrick. He said: "At this half-century anniversary, the name of Angus Gray should be remembered as an instructor in a labour camp in the vicinity of Nairn Centre during the winter of 1902–03. He was the first to undertake manual labour during the day while teaching at night."

Because of Gray's pedagogical innovation, the employment advertisements for instructors had to change. In the *Ottawa Citizen* in late 1902, the call for worker-instructors was titled "Bush Teachers Wanted." It read: "Men are scarce in the woods and wages run from $25 to $30 per month, with board, according to the ability of a man to handle an axe, saw, or drive a team. Through the kindness of employers, the association is able to place a dozen good men at from

$25 to $30 per month." The ads also noted that for teachers or college graduates who were out of work and were willing to do manual labour during the day and conduct classes at night, "the Association will pay from ten to twenty dollars per month additional." The association guaranteed five months' work only but would try to get the teachers work in the summer months in sawmills, mines, and railway construction. The advertisement closed with "Candidates who speak French are preferred. A. Fitzpatrick, Nairn Centre, Ontario."

Not surprisingly there was not a stampede of young men to Nairn Centre. In the winter of 1902-03, ten worker-instructors were placed, four of whom were from Alfred's alma mater, Queen's University. In the years to come, students in arts, medicine, and science from universities like Dalhousie, University of Alberta, University of Toronto, and, of course, Queen's would become for a period of several months a logger, navvy, swamper, teamster, log sorter, slab cutter, and on and on. But the fundamental two principles of adult learning in such an environment or perhaps any environment were for the instructor to accept the ideas and worth of all the learners as to what they wished to learn, and, in return, the instructors must show their ability and their worth in the learner's domain of labour. Do not just live with the learner but share their work experience.

Alfred opposed the use of tobacco or liquor or stimulants in any shape or form for either the men in the camps or his student instructors. It is clear that he followed the tenets of his Presbyterian faith, which greatly influenced how he perceived the "sins of the day." He once wrote: "The great majority of women and all sane men believe the use of tobacco and alcohol to be injurious and unnecessary." No doubt the wealthy men who ran and owned the camps and who demanded as sober and steady a labour force as they could hire would agree with these sentiments, though perhaps not for themselves.

As the Reading Camp Association was taking shape, Alfred also had personal and family matters to attend to back home in Millsville. His father had died in 1897. Consequently arrangements had to be made to care for Alfred's mother, Mary, and Thomas, his brother who, due to his head injury, was not capable of running the farm. It was necessary to find ways to safeguard the homestead and look after Mary and Thomas. Alfred's brother James William (1850–1928)—namesake of the first Fitzpatrick in Pictou, his grandfather James—took up the family responsibility. James W. was financially the most successful sibling in the family. Beginning his career as a teacher at eighteen, he became principal of a school in Port Morien, Cape Breton, then by the early 1880s attended law school at Dalhousie University in Halifax. He paid his way by selling insurance for the Mutual Life Insurance Company of New York, self-described as the "Largest Life Company in the World" with advertised assets of $400 million by 1887. J.W., as he was known, moved his wife and family to Portland, Maine, where over the next two decades he sold Mutual Life insurance. With his father's death, it was clear J.W. was the only brother in the family able to provide the leadership necessary for the Fitzpatrick family to maintain the farm. According to family oral tradition, he convinced his younger brother Walter, who worked as an itinerant tanner in various locations in Massachusetts, to return to Millsville to care for Mary, Thomas, and the farm, in exchange for owning half the farm with Thomas and Mary holding the other half. Together, Alfred and J.W. persuaded Thomas that he should accept this proposal.

The scheme did not work out as planned. Walter was willing but was a poor farm manager and was unable to run the farm. Mary died in 1902, then Walter died in Millsville in 1903 at the age of forty-five. With Walter gone, Thomas, now close to fifty, moved to Northern Ontario shortly thereafter to be cared for by brother Alfred for the rest of his life. In Millsville, the solidly constructed frame farmhouse, which Alexander had built with his own hands in the early 1850s and in which he and Mary had raised their large family, lasted another fifty or so years. But in the absence of inhabitants, repair, and care, it collapsed in on itself and was torn down in the 1950s.

Alfred was now in his early forties. Tall and slim, he favoured a full moustache that covered his upper lip and extended past the corners of his mouth. With wire glasses or a pince-nez, piercing blue eyes, and a hairline that seemed in constant retreat, Alfred was always well turned out. He wore his single-breasted wool suits, perhaps Etonian serge (as advertised in the 1900 edition of the Eaton's catalogue for $12.50) with tie, white shirt, and starched white collar. His later associate, Edmund Bradwin, would comment sardonically that Alfred dressed as if he was principal of a ladies' college. Even in the handful of photos that are available, he appears ever in the background in a dark fedora, white scarf, and jacket likely dark blue or black. There are few pictures of him smiling, although it is said he would often tease the female staff in letters and conversations, so he did have a sense of humour. Although his photograph appeared in several newspaper bylines and articles, it was always the same head-and-shoulders shot that would have been included in a press kit and on file. With this photograph, it would seem that, like Oscar Wilde's Dorian Gray, Alfred Fitzpatrick would never age.

By all reports, Alfred was a shy, retiring person who was not comfortable with a large audience. Following an address to a church congregation seeking support for the association, he was described by the minister as soft-spoken and plain in language, though he spoke with great precision. Alfred's passion and intensity for his chosen work of "literacy for all" was evident in one-on-one or small-group conversations. These were frequent, as he continued to request support—moral, physical, financial, and any in-kind contributions that could be spared. Alfred did not like to ask for financial support; nevertheless, it was clear that he must.

In the *Mail and Empire* (Toronto) newspaper of September 1903, in an article titled "Backwardness of Church," Alfred was described as just having returned from British Columbia and was quoted as saying that employers were prepared to help, but church and state were "indifferent." He continued: "The churches are too busy in a humiliating competition for the building up of sectarian churches and other institutions," and they were committed to raising $150,000 for a church in a crowded city but not prepared to expend $150 for a reading room. In the years to come Alfred would frequently come back to this urban–rural contrast of wealth and the role of church and state. He declaimed about men huddled together like galley slaves. It was impossible to keep themselves clean. "Every man should have a spring bottom bed and mattress to himself." Alfred was not just addressing the lack of literacy in his lectures but challenging businesses, churches, and politicians to address the social and economic welfare of these "galley slaves."

Through public lectures, letters, editorials (written about and in some cases by him), books, pamphlets, and personal persuasion, Alfred would become, over the next three decades, a constant advocate for literacy, better working conditions, and simple social justice for those who could not access those societal norms. But he never knew where support would come from for his cause.

In his correspondence, Alfred was direct and to the point, rarely going beyond a businesslike page or two. Nevertheless, at times his passion for "the work" would show itself. In a several-page 1903 letter, he briskly reprimanded a young new instructor: "You cannot expect to have everything as convenient in [a] lumber camp as in a city, and you will find it more satisfactory to adapt yourself to existing conditions." He closed the letter by adding that if the instructor didn't like the conditions, Alfred would get another man to take his place. "In which case you will not get your fare paid back from camp. This is the universal." And it remained "the universal" until well into the last half of the twentieth century. Alfred could not afford to risk losing the reputation of the association to any person whose actions might shake the confidence of camp owners or potential financiers.

For much of Alfred's thirty plus years in the literacy field, financial security would be an issue. As noted, it took five hundred dollars of his savings in addition to public donations to build the three log reading rooms in 1900. As Alfred dedicated more and more of his time to literacy and the campmen, by 1902 he had ceased being an active minister in the community and thus cut himself free of his church salary; he is listed in the church records as "W.C. (Webbwood)," meaning "without charge." Family assistance was forthcoming but sometimes there was a catch. His cousin, A. P. Willis, founder of Willis & Company Ltd. in Montreal, wrote to him in December 1900 inquiring if Alfred would like to be a "Willis representative" and sell organs to the many camps he was visiting. Each organ would bring a commission of twenty-one dollars for himself. Willis & Company had developed a thriving piano and organ retail business across Canada in the 1880s. In 1907, for example, the company sold two thousand pianos. Alfred's brother J.W. had been a very successful regional salesman in Halifax and Saint John in the 1880s, and Willis, no doubt, hoped Alfred would be as successful. However, Alfred did not have his older brother's business acumen. Over a two-year period, Alfred succeeded in selling only one organ. It was clear he didn't think much of his own capabilities as a salesman. He sold a total of two overall then gave up.

Although frequently in debt, Alfred did have a reputation for paying what he owed as soon as possible. He would often use the gold watch and gold coin his father had left to him upon his death as collateral when he borrowed money. Well into the 1930s Alfred still had the watch, and the coin his father had given him was among his meagre possessions when he died.

Although the Ontario Minister of Education, Richard Harcourt, said glowing things about Alfred and the "travelling libraries" concept, the Ontario government gave support to the association somewhat grudgingly. Still, the grant of one hundred dollars each year from 1901 to 1903 was raised to five hundred in 1904. Despite this raise and Alfred's best efforts, these funds were not from a government budget line but solely based on Harcourt's admiration for Alfred and his mission. That amount together with donations would not keep the association afloat. Obviously, Harcourt would not be there forever and a new ally had to be found. Alfred would have to engage in some political lobbying.

In December 1904, Alfred wrote to J. P. Whitney, Conservative MPP in the Ontario legislature, thanking him for his support in getting the provincial grant raised to five hundred dollars. Alfred outlined the needs and requested three thousand dollars; if granted, Alfred promised he would do all he could "to secure your return to power." Whitney's response was naturally political as well. He would offer support of one thousand dollars, which he announced on the floor of the Ontario legislature, but anything more was questionable. He added, "I am glad that you have decided to help us in the present struggle" and inquired if Alfred would assume a more partisan position. Alfred responded quickly that he was grateful for the support, but he had no inclination to engage in politics, as he had never been bound to one party.

By January 1905, Whitney was premier with a forty seat majority, and Fitzpatrick had only received five hundred dollars. He then wrote a biting letter to Whitney expressing the view that it would have been better for the association if the old government had been returned to power. He had already contacted the *Globe* about the shortfall. Alfred had also just published an article in the *Canadian Magazine* about the association and its needs. The *Toronto News* recommended in an editorial that the government provide twenty-five thousand dollars to the association. In July 1905 an order-in-council passed an additional grant of five hundred dollars for the Canadian Reading Camp Association. Principal Grant had correctly warned Alfred not to expect support from government but just to trust the public. Alfred's victory was somewhat tarnished. And this was only the first struggle he would have with the Ontario government over funding.

In 1905, the *Globe* reported that after Alfred's address at a recent convention of the Dominion Educational Association, a motion was passed in support of his Reading Camp Association, and the educational association urged governments (not just Ontario) to provide travelling libraries and elementary instruction. With such results, Alfred was clearly a convincing speaker. He took his message abroad as well, to England and the United States, and succeeded in attracting both American and British students to the association as labourer-teachers. In 1905, with the title "Aiding Camp Men," he addressed the American Library Association's annual meeting in Waukesha, Wisconsin, and urged support for travelling libraries and basic literacy for those in isolated locations.

Alfred also published pieces in one of the more popular monthlies of the time, the *Canadian Magazine of Politics, Science, Art, and Literature.* This magazine was widely read by an upper- and middle-class audience. In addition to raising public awareness of the association, such articles would also assist him in his lobbying and fundraising efforts among the moneyed classes.

In May 1905, a six-page illustrated outline of the association's work, entitled "The Neglected Citizen in the Camps," appeared in the *Canadian Magazine,* followed two years later by "Life in Lumbering and Mining Camps: A Plea For Reform" (May 1907) in the same magazine. Both articles stressed similar themes. First, the inadequate and transitory role of the clergymen in camp situations, as they come and go and are "never known by the toilers." Second, as "the state takes much from them and gives little in return," it must in turn play a more prominent role in assisting the men in these camps; the exploitation of the natural resources without some consideration for the spread of disease and the lack of intellectual and moral value to the workers "ought not to be left wholly to the capitalist." Third, the unsanitary condition of the camps and the presence of contagious afflictions like smallpox, tuberculosis, and fever must be addressed; therefore, Alfred sought to recruit more medical students to volunteer. He proposed that he would approach the university medical councils and suggest that they allow students the option of spending the fifth year of their program in the camps. Finally, Alfred continued to emphasize his overriding conviction that "Education is the God-given right to every man, not the exclusive privilege of a few favoured persons," and that this right can only be accomplished with a greater diffusion of education. Given all of the above, as Alfred summarized bluntly, "These toilers of forest, mine, and railway construction are being robbed."

Alfred's strategy had to be multi-faceted. His talks, letters, articles, and lobbying were all vital. Similarly, the association board had to be diverse. From its earliest formation it would include a variety of politicians, businessmen, and wealthy citizens. There were no religious leaders on the board. To add a patina of respectability, which was very important for fundraising at the time and remains so today, he sent annual reports to the Governor General of Canada, who was described as an "energetic and keen imperialist." In a letter dated February 5, 1906, Alfred asked for his support. Lord Grey answered that he would like to meet Fitzpatrick when he was next in Ottawa. By 1909 His Excellency, the Right Honourable, the Earl Grey, P.C., G.C.M.G., G.C.V.O, Governor General of Canada had become a patron of the Canadian Reading Camp Association and would remain so until his departure for England a year later.

In 1907, according to the *Orillia Packet* newspaper, Alfred addressed the local Canadian Club on the "Duty of the State to the Frontier Laborers of Canada" along non-denominational lines. The paper described Fitzpatrick as a moving speaker who connected one-third of Ontario's wealth to its forests and mines in Northern Ontario. This wealth, however, went to the public schools, libraries, and colleges in the towns and cities to the south. The sons and daughters of the wealthy had too much education while young men in the woods were largely ignored educationally and ostracized socially. The mayor of Orillia, who was chairing the meeting, called a vote to send a "memorial of remonstrance" to the Ontario government in support of Alfred Fitzpatrick's mission. It passed unanimously.

It is somewhat ironic that the very people that Alfred was approaching for large financial donations were also the ones he was most critical of in his writings. He would often decry the financial support given to universities compared with the lack of financial support for his educational venture. He was likely not impressed with financier Andrew Carnegie's matching grant of $350,000 in 1903 for a new library in Toronto while Alfred had his libraries in tents, log cabins, and boxcars, without any such contributions. But the work went on and fortunately was faithfully recorded from its beginnings by annual reports.

The first annual report of the newly established Canadian Reading Camp Association made its appearance in February 1901. It was a brown booklet of some thirty pages entitled *Library extension in Ontario: Travelling Libraries and Reading Camps*. The cover of the annual reports that were to follow over the next several years often featured a quote from Alfred's favourite authors, such as Thomas Carlyle, Robert Browning, and Ralph Emerson, regarding literacy, work, and the importance of intellectual development. On the cover of this, the first report, there was a single line from nineteenth-century American clergyman Henry Ward Beecher: "A library is not a luxury but one of the necessities of life." In addition, beneath the title was a more extensive quote: "The men of the book are still there in mines and lumber camps of the mountains, fighting out that eternal fight for manhood, strong, clean, God-conquered." This quote is taken from the preface to *Black Rock*, Ralph Connor's popular 1898 novel about the mines and lumber camps of Western Canada. Alfred no doubt identified with the young, dedicated college graduate missionary who was featured as a hero in so many of the early works of Ralph Connor, pseudonym for the Reverend Charles W. Gordon. The hero's struggle was to bring Christianity to the isolated settlements, raucous labour camps, and the First Nations Peoples of the West while at the same time facing daunting challenges of health, isolation, and climate.

The first annual report focused on the need for the extension of libraries to the isolated communities and camps in Northern Ontario and to "make systematic home study possible for all workmen... [e]ven those whose conditions are the most adverse." At this point, Alfred's vision was of a passive opportunity for men to self-improve intellectually with access to books. The library board in Little Current, the report noted, had already sent small branch libraries into the nearby camps, but much more could still be done across the province.

The introduction to this report touches on several common themes that were discussed in succeeding annual reports: that the Government of Ontario take responsibility for the establishment of a system of travelling libraries, or as Alfred called them, supervised reading rooms; that the literature be non-religious but good literature like *Robinson Crusoe* or *Swiss Family Robinson*; and that the provincial effort be supported by lumber company owners, churches, and individual donations. Alfred was particularly complimentary about the support of the Woman's Christian Temperance Union, the Lady Aberdeen Association, which had supplied the workers with comfort bags, and of course the CPR for its "free of charge" rail passes.

In his report Alfred confronted head-on the arguments from influential corners that opposed the project: that many of the men would not use the libraries because they could not read, and that after a ten- to twelve-hour day of labour, the men would be too tired to read or study. To the second point, Alfred responded that the hours of labour for all working men should be shortened anyway so the men could have more leisure time. In the years to come he would frequently raise such objections to long hours of work.

In the final section of his "Introductory," under the title "Object of the Experiment," Alfred declared the object to be that the Ontario government, which received such a large revenue from the timber and mines of the province, should be prepared to set aside a small portion of this revenue for the benefit of the woodsmen and the miners. Alfred then provided a short financial statement that listed cash contributions for the first year, 1900–1901. It is indeed a short list, as it totals $49.50 with no expenses recorded. This list of donations would expand greatly in the years to come and be an integral part of the budget.

It is important to note that for those who gave what they could afford to support the association in the early twentieth century, whether it be fifty cents, a dollar, or more, there was no government recognition of charitable donations to be taken into account. Income tax would not be implemented in Canada until 1917, and the charitable donations deduction would not come into effect until 1930, so what was donated was not for a tax writeoff but because donors believed in the association.

There follows fifteen pages (half the length of the report) of endorsements from supporters, including quotations from mill owners, Protestant and Catholic ministries, newspapers like the *Globe* and the *North Boy Times*, universities, and of course, his mentor George Grant, principal of Queen's, who included the suggestion that "an indispensable requisite is the right man to supervise" and to keep the library running given "the actual conditions and temperament of miners and lumber workers."

In succeeding years, the annual reports would reflect in detail the efforts and changing nature of the Canadian Reading Camp Movement, as it would be named by the second annual report (1901–02); a year later it was finally named the Canadian Reading Camp Association. There was a certain format that was followed in these reports, each reflecting in its title the basic goals of the organization: "Home Education Expansion"; "Education of the Frontier Laborer"; "Reading Camp Association: Entertainment and Culture for Manual Laborers"; "Canada's Frontiersmen"; and "Camp Education by Contact." The words *camp* and *education* were usually on every title page. There was one mention of camp churches in the third annual report (1902–03), but it was noticeably absent in subsequent reports. As noted, the cover also frequently included an appropriate quotation related to education and labour: "It spoils my enjoyment of anything when I am made to think that most people are shut out from it" (George Eliot); and "That should there be one man die ignorant who had capacity for knowledge, this I call a tragedy" (Thomas Carlyle). As a reflection of what he was trying to do, Alfred included the entreaty of Nova Scotia's most prominent politician, Joseph Howe: "The time will come in Canada when the question you will ask people is not what party you belong to but what good movement have you assisted." Given his apolitical nature, this was likely Alfred's favourite.

Through the years to come and in report after report, Alfred, as Superintendent of Camp Education (so named by the Canadian Reading Camp Association board in 1904), presented his rationale for the importance of the association. He lobbied for the shortening of the working day to eight hours and linked this additional time to providing the means of self-improvement, with the most urgent need being intellectual development. He continued to call on the government to provide such educational access for the men. In his view, the Church meant well but had little if any influence in the isolated camps of Canada. The missionary might as well "save his elbow grease to sow the seed" in the more "cultivated" soil of the towns and cities. Thus, the responsibility must fall on the owners of industry, the departments of government, and the support of the Canadian people.

Like the first report, subsequent annual reports included letters of support from a variety of politicians and businessmen. For example, the president of the Georgian Bay Lumber Co., W. J. Shepherd in Waubaushene, Ontario, promised to supply a reading camp and "perhaps far more than one next year." Edmund Hall in Nairn Centre said he would pay his own money to build a reading room. No doubt there were many other businessmen who objected to this intrusion into their camps; literacy might give the men ideas.

Throughout his career, Alfred showed himself to be a very good "media man" with the newspapers. In his first report, he quoted the *Globe*, which had written in its "Press Notices" section of October 3, 1900, about his initiative. "It is a good plan, and we hope to see it working in time for the coming winter." Nearer to Nairn Centre, the *North Bay Times* touted the association's plan as one where men would be able to procure wholesome reading. It was a concept that should be welcomed and endorsed by every lumberman, said the *Times*. The *Renfrew Mercury* called it "the most sane mission work that we have heard of." There was also support from Quebec. *La Presse* wrote: "Cette oeuvre est appelée à faire beaucoup de bien, c'est pourquoi elle merite tout l'encouragement possible." Ontario's education department offered somewhat tepid support of it as long as the books were "properly selected."

In this period of early development, Alfred realized that an "illustrious" board with strong name recognition was essential. Although he had W. J. Bell of Nairn Centre, a prominent lumberman in the Algoma region, as the first treasurer in 1902, it was not until 1904–05 that the CRCA board really began to take shape. It included notable businessman A. P. Turner, president of the Canada Copper Company in Copper Cliff near Sudbury, as CRCA president; the afore-mentioned W. J. Bell as treasurer; and Speaker of the legislative assembly of Ontario, William Charlton, who was also a lumber merchant, as vice-president. Soon the board would expand into a more national body as the appeal for support for the organization went well beyond Northern Ontario.

As we have seen, the finances of the CRCA were precarious from its very beginnings, despite the presence of captains of industry on the board. As noted, the first year brought in meagre support, but as the profile of the association increased, due to Alfred's incessant lobbying, the contributions increased. Who were these contributors?

Fortunately, meticulous financial records were kept in the annual reports, and it is clear that the association had donations from a great variety of individuals, organizations, and governments across Canada and beyond. The amounts varied: one dollar from "a friend" in Alfred's old pastoral charge in Kincardine, and many, many fifty-cent, one-dollar, and two-dollar contributions from the small villages and towns of Canada. The first complete list, which was in the 1901–02 report, itemized the cash received in chronological order and totalled $1,538, including a donation from Alfred himself for $15.80. At this early stage, Alfred was only being reimbursed for his expenses, as he was still receiving his minister's salary, but that ceased in 1902. The total donations for 1902–03 amounted to $1,938.56.

By 1905–06, total donations had climbed to just over $3,900. The grant of one thousand dollars from the Ontario government in 1905 was particularly welcome.

Each report listed the names of the instructors, their university affiliation, and their various postings to such places as the Grand Trunk Pacific Construction in Touchwood Hills, Saskatchewan, or lumber camps in New Liskeard, Northern Ontario. In these early days, most instructors were undergraduate men from various universities such as McMaster, McGill, and Toronto. Each year thirty or forty were sent to the lumber camps for the winter, while some spent their summers working on railway construction and repair. Occasionally the yearly reports included the location and number of reading camps. In 1906–07, over twenty reading rooms, reading railway cars, and reading tents, all with "Everybody Welcome" signs at the entrance, had been established between Parry Sound, Ontario, and Regina, Saskatchewan. In addition, fifteen clubhouses and reading rooms had been built by companies, with employee assistance. These were in the coalfields of Alberta and the Creighton mines near Copper Cliff, Ontario.

To illustrate the work and camps, each report included an abundance of photographs—usually thirty or forty—of the instructors, the working men, the location, the classroom and camp structures, and how the work was done. Each photograph was captioned and in most cases had been taken during the year of the report. During these early years, these visuals—"Galicians Working on the Grade, G.T.P. Railway, Sask"; "Loading a Gravel Train"; and "The Water Tank used in making ice roads, Wahnapitac"—were usually taken by the instructor and provided valuable portrayals of the life and work conditions of Canada's scattered "peripheral" workforce in the first decade of the twentieth century. They were illustrative of the conditions that Alfred Fitzpatrick, through the association, wished to change.

Two stationmen at work in the Abibti District, Ontario, circa 1909. (LIBRARY
AND ARCHIVES CANADA/FRONTIER COLLEGE FONDS/A061813)

Photographs of board members were non-existent in these reports,
and Alfred himself rarely appeared. He remained in the background,
watching a class, for example. By contrast the instructors received
pride of place; there were numerous photographs of instructors
labouring or teaching. This reinforces the notion that Alfred was a
modest man who avoided the spotlight and was more comfortable
working behind the scenes.

Alfred distributed these increasingly detailed and illustrated
reports as he approached donors and sought to raise money for his
mission. He was no doubt aware just how taxing and difficult his
mission was becoming.

The year 1906 was one of self-questioning by Alfred Fitzpatrick. Certainly there had been successes: instructors had been deployed to Ontario in 1900, the North-West (soon to be renamed the province of Saskatchewan) in 1903, and Manitoba in 1906. In the annual report of 1905–06 entitled *The Frontier Laborer*, Alfred counted eight reading camps (i.e., reading rooms with instructors), one railway reading car, and sixteen reading rooms from Ontario to British Columbia. The "rooms" did not have instructors but were built "by the respective firms co-operating with their employees."

In 1906, the CRCA board was in place, with George Grant's friend Sir Sandford Fleming as honorary president and all the officers being men of position in the lumber and mining industry. As for Alfred, whereas he had served as General Secretary of the board since the founding of the association, as of 1904–05 his contribution to its success was rewarded with a new, more permanent position. At the bottom of the list of board members in the 1906 report appears "Superintendent of Camp Education, Alfred Fitzpatrick, B.A."

The 1906 report featured comments and descriptive memos from the field. Some, while positive, revealed the anti-ethnic attitudes of the time: "I had 12 Italians who came to the car for arithmetic, writing, and reading...I had 12 who came regularly and got along with the work rapidly, much to the surprise of the English spectators, who thought the [Italian] stronghold was the shovel and nothing higher. – A.J. Keeley, Reading Car, T.N.O.R'y 1906." Another comment demonstrates the great value some workers saw in the instruction being offered: "A miner, living in the country not a great way from the camp, gave up a job at $3.00 per day, that he might bring his boy to this camp 'to get more schooling,' as he put it. – Joseph Wearing, Conger Company's Camp, Parry Sound, 1906." That sentiment is echoed in a third comment: "With the present state of the 'Cobalt Fever' [gold had been discovered in 1906 in Cobalt], these Instruction Classes, as an aid to the hundreds of intending prospectors, have been much appreciated. – E. Bradwin, Cobalt, 1906."

The last excerpt refers to the instructor as Dr. Goodwin, of Queen's University, who was a geology professor as well as an assiduous extension educator for the university in his spare time. It was written by Edmund Bradwin, a tall, gangly University of Toronto dropout who would much later replace Alfred as principal of Frontier College.

On the financial side, Alfred, despite his lack of confidence in his fundraising capabilities, had collected almost five hundred separate donations in 1905–06, totalling $3,914, well above the first difficult year of activity. However, there were only eight instructors, and these were all from Ontario and all serving in the reading camps of that province. Not a healthy sign for a national organization.

The funding situation was still a disappointment to Alfred. He had lobbied the provincial governments for sufficient operating money and urged them to take over the responsibilities of the project. But he received only one thousand dollars in provincial government funding in 1905–06 and barely five hundred by early 1906 with the implied quid pro quo from Premier Whitney that Alfred run for office for his party. As noted earlier, Alfred rejected this offer out of hand.

Alfred had been successful in setting up the travelling libraries to the work camps; innovating with the concept of the worker instructor (later called labourer-teacher); and establishing reading rooms from Ontario to the Pacific. It had always been his goal to take the concept across the nation. His priorities as he stated them were to make reading a possibility, to inculcate morals and citizenship, to provide entertainment, and most importantly, to promote learning.

Despite all of his best efforts, or perhaps because of them, Alfred's correspondence began to reflect a weariness with the work, a sense that he had done all he could and could do no more. It is worth noting that for Alfred, forty-four years old in 1906 and clearly not especially well off financially, this was the longest period of time he had spent in one place. Perhaps it was time to move on.

Some insight into Alfred's discouragement appears in a letter (circa 1906) that he received from his nephew Reverend Luther Young who was serving as a Presbyterian missionary to the minority Koreans in Japan. In it, Young is obviously responding to an earlier letter from Alfred in which he complained about not accomplishing anything in his life. His nephew told him not to worry over his past and added, "You have lived a much better and more useful life than most men." Luther then went on to say that if good works meant salvation, then Alfred would have a better chance than the majority of men. He concluded with the observation, "thank God salvation is by faith," which was all that was needed for "time or eternity." Given that Alfred had ceased being a Presbyterian clergyman four years earlier, these words might not have been reassuring or comforting. It seemed, though, that he didn't need reassurance about his salvation or his faith. He wanted change but not the kind that would necessarily include his religious beliefs. In 1904, the Presbyterian Church had offered to assume responsibility for Alfred's work in the camps. Alfred rejected this proffered assistance unless the Church agreed to be non-sectarian, which, of course, the Church could not and would not agree to.

In February and March of 1906, Alfred exchanged a number of letters with his Queen's University classmate and roommate Reverend John Millar, who was now in Nanaimo, BC. Alfred wrote that he planned to resign his position and asked Millar to take up the work, as he did not wish to carry on. He then went on to outline why he wished to step down and what needed to be done to keep the CRCA alive. His major complaint was about financing. He was constantly borrowing money wherever he could get it. Over the previous four years the association had only compensated him for expenses. The association desperately needed a "strong financial committee," as he felt he was too disorganized to fulfill his financial duty. The Ontario government must be forced to fully support the CRCA. One strategy Alfred suggested was that if Millar agreed to assume the leadership role, Alfred would be prepared to become a long-term settler in Northern Ontario, and then he would be eligible to run for political office. If elected, he could pressure the education department "to take full responsibility." Alfred would also be free to carry out his experiment in literacy. If he stepped down, he and his wealthy brother, James William, would act on their plan to acquire a small lumber camp in Northern Ontario by the fall. They would hire fifteen to twenty men who would cut timber for not more than eight hours a day. The men would also have to agree to two hours a day of "intellectual labour." He wrote that men were currently working for ten, twelve, fourteen hours a day and were "kicked about like horses and dogs." Ever the optimist, Alfred added that when his experiment worked, he would pressure the Canadian government to make the scheme universal across the country.

Not surprisingly, Millar was hesitant and very reticent to assume such a position. He was already well-established in his church in Nanaimo and he expressed his doubts that the association was viable. In his reply, Alfred noted his lack of enthusiasm and urged him to take "divine guidance." The files contain no further exchanges of correspondence between the men, although Reverend Millar's name does continue to appear as a donor.

It is clear then that by 1906 Alfred had made some headway, but he was weary of the work. His major problems of administration and finances had to be faced or he could not go on. In the next couple of years, Alfred addressed these matters in surprising and quite unexpected ways as the mineral wealth of Northern Ontario allowed him to earn more money than he had ever seen.

CHAPTER 4

REVIVAL: ENABLERS OF ALFRED'S PASSION 1906–1914

J. W. FITZPATRICK

IN THE FIRST DECADE OF THE TWENTIETH CENTURY, RAIL connections ran northward from Union Station in Toronto to North Bay then on via the Temiskaming and Northern Ontario Railway to Cobalt and New Liskeard in the "New Ontario." At the turn of the century, passenger trains carried the gold watch–fobbed wealthy and the flannel shirted hope-to-be wealthy to the vast forests and potential riches of the gold and silver mines of Northern Ontario. Alfred's older brother James William, known as J.W. ("Uncle Jim" to the Fitzpatrick clan), was one of those speculators.

In 1903 during the construction of the Temiskaming and Northern Ontario Railway, high grade silver was discovered in the bedrock as the labourers felled trees and dynamited the granite that littered the landscape like blocks in a giant's playroom. By 1904 the silver rush was on, and a town called Cobalt, named for the by-product of silver, soon came into existence four hundred kilometres due

Cobalt, Ontario, 1906. The wooden building to the right is being constructed to house the classroom and office of the Reading Camp Association. (LAURENTIAN UNIVERSITY ARCHIVES/P230 PETER FANCY FONDS)

north of Toronto. In 1906, the year that Alfred Fitzpatrick sought to wind up his work with the Reading Camp Association, forty-four stockbrokers from New York took a week-long round trip expedition in three luxurious private railcars to investigate the potential of the silver boom and perhaps invest in the "tent city" of Cobalt. This particular excursion began in New York and likely picked up a number of eager moguls in Toronto as well. The moneyed interests of Toronto were now bound by these sturdy bracelets of steel to a booming financial frontier that would produce over eight million dollars of silver ore by 1906. Within two years, by 1908, with a flood of speculators and prospectors seeking to tap the wealth of the wilderness, the Cobalt area became the world's largest producer of silver.

In his classic *Sunshine Sketches of a Little Town* (1912), humourist Stephen Leacock described life in the fictional small town of Mariposa, Ontario, situated north of Toronto and believed by many to be based on the real town of Orillia, one hundred kilometres north of Toronto between Lake Simcoe and Lake Couchiching. Here Leacock, who taught political economy at McGill University in Montreal, would spend his summers writing from his summer house at Old Brewery Bay. In *Sunshine Sketches* he described the night train express through Mariposa as it steamed north with flashing windows of brilliant light. Within the Pullman coach, "a vista of cut glass and snow white table linen, smiling negroes and millionaires with napkins at their chins" whirled past.

J. W. Fitzgerald could well have been on one of those flashing trains. In the early twentieth century, J.W. decided to retire from the Mutual Life Insurance Company and move back to Canada. He had amassed a considerable fortune for the time—well over three hundred thousand dollars—but he still continuously sought new investments. Northern Ontario seemed like a sure thing. J.W. was an aggressive and fiery-tempered man, and his photographs reveal a commanding presence behind his white handlebar moustache. He no doubt believed he had an advantage in that his brother Alfred had established a reading camp in the centre of the boom town Cobalt and thus would be well informed as to the investment possibilities there. On his journey north from Toronto by rail, J.W. was greatly impressed by the economic future of New Ontario—the wealth and variety of forests, the neophyte mining possibilities, and the clay belt of prime farmland beyond Cobalt where lay New Liskeard and Haileybury.

J.W. was soon financially involved in the region. Photos show the rapid development of Cobalt from a number of tents and shanties around a railway station in 1905 to several framed three- and four-storey buildings along the rail tracks the next year. By 1909, Cobalt had a population of over ten thousand people with a two-storey Bank of Commerce in the town centre. Right next door was a Reading Camp Association structure, well positioned for any "literacy drop-ins."

J.W. realized very quickly that new logistics would be crucial to the success of the mining industry and began construction of the Nipissing Central Railway, a "street railroad" that ran north some five miles to Haileybury. J.W. became president of the railway, which would later be sold and added on to the Temiskaming and Northern Ontario Railway. He also bought property on the Wendigo River so he could control the waterfalls, intending to produce electric power, which, with the mushrooming community, would be in great demand. He would lose out on this venture in a celebrated court case some fifteen years later as the Government of Ontario won its claim of a right to all waterfalls. J.W. was also somewhat less successful with his and Alfred's mining initiatives.

Oral tradition about their venture capitalism collected from Jessie Lucas, later administrative secretary of the Reading Camp Association, recounted that around 1906 J.W. had acquired a promising property near what would become Timmins, Ontario. Both silver and gold fever was rife, and J.W. and Alfred were each interested in success for different reasons: J.W. to secure his retirement, and Alfred to achieve some financial stability for his Reading Camp Association and perhaps for himself as well.

It is clear from Alfred's correspondence through the years that he hated to fundraise and accepted that he did not have the personality to be successful. He was big on ideas and vision but not so much the practical, everyday means of fulfilling what was required financially. If this property near Timmins proved to be a "strike," his financial difficulties would be a thing of the past.

J.W. and Alfred sought the best advice they could obtain and brought in a "mining man" from Harvard University to advise them. This geologist reported that there was gold but not in paying quantities.

Discouraged, they dropped the project and sold the property, which eventually fell into the hands of Benny Hollinger. In 1909, Hollinger discovered gold-bearing quartz on the property that became Hollinger Mines. Hollinger Mines was incorporated in 1910 under a new president, Noah Timmins. Within a decade, it would become the largest gold mine in the British Empire with annual dividends of five million dollars. Not surprisingly, in 1912 this company town was named Timmins.

It would appear that the Fitzpatrick brothers had lost out on their big strike. Nevertheless, there must have been a few financial successes. Over the next three years, Alfred had enough funding to support many of the Reading Camp Association's initiatives either with the money he had earned from various mining ventures or in collaboration with J.W., although how much came from his brother is not known. In the treasurer's report of the association's yearly financial statements from 1907 to 1911, "A. Fitzpatrick" is listed as providing loans to the association amounting to over twelve thousand dollars. Alfred, in a financial statement written in the 1920s, noted that he also lost some of this money when his business associates did not pay the men for their work; as he felt he had a financial and ethical obligation, Alfred paid them himself. There is no record of J.W. providing support for Alfred or his association at this time, but given that Alfred had committed himself to looking after their brother Thomas, who now lived with him, presumably J.W. was supplying surreptitious additions to whatever money Alfred was able to raise to keep the association afloat and provide for Thomas. Really, there is little evidence to support this conclusion. J.W.'s name would appear on the list of donors only once in the years to come—in 1921. There, it was noted that he lived in New Liskeard and that he made a donation of six dollars.

In 1910, J.W. had begun to withdraw from speculative undertakings. He was now sixty and he decided to fully settle in the area around Cobalt. He purchased a 330 acre property that year at Dawson's Point on the shores of Lake Temiskaming, and recalling his roots in Millsville, turned his hand to farming the extensive clay belt around New Liskeard, an area that he felt had a splendid farming future. In succeeding years, 120 acres were cleared and a house, two barns, and stables were built. It was said to be the best equipped farm in Nipissing district with running water in every barn stall and up-to-date machinery—tractors, a binder, and a threshing machine—making it a very modern farm for its time. Long after Alfred and Thomas moved to Toronto, J.W. remained in New Liskeard on his farm. Alfred would visit him whenever his travels took him north. J.W. died in 1928. The Reading Camp Association office of his brother Alfred had long since moved on.

It used to be said of Alfred Fitzpatrick that he didn't have an office, merely a vest pocket from which the association operated. He was a man always on the move, but the more he visited Toronto, the more he realized that he and his office would have to relocate. From Toronto, it would be an easy train journey to Northern Ontario and beyond. A considerable number of his many wealthy benefactors had their head offices in Toronto, the major newspapers with whom he had close relations were also there, and finally he would be closer to the provincial department of education, which he could continue to lobby even more intensively.

In 1906, Alfred and his "vest pocket office" was operating out of 98 Walker Street, south of St. Clair Avenue West just off Yonge Street, Toronto's main north-south corridor. It was not exactly downtown in 1906 Toronto and therefore not expensive. Alfred stayed for a few months and then returned to Cobalt with the association and worked out of his brother's house on Dawson's Point.

It was during this time that the silver rush increased its momentum, and he and J.W. became deeply involved in speculating for wealth. Within two years the mineral wealth seemed to be exhausted, and the Reading Camp Association moved permanently to Toronto, opening an office in the Traders Bank Building, 67 Yonge Street. This was a more central and prestigious location but was also a more expensive location. Alfred, however, could afford this new placement because of the wealth he and J.W. had acquired.

Together with his brother, Alfred was listed as a director on the board of their Searchlight Larder Lake Mines Ltd. with the title "Educationist" in subscript beneath his name in the company brochure of 1907. By 1908, the City of Toronto Directory shows that Suite #1123 of the Traders Bank on Yonge Street housed the Reading Camp Association as well as the Searchlight Larder Lake company and J.W.'s other company, Combined Goldfields. This location was quite convenient for the peripatetic Alfred as the Canadian Pacific Railway pass department was right next door. By 1909, another Fitzpatrick company, Cobalt Mines, was added to the door plaque.

A year later, 1910, as investments showed little improvement, the association and the companies vacated the Traders Bank Building. Alfred's financial situation was no longer as promising as it had been, and so the new office for the association, without the mining companies listed, was now in a less favourable location, namely 43 Victoria Street on the corner of Victoria and Adelaide Street East, a number of blocks away from the prime location on Yonge Street. It was clear from the association's budget that the family "boom" had become a "bust," and Alfred had little financial wherewithal to continue to lend money to the association.

Never a spendthrift, Alfred was quite abstemious in this period and in the succeeding years. Throughout his life, he never owned a house and always lived in rented rooms or stayed with friends.

Between 1906 and 1913, true to his nature, he moved five times and would continue this pattern until his death in 1936. He never seemed settled in Toronto as his focus was always on the isolated men far removed from the towns and cities. Cities like Toronto, in Alfred's view, enjoyed the abundant wealth that "his campmen" produced but did not share it. Passion and compassion would, he believed, make their situation better. He would soon have a like-minded partner in this regard, who had already been hired by the Reading Camp Association.

EDMUND BRADWIN

Edmund W. Bradwin joined the Reading Camp Association in 1903 and over the next three decades would become the enabler of Alfred's ambition, first as a labourer-teacher, then assistant, associate, and finally an equal. Bradwin would in the end disavow Fitzpatrick's aspirational goals in 1931. Of the many, many acquaintances in Fitzpatrick's life, Bradwin was the closest to an alter ego. Each of them shared a passion for literacy and a sympathy for the manual worker and the underdog.

Edmund Bradwin was born in 1877 in the small community of Lynden, twenty-five kilometres southwest of Hamilton, Ontario. At a young age he moved with his parents to Wingham, 160 kilometres west of Toronto, where he completed his public school and high school education. Wingham was settled in the 1850s and was incorporated as a town in 1878 with a population of close to two thousand. With the railway expansion in the 1870s and 1880s, it became an important supply and distribution centre to the burgeoning lumber woods in the hinterland of the town. By 1898, the new factory of the Conestoga Chair Company was turning out hardwood chairs, and soon a door manufacturing company was established. Like the other settlements of Northern Ontario, Wingham was very dependent on the timber trade and the woods workers who frequented the town on the weekends.

After graduating from high school, Bradwin took a course in teacher training in the Model School in Clinton, some thirty-five kilometres from Wingham. After completing this course, he taught at an upgraded school in Culross Township, ten kilometres north of Wingham, for five years. Whether he walked home each day to Wingham or boarded in Culross Township is not known, but Bradwin was known to be close with his money, and by 1901 he had saved enough to enrol at the University of Toronto.

Between 1901 and 1903, Bradwin engaged in two different attempts to study chemistry and mineralogy at Victoria College, University of Toronto, which he'd been told was the "manly" thing to do. However, his interest in English and history led him to spend long periods of time in the library at the expense of his studies in science. By 1903, he decided to discontinue his studies due to his "broken courses," as he called them. In other words, he "flunked out." Ironically, a half century later he would receive an LL.D. from the University of Toronto in recognition of his work with the organization that he was about to join, the Reading Camp Association, precursor to Frontier College. He would work with the association/college until his death in 1954.

Somehow Bradwin learned of the association and by late 1903 he was a swamper removing the mud and muck from swamps and bogs for the roads of the Conger Company lumber camp in Parry Sound, two hundred kilometres south of Nairn Centre, and instructing the men he worked with at night. This, he wrote, he would rather do than the more regular class routine. In fact, he once remarked that he would rather teach than eat. A tall, well-built man, Bradwin would go on to be a navvy, the term used for unclassified labour, with the Temiskaming and Northern Ontario Railway camps near White River from 1904 to 1906 and a navvy and packer (or carrier of supplies) in various lumber, mining, and construction camps from 1906 to 1911.

Working in the lumber woods was not the destiny that Bradwin had imagined for himself. In fact, he confessed twenty years later in his book *The Bunkhouse Man: A Study of Work and Pay in the Camps of Canada, 1903–14* (1929) that before his involvement with the association in 1903–04 he had never seen the inside of a lumber work camp. In the book he explained that his attraction to the work was due to the "appeal of a new endeavour" to a young man and "the challenge of serving as a preceptor and teacher to the men of the bunkhouse."

Within two years he became both worker in camps and supervisor of other instructors in Northern Ontario and Northern Quebec. Being a supervisor meant packing and carrying books, magazines, and other supplies with "tump-and-line" to isolated camps and solitary instructors, thus gaining a practical knowledge of various camp work tasks and, more importantly, how the instructor-worker was coping with his environment, his employment, and his students. This decade-long experience of supervision would have a lasting impact on Bradwin's later interaction with the ongoing operations of the Reading Camp Association. In that regard, between 1907 and 1914 he built two dozen log buildings to serve as centres of instruction in the various bush camps north of Georgian Bay. Many tents were erected and box cars reserved for the same purpose. His travels would also provide Bradwin with the research information that would form a major component of his doctoral studies at Columbia University, some twenty years later.

But first things first. Bradwin needed an undergraduate degree in order to go on. That would be the challenge.

By 1907, Bradwin was thirty years old and was in no position to go back to university. Few universities in Canada at that time engaged in extension teaching or adult education. The circle of camps that Bradwin orbited throughout Northern Ontario were a long way from the academic cloisters of his original university of choice in Toronto, and Toronto did not offer any extramural courses. A complete extramural degree would be impossible. Those universities that did offer such courses insisted that the student complete at least half of their degree studies on campus. As prominent Canadian adult educationalist E. A. Corbett remarked about the mindset of higher education in the first three decades of the twentieth century, "adult education had no name and no social standing." Fitzpatrick himself wrote that adult education was a "daydream of visionaries."

In terms of extension courses, there was one definite option for Bradwin and that was Queen's University in Kingston. Being an alumnus and very aware of the university's program, Alfred convinced Bradwin that Queen's was his best choice, and by 1907, Bradwin had been accepted by Queen's and was studying part-time. With Alfred granting him time off from his duties, Bradwin completed a Bachelor of Arts in 1913 with honours in history, his favourite subject, and economics. A year later, in 1914, he received his Master of Arts—both degrees without ever attending a class at Queen's. This academic success, receiving two degrees by extension studies, was a harbinger of things to come for the Reading Camp Association as it evolved into Frontier College later in the decade. Bradwin's successes, however, would also raise considerable tensions between Bradwin and his boss, Alfred, which are detailed in the next chapter.

Much that was known about the difficult conditions in the work camps of Canada in the first fifteen years of the twentieth century can be attributed to one of the few eyewitnesses to provide a detailed account—Edmund Bradwin. Having completed his M.A. at Queen's

Edmund Bradwin, circa 1914. (**LIBRARY AND ARCHIVES CANADA/ FRONTIER COLLEGE FONDS/C-47542**)

in 1914, Bradwin was accepted for a doctoral program at Columbia University in January 1915. He took time off from his duties at the association and enrolled in the fields of economics and industrial history and studied economic theory, sociology, and Marxian socialism. This last course was especially important as it was related to what was happening in Europe following the Russian Revolution and to the distinct possibility of social unrest in the Canadian work camps. So Bradwin took the course not to be radicalized but to counteract those who, in his view, were. By 1922, he completed his coursework and began to write his dissertation, still fully employed by what had become Frontier College. His topic was a study of work and pay in the camps of Canada from 1903 to 1914, no doubt based on his personal experiences in such camps during that time period. His dissertation entitled "The Bunkhouse Man," was accepted in 1922 and in 1929 was published in Columbia University's *Studies in History, Economics and Public Law*. Reviewed widely by both academic and popular press that year, it was praised with comments like "vivid pictures of the life of the camp men" and "their conditions are far from that which is to be desired."

"Canada is still a land of camps!" Bradwin would often declare. He observed that there were some three thousand large camps in operation throughout Canada whose activities included logging, mining, railway work, and hydro development. On average well over 250,000 men in a country with a population of five million were employed at one time or other in these camps. Few Canadians realized the debt owed these workers or the great responsibility for health and education that had not been provided for them by the companies or the shareholders. He concluded that there were definite tendencies in these camps for owners to maintain conditions that were "lesser forms of serfdom," as Bradwin put it. Indeed, as Donald Avery observed in his *Dangerous Foreigners* (1979), these workers, the majority being immigrants, "existed near the border between subsistence and destitution." Bradwin's goal in raising these issues was to obtain for the migratory worker more security for their jobs, their pay, and their health.

Who were these workers?

When Alfred Fitzpatrick began his efforts in the camps of Northern Ontario in 1900, the Canadian labour supply was on the cusp of change. Canada's Minister of the Interior, Clifford Sifton, had urged the Canadian government in the late 1890s to accept east-central Europe's "stalwart peasants in sheep-skin coats" to settle and farm western Canada. In Rome in 1906, Sir Wilfred Laurier, the Canadian prime minister, said to his Italian hosts, "Vous avez une belle race. We require good European arms; this year we need at least fifty thousand immigrants to help build new Canadian railroads." Workers were needed for other purposes as well: the harvesting of natural resources like lumber, wheat, and minerals; the building of a system of trains and roads; and working in the industries, factories, and workshops of the urban centres. Between 1900 and 1914 the Canadian government was attracting both agricultural settlers and, just as importantly, an industrial proletariat. In this transatlantic, mobile labour market, the migrant labourer would work for a short period in Canada and then move on to work in other parts of the world. Eventually some of these immigrant labourers settled in Canada. In the decade between 1896 and 1905, the annual number of immigrants arriving in Canada increased by almost 800 percent from 16,835 to 141,465, and in the years to follow many, many more would be part of this economic wave from Europe that washed over the beckoning frontiers of a rapidly industrializing Canada. This would soon require not only economic accommodation but social and cultural accommodation as well.

A vociferous public debate about immigration and what type of society Canada would become dominated the media and preoccupied the literati of the early twentieth century. Canadian historians,

Lumber camp workers travelled along the "tote" road daily, going in and out of the woods. Photo taken circa 1910. (**LIBRARY AND ARCHIVES CANADA/FRONTIER COLLEGE FONDS/PA-079006**)

like Howard Palmer in his essay in *Immigration in Canada*, stated that twentieth-century Canadian society maintained three progressively changing attitudes to the new immigrant—conformity, assimilation, and later, multiculturalism. The first was an expectation of "Anglo-conformity" in the face of large-scale immigration in the early twentieth century—a migration that confronted Canadians for the first time with extensive ethnic diversity. By 1911, the percentage of recent immigrants within the Canadian population reached twenty-two. Public reaction was increasingly an ideology of assimilation—a strict conformity to the Canadian "norms" of a Christian God, a British king, and an assumption of white Anglo-Saxon male authority.

According to many, there were desirable immigrants who were judged to be culturally similar to the Canadian norm, like the Northern (Scandinavian) and Western European. Below that line, as reflected in the much-cited book *Strangers Within Our Gates* (1909) by Methodist minister J. S. Woodsworth, were the "others"—those from southeastern Europe, the Balkan states, Levantine races, "Orientals," "Negroes," and East Indians, in that order. Although sympathetic to the individual immigrant, Woodsworth cast them into nationality molds of stereotyped group characteristics. These attributes, as described by Woodsworth, reflected the tenor of his times, a time when the ethos of the Canadian nation, at least among English speakers, was Anglo-Saxon, Christian, and imperial. At the beginning of the twentieth century this was the social milieu in which well-read English-speaking Protestant Canadians, like Fitzpatrick and Bradwin, worked and lived.

Bradwin's dissertation for Columbia University described in minute detail just how the camps functioned, everything from the job of the "chore boys" to the dimensions of the bunkhouse—average size 34 by 52 feet. He described bunks bedded with hay, rampant with vermin, and dark, dungeon-like buildings without windows and with leaky roofs. In such an environment, with ten to twelve hours of labour a day, "there is a weariness of heart, a blank feeling." It was also a dangerous life. In *Dangerous Foreigners*, Avery writes that between 1904 and 1911 there were almost ten thousand fatal industrial accidents (recorded) in Canada; 23 percent of these were related to the railway industry. Government inspection was infrequent or non-existent in the more isolated camps, and even if there was a complaint, the response was "love it or leave it." Many workers did jump camp, but as immigrant, unskilled labourers they had nowhere else to go but to another camp. It was not a huge problem for the owners as new immigrant labour was arriving daily in Montreal or Halifax on ships from Europe. Once they stepped ashore they

The small lumber camp bunkhouses accommodated up to eighty men in close quarters. Photo taken circa 1925. **(LIBRARY AND ARCHIVES CANADA/FRONTIER COLLEGE FONDS/C038620)**

could be easily recruited by private contractors. Desperate for work, the newly arrived immigrant soon signed a contract, sealed with a handshake, and in a matter of hours was on a train to a hay-strewn bunk in the Canadian bush. Bradwin described this individual as Canada's national asset; he deserved fair pay, fair work hours, and an equal opportunity for social improvement. Fitzpatrick had indeed found a partner for his cause.

THE LABOURER-TEACHER RECRUITS

Fitzpatrick and Bradwin now urgently sought "junior partners" to pursue this goal of social improvement for all, as Bradwin described it. These labourer-teachers were required to meet a strict criteria. Recruited from large universities (50 percent in the first twenty years were from U of T and Queen's), they were young males, usually in an arts program or possibly a medical student, Christian (or at least a nominal one), strong and physically fit, and prepared to undertake, as Bradwin would later describe it, "Hard work, low pay, and the experience of a lifetime." They should be prepared for isolation as well as for a true test of their physical and mental endurance. They must also be devoted to social justice and the importance of literacy skills and, as one writer put it, be a bit left of centre politically. One such recruit, Norman Bethune, was thus an ideal candidate.

A second-year medical student at the University of Toronto and a Presbyterian "son of the manse," Bethune was certainly qualified. In October of 1911, he arrived at his Reading Camp Association posting at Pinage Lake, a logging camp close to Whitefish, near Sudbury, Ontario. He was no neophyte to the woods camps of Northern Ontario, as he had previously found work in the construction camps of Algoma District in 1907 and 1908. As a seventeen-year-old he had worked with the men a standard six days a week, ten hours a day, and slept and ate in the drafty log bunkhouses in a fog of sweat, smells, and smoke. In order to earn enough money to attend university he took a teaching position in a one-room school in Edgeley, just northwest of Toronto, in January 1909. Thus, he had the necessary requisites of a camp instructor—a strong back, teaching experience, work experience, and a commitment, as he would later write, to teach the men the English language before they left the camp in the spring. By October 1909, he entered the University of Toronto, intending to enrol in the faculty of medicine. However, after two not very successful terms he decided to return to his beloved Algoma

District to earn his university tuition and perhaps refocus on what he really wanted to do. The Reading Camp Association provided him the opportunity to do both.

The camp in Whitefish, Martin's Camp, was one of many owned by the Victoria Harbour Lumber Company, which was situated in Victoria Harbour on the southwest tip of Georgian Bay. Founded in 1886 by Toronto-based businessman and federal politician John Waldie, the company was, according to one writer, considered one of the "pioneer lumber manufacturing companies in Georgian Bay district," harvesting the extensive white and red pine of the Great Lakes–St. Lawrence forest region and controlling the many subcontracted lumber camps situated on the north and northeast shores of Georgian Bay. In the three logging seasons of 1904 to 1906, for example, almost half a million logs were cut, amounting to twenty million board feet. Crown land had been purchased from the Ontario government by many such companies, which succeeded in transforming the timber value of Crown land into cash revenue for the provincial treasury. Between 1900 and 1920, revenue from timber amounted to 20 percent or more of Ontario's budgetary income.

As for the Indigenous Peoples of Northern Ontario, whose values and cultures were intimately bound with the forests, they received little consideration or compensation. Treaty 9, the James Bay Treaty of 1905–06, had been negotiated by the governments of Canada and Ontario with the Cree, the Anishinaabe (Ojibwe), and other Indigenous Peoples who occupied the land. Thirty years before, these Peoples had protested the increasing presence of non-Indigenous trappers and prospectors on their land. With Treaty 9, the great wealth of forest, minerals, and streams passed out of their hands and they were confined to reserves, land chosen by the Ontario government. By order-in-council in 1905, the provincial government announced its intentions to open Northern Ontario—233,100 square kilometres of it—to settlement, trade, mining, lumbering, and immigration. Treaty 9 was finalized in 1906; clearly the Cree and Anishinaabe were not considered a part of Ontario's future. They were limited to resource collection, and a few got jobs in the scattered logging camps. One or two Indigenous people appear in the iconic photograph of Bethune and other workers in 1912, and others are listed in the attendance records of the CRCA instructors.

The area around Pinage Lake where Martin's Camp was situated was purchased by John Waldie for one million dollars. According to the *Orillia Times*, 1911 promised to be "one of the best seasons for the company in years." It is very doubtful that Norman Bethune knew any of these particulars about the Victoria Harbour Lumber Company when he arrived in October 1911 for a winter's work of logging and teaching. Given his later experiences and political commitments, if he had known, he may well have decided not to participate in the company's work.

By all accounts Bethune's employment at Martin's Camp was a success, and his activities mirror what many Reading Camp Association instructors across Canada had done and would continue to do in the years to come. Fortunately, the exchange of letters between Bethune and the association in Toronto have survived, and they detail the activities of a typical instructor.

Alfred Fitzpatrick had lobbied the various railway companies in Canada to provide free transportation for instructors to their work sites, so Bethune, armed with a CNR pass, two letters of introduction to the company foremen, and of course lugging two boxes of books and magazines, arrived in early October at the beginning of the winter woodcut. His first week was spent laying in a supply of wood, plastering the holes in the roof and log walls of the reading room, and arranging shelves, desks, and benches. The first couple of weeks were also spent getting accustomed to the long, difficult days of work, which earned him sore, blistered hands and "fully-developed symptoms of a kink in my vertebral column." However, he wrote of enjoying the experience and set about providing for his students by ordering notepads, a small English dictionary, copies of the *Illustrated London News* and other magazines, as well as a selection of records for the wind-up phonograph. He also sent for instruction books in German, Polish, Hungarian, and French for at least a dozen of the men in camp who could not speak English. In late December 1911 he helped transport a "Pollack" who had broken his leg by horse team to Whitefish, then by train to hospital in Sudbury. There are few observations by him about his interactions with the men out of class or on the job; however, his reading camp assessment included references to him leading the men in Saturday night singsongs and a Sunday service. Indeed, as woodsmen often composed their own songs, he may have heard or even led one such composition about their bosses, Robert (Bob) Waldie, owner of the Victoria Harbour Lumber Company, and Manley Chew, a lumberman who owned sawmills in Midland at the southern end of Georgian Bay:

Who feeds us beans? Who feeds us tea?
Manley Chew and Bob Waldie,
Who thinks that nothing else will do?
Bob Waldie and Manley Chew.
We make the big pines fall kerplash
And hit the ground with an awful smash
But for the logs, who gets the cash?
Manley Chew and Bob Waldie.

Prince Edward Island songwriter Larry Gorman (1846–1917), also known as "the man who made the songs," once said that the lumberman's life is of short duration, "made up of tobacco, hard work, and bad rum." Music and satirical singsongs may have helped them live longer.

By the end of the year, Bethune reported that class work was going well although his class numbers declined greatly due to the usual "jumping" (leaving the camp) around Christmas by the migrant workers who sought better work conditions or simply moved on.

Both Bradwin and Fitzpatrick visited every instructor in their workplace, and Fitzpatrick arrived on February 16, 1912, to see Bethune. As can be seen by the many photographs in the association's annual reports and the several thousand in the Library and Archives Canada collection, Fitzpatrick made every effort to record visually where his instructors were and what they were doing for his yearly reports and fundraising. Thus, when he arrived in Martin's Camp, he had a professional photographer with him who promptly composed and shot perhaps the most viewed photograph in the Frontier College collection. Standing with a group of men, there is Norman Bethune, in the vainglorious stance of a twenty-year-old, arms akimbo, legs spread, and head thrown back—an intimation perhaps of what was to come in his life. By contrast, behind him, third man from the right, Alfred Fitzpatrick stands in the background, modestly blending in. He reported back to the association office that "Bethune is getting along OK."

In mid-March, the snow and ice began to melt. The winter work season was completed, and Bethune travelled to Toronto to receive his pay from the association for teaching—$120 for the winter. He had already received his monthly pay from the lumber company of $25 to $30 a month, plus board. He did request a summer appointment with the association on the railway or in a construction camp, but no positions were available. October 1912 saw him back at University of Toronto to pursue his medical studies.

What long-term influence his experience at Martin's Camp had on Bethune is impossible to say. He would go on to serve in the First World War and in the Spanish Civil War as a medic. Recognized as a medical innovator for having developed a mobile blood transfusion

Norman Bethune, fourth from the left, proudly poses at Martin's Camp in 1912. Alfred Fitzpatrick stands to the side, third from the right. **(LIBRARY AND ARCHIVES CANADA/FRONTIER COLLEGE FONDS/C056826)**

service on the battle front, Bethune, by now a prominent communist, travelled to China and served the Communist Party and China's Eighth Route Army until his death from blood poisoning in 1939. Bethune once stated, "Let us say to the people not 'How much have you got?' but 'How best can we serve you?'" Fitzpatrick would have agreed.

It is beyond the scope of this book to detail the work of the many other instructors for the association. Their motivations, goals, and values are as difficult to ascribe as it is to measure what impact if any their work and teaching responsibilities had over the long term on them and those they taught. Bethune's experience has been detailed as a case study, but conditions would vary with each individual and each locale.

Still, the responsibilities remained the same, and as would be expected the outcomes differed dramatically. Below are three more examples.

Joseph W. Noseworthy, a student at Victoria College, Toronto, worked for the association as a carpenter in Port Nelson for the Canadian Department of Railways and Canals in 1914, then spent three summers with the McIntyre Mine, Schumacher, Ontario, also as a carpenter, and completed his last summer in Timmins. Born in Newfoundland, Noseworthy went on to teach high school, and in 1942, as a member of the Co-operative Commonwealth Federation (CCF), later the New Democratic Party, he defeated former Canadian prime minister Arthur Meighen in a by-election in York South, Ontario. He served for ten years as a Member of Parliament in Ottawa. He frequently defended the rights of immigrants and minorities until his death in 1956.

At the age of nineteen, John P. Bickell was posted to the Rat Portage Lumber Company at Lake of the Woods for the winter of 1903–04. "Jack" was also a "son of the manse," his father being Presbyterian minister Reverend David Bickell. Jack's time with the association introduced him to the opportunities of wealth in Northern Ontario. In 1911, he became involved with the gold mining industry in Cobalt and invested in McIntyre–Porcupine Mines Ltd., of which he later became president. Over the next three-quarters of a century, the company produced over ten million ounces of gold and became one of Canada's most successful mines. Jack had started his own brokerage firm in 1907, and with the success of the McIntyre–Porcupine Mines Ltd. he was a millionaire by the age of thirty. Bickell would be of great assistance to Frontier College in later years as donor, fundraiser, and lobbyist. John P. Bickell died in New York in 1951.

Finally, there was young James Ralph Mutchmor, who was interviewed by Edmund Bradwin in 1911 for a railway job with the Grand Trunk Pacific Railway. He was asked his first name by Bradwin and he replied "Ralph." Bradwin frowned and asked if he had another name. "Jim" was the response. "Jim is a better name for the railway," Bradwin directed. In time, "Jim" Mutchmor, instructor, would become a Presbyterian minister, an outspoken humanitarian, and eventual Moderator of the United Church of Canada. His experience with the Reading Camp Association was definitive. In his autobiography, *Mutchmor: The Memoirs of James Ralph Mutchmor* (1965), he wrote: "My five summers on railway construction put into my soul the iron to resolve to stand up for the working man. To sleep in lousy bunkhouses, to be forced to eat salt pork, vulgarly called sowbelly, to be pushed around and sworn at, and to be ordered when very tired to do overtime at ordinary pay, had only one dividend for me: a determination to get a square deal for the low-paid worker."

Mutchmor spent five consecutive years as a navvy in places like Cochrane, Fauquier, and Renfrew in Ontario. Later he would write of the men, generally the Slavs, who did much of the work for very little reward. They had nothing to sell but their labour and were often paid by contractors "whose loaded guns were on the table. ... It was take it or leave it." Mutchmor remarked that these men would become early members of the newly formed Communist Party in northern Winnipeg by the 1920s. As a graduate of University College, Toronto, Mutchmor attended Columbia University in 1914 for his M.A. and Bachelor of Divinity and became a prominent and controversial voice of the United Church, leading a number of delegations to the federal government well into the 1970s demanding improved social conditions.

In the first half-century of the Reading Camp Association / Frontier College (1900–1950), on average over seventy instructors or labourer-teachers served each year in winter and summer employment. Several thousand men were enrolled in regular classes, thousands of discussion groups were held annually, and four million magazines and one hundred thousand books were distributed. It would be impossible to measure the impact of this experience on all these young men and the approximately twenty women who were posted. For some it may have simply been a summer job, for others a way to travel to parts of the country they had not seen. There were also many like Bethune, Noseworthy, Bickell, and Mutchmor whose time with the Reading Camp Association was a life-changing experience that shaped their destinies.

Unfortunately, the documents available do not allow for a similar analysis of those that were taught. Illiteracy and lack of language skills play a large part in this. Still, most instructors maintained a list of their students' names with observations about their progress. A table in Appendix B of Alfred Fitzpatrick's *The University in Overalls* (1920) included a cross-section of the average pulp and paper camp students with name, nationality, language, age, time in camp, use of reading room, and progress of student. It included names like Roudolph Lausch (German), Aaron Swanson (Swede), and John Shaganash (Indigenous). Of the eighty men listed, the ages varied from sixteen to fifty-seven, and 50 percent had left camp after one month of work for another camp, other work, or home. Many made use of the reading room, and their progress, where noted, was "slight," "fair," "good," or "very good." Fitzpatrick stated that all universities owed something to these men and that they should assist in providing a well qualified instructor (either faculty member or student) in every camp. What the long-term impact was on the workers that were taught cannot be known.

The documentary evidence is scattered and fragmentary. In addition, too much time has passed for any oral history collection from the workers of this period. However, there does exist the extensive Frontier College document and photograph collection in Library and Archives Canada.

By 1910, the Reading Camp Association office was established at 43 Victoria Street, Toronto, in what they hoped would be a permanent home outside of Fitzpatrick's vest pocket. The record of the ninth annual general meeting of the association, held in 1910 in the Aberdeen Chambers, was written in a clear pen script and represents the first minutes to survive from that initial, somewhat nomadic decade of the organization. It was a small, rather intimate gathering commencing at twelve noon and presided over by the association president, H. L. Lovering. Lovering was the wealthy owner of the H. L. Lovering Lumber Company in Coldwater, near Orillia, Ontario, established in 1882. He had been association president for four years. Others sitting around the table in the office were Lt-Col. D. M. Robertson, treasurer, who was widely known in the mining and paper industries of Toronto as a prominent barrister and solicitor; Alfred Fitzpatrick, Superintendent of Camp Education; and two of his staff, Ed Bradwin, Ontario Secretary based in Cochrane, Ontario, and Joseph Wearing, Associate Western Secretary, Toronto. The board also consisted of a veritable who's who of businessmen, railway presidents, and politicians, all of whom, despite their absence that day, were quickly reconfirmed as board members. Their role was usually perfunctory and well understood—to provide financial support, to lobby government and industry on behalf of the association, and to ensure that positions were found for working instructors.

The officers on the board that year included lumber company owners, railway executives, and mining entrepreneurs. Men like James Playfair, president, Midland Navigation Company of Ontario; W. J. Guest of Guest Fish Co. in Winnipeg; J. B. Miller, president, Polson Iron Works, Toronto; and Duncan McMartin, who is listed simply as "Capitalist Montreal." McMartin was somewhat of a "wunderkind" in the mining community of Northern Ontario. *Maclean's* magazine hailed him as "The Cobalt Millionaire" in a January 1909 feature, as he had made his fortune within six years at the age of thirty-six in the silver mines of Cobalt. In 1910, McMartin donated $100, his only donation, to the association. Compared to other donations, it was a substantial amount for the time but hardly anything relative to his wealth.

In addition was an alphabet soup of the major railways in Canada and their presidents or vice-presidents. Among this board of directors were Charles Hays, president of the Grand Trunk Pacific Railway (GTPR); the first vice-president of the association was D. B. Hanna, vice-president of the Canadian National Railway (CNR); and the honorary president of the association was William Whyte, vice-president of the Canadian Pacific Railway (CPR), based in Winnipeg. In all, four provinces were now represented on the board: Ontario, Quebec, Manitoba, and Saskatchewan. These representatives would be of great benefit to Fitzpatrick when he approached the various provincial governments of Canada. Financial support had already been received from every government west of Quebec. In all of Alfred's lobbying, it was always very useful to have a prominent Canadian as a patron whose imprimatur would add to the respectability and legitimacy of the association. In this regard, Alfred had convinced Reverend George Grant's lifelong friend Sir Sandford Fleming to be "The Patron" in 1905. By 1909, due to Fitzpatrick's lobbying, Lord Grey, Governor General of Canada, had replaced Fleming. With the association in such august company, how could any potential financial contributor refuse?

Beginning in 1908, the annual reports of the association included an extensive list of the geographical locations of donors and the amounts they contributed. Donors came from across Canada and beyond; the list in each report provided some evidence as to how far "the work" and its literacy message had spread. In 1908, for example, the Ontario government grant amounted to five hundred dollars, and from Saskatchewan came two hundred and fifty dollars. Prominent men of wealth like Joseph Flavelle and J. B. Osler of Toronto as well as the aforementioned board members like McMartin and Playfair gave contributions between fifty and one hundred dollars or more. The rest came from a variety of sources. Methodist, Presbyterian, and Roman Catholic churches sent funds collected at special Sunday services. Even collections from various labour camps were received. From Halifax to Victoria and in communities like Peveril, Quebec; Moose Jaw, Saskatchewan; Fort Rouge, Manitoba; and Edmonton, Alberta, small amounts of one, two, and five dollars were being received. By 1910, financial support was being collected from Ireland, England, Scotland, and the United States as Alfred spread his message as far and wide as possible.

With a capable staff like Bradwin and Wearing placing the instructors and an efficient secretary, Frances McMechan, B.A., in the Victoria Street home office, Fitzpatrick's tasks were clear: to publicize, collect donations, and promote the association at every opportunity. This meant he would have to forego any plans he had for further self-education, at least for a while. In 1908 he had applied to and been accepted by McMaster University, a Baptist institution on Bloor Street West near the University of Toronto. McMaster did not offer extension programs, so perhaps Alfred hoped that he would have time to attend classes. However, his constant travelling and his declining prosperity meant that he had to withdraw from McMaster within a year.

Fitzpatrick would often complain that he was a habitual letter writer as well as an inveterate traveller. Fortunately, some of his extensive correspondence with Miss McMechan, or "Miss M." as he called her, survived, and a survey of the correspondence from 1910 to the First World War provides some insight into his many travels and his many concerns for the Reading Camp Association. The major worry was the success or failure of the instructors in the field, and so he visited every instructor that had been posted to isolated locations. He was also concerned about reaching out to immigrant labourers often shunned by Canadian workers. In 1911, he directed McMechan to send a letter to each instructor asking them to pay attention to foreigners that did not come to the reading tent, as they were often discouraged by the English-speaking workmen. He added "you should go to their sleep camps and bunkhouses and interest them there in the privacy of their own tents." With his eye ever on raising both funds and the awareness of his audience, he added "this part of our work appeals to the public."

The money issue comes up frequently in the correspondence. Alfred wrote from Red Deer, Alberta, in the fall of 1911 that he was attempting to sell his empty town lot in Wapella, Saskatchewan, where he had been a minister in the late 1890s, in order to raise funds for the association. "It is hard to finance our work when we have so many disappointments, but 'failure' is not in the dictionary of the Reading Camp Association." Alfred then goes on to say that if he couldn't sell the lot he would have to "collect" for two weeks for the association before going west. In response, McMechan, well aware of the shortages, wrote "the bank account was alright today without a deposit." Keep on advertising, Alfred exhorted, as he didn't "worry about anything except my bank account and bad heart." He even suggested street car advertisements featuring the Reading Camp Association in all major cities. As noted previously, the annual reports reflected a large number of small contributions, from one dollar to five dollars; Alfred directed, in early 1911, that a copy of a financial letter of inquiry be sent to all contributors of five dollars or more. A year later he was in Montreal and borrowed a couple of hundred dollars from his cousin A. P. Willis. In Quebec City in November 1912, he wrote, "I am going to try to raise some money this week but am not sure where."

In his search for support, Alfred did not confine himself to Canada. In July 1910, he travelled west on a fundraising trip. By August, he had made his way to Mendocino City, California, near his former missionary posting of Little River over a decade previously. There he visited camps where he had once served and while "talking with the old timers" (as Alfred put it) described the association and its activities with the hope, perhaps, of a donation. His occasional trips to England to collect for the association made him aware of other like-minded organizations. There were also a few scam artists like "a McCormick of the Navvy Mission" who came from Canada, circulated among the various English churches, and "cleaned up thousands of dollars" that should have gone to the association. "The English don't know one from the other," Alfred remarked. Not surprisingly, Fitzpatrick went in the hole during that trip.

At other times, Alfred had "no time to write" and was "hard to locate. Walked 18 miles yesterday." Not surprisingly the association office secretary received a letter from an exasperated J. W. Fitzpatrick in New Liskeard who complained of having written "brother Alfred" twice with no reply: "is he in Toronto or where and when was he last home," he wanted to know.

Alfred's travel correspondence also brings moments of panic. For example, in early July 1911, a huge fire swept through Porcupine, Northern Ontario, a major centre of the association's work. Joseph Wearing, Western Secretary, sent a night lettergram to Fitzpatrick in Burbank, California, about the tragedy. "Impossible to leave office...

Don't know what to do. Got fourteen dollars yesterday... Could do nothing... Bradwin lost everything...." In addition are letters that must have been discouraging, given all that he had done. In February 1913, W. C. Edwards of W. C. Edwards and Company, Lumber Manufacturers, Ottawa wrote that he would be glad to help if he thought Alfred was doing anything meritorious or useful and added "I think that it is very much to be regretted that a man of your ability and education is not applying himself to some useful purpose."

Finally, through his letters to Frances McMechan, Alfred's travel correspondence provides some personal insight into his relations with and opinions of women. He relied frequently on Frances using her best judgment in most administrative matters and gave her leeway in early 1914 to write to leading universities in Russia and Argentina to find out what extramural/extension work they were doing in their "underdeveloped hinterland." He also had an at times teasing, paternal relationship with McMechan, as well as other secretaries, telling her she must devote her heart, soul, mind, and strength to the association in office hours and not allow any young man to waste her time. At times he would also ask her to write "sisterly" letters to discouraged instructors and to urge them "to dig in and be a man." During the First World War, Alfred was quite prepared to send a female graduate to teach a class of foreigners at the munitions camp at Energite in Renfrew, Ontario. With a combination of enthusiasm, confidence in her abilities, and what today might be called sexism, he told McMechan to go after Ontario Deputy Minister of Education A. H. S. Colquhon for boxes of books as "You have a better education, a better cause, a better record, and a better face than he, so go in and win." After a visit to Ottawa, Alfred described Sir Robert Borden, Canada's First World War prime minister, as a fine-looking man who "fixes a big curl on the front of his head. So even he is human" and goes

Ed Bradwin, fourth from the right, at a railway construction camp in British Columbia, circa 1912. **(LIBRARY AND ARCHIVES CANADA/FRONTIER COLLEGE FONDS/C-046154)**

on to write that in twelve to fifteen years Canada would have a woman for prime minister. "I think that she will not be given to such vanity."

To use a biblical analogy that Fitzpatrick might appreciate, he'd had seven lean years (1899–1906) and now had seven years of accomplishments (1907–1914) for the Reading Camp Association. He was now established in downtown Toronto in an office with competent and devoted staff, one of whom, Bradwin, had completed his B.A. (1913) and commenced his master's studies. His networking had brought together a number of wealthy benefactors well beyond the city of Toronto and the province of Ontario. The association by 1913 had instructors in eight of the country's nine provinces, all but PEI, and the influx of immigrants had brought an enhanced focus as to what the association's goals were. Toronto and its confluence of railways gave access to the country's farthest borders, and the many voices of the print media allowed Fitzpatrick a megaphone for his message. Although his very small fortune invested in the Reading Camp Association was now gone, the association found itself in a much better financial position than it had been in the midst of Alfred's discouragement in late 1906. Things were looking up economically, politically, and socially. However, change was about to come. To use another religious saying that presumably Alfred knew well, "What man proposes, God disposes."

In mid-July of 1914, Fitzpatrick's letter to McMechan was about Bradwin: "Ed is the one soul in Reading Camp work who is fit for the kingdom of Heaven and, notwithstanding that, we cannot part with him." Within a few months, Fitzpatrick may have wished he could take those words back as he and Bradwin battled over the leadership of the association. There was, however, a much larger conflict that would deeply affect the association's work. On August 4, 1914, Canada entered the First World War, and the "Guns of August" would echo down the next four years. The association was now faced with another challenge to its survival.

CHAPTER 5

NEW INITIATIVES AND THE GREAT WAR 1914–1918

EDMUND BRADWIN

EDMUND BRADWIN WAS STILL UPSET WHEN HE ENTERED THE *Reading Camp Association office on Yonge Street the morning of October 28, 1914. He pulled his chair out and sat at his desk, ruminating on how he had been verbally accosted the day before by his boss. The argument had been somewhat one-sided, so now Bradwin wanted to collect his thoughts and refute Alfred's accusations on paper. There had been so many of them yesterday that it was difficult to know where to begin. Alfred Fitzpatrick, usually a mild-mannered, if at times scatter-brained employer, had obviously been hiding his anger and frustration for years. It struck Bradwin as a rage rooted in jealousy.*

Bradwin, ever logical and systematic, waited until he had calmed himself. He was now ready to carefully list the accusations and respond in writing to each one. He would later decide how he would convey this to Alfred, either verbally or in written form. He was too committed to this association, for which he had worked for over a decade, to quit, but he could not continue to work with Alfred until he could at least try to clear the misunderstandings between them.

Bradwin's handwritten response in draft form to Alfred's accusations reflected both his shock and his anger. Alfred's unexpected outburst had struck him "like a bolt from the blue." He continued, "I find myself accused of things directly which would shame the workings of a German spy."

In his twelve-page letter, Bradwin enumerated the various accusations and admonitions that Alfred had made, and Bradwin refuted each in turn. The charges included:

1. that Bradwin wished to publish data about camps in *Queen's Quarterly*, an academic journal;
2. that Bradwin was keeping the best photographs of the work to himself;
3. that Bradwin, although working for the association, was collecting research material; and
4. that Bradwin was not to publish anything without talking it over with Alfred first.

Bradwin's detailed responses, which included marginal notes, constituted about ten pages of the letter, denying in turn each of Alfred's complaints. Bradwin did not directly refute the accusation about collecting research material, but he did write: "That is too ridiculous for anything as I have had no such intention, and do not know what you are hinting at. My room, and books, bags, and trunk, lie open, and unlocked. I have no secrets to hide, not anything hidden."

In his conclusion, he expressed his frustration that such accusations would be made after eleven years of service "through thick and thin." He added in an effort to ameliorate the tension between them that he had always held up the work as Alfred's idea and Alfred's alone. He explained that one of the rationales for doing his M.A.

thesis at Queen's was so he could have a job if the YMCA took over the association, fearing they might "throw me out" and he'd be "forced to settle in Toronto and keep my old folks."

The timing of Alfred's confrontation with Bradwin is crucial. It was late 1914, the First World War had broken out, and the association was beginning to incur financial problems. Perhaps Alfred was beginning to wonder and worry about his own future. He had been nothing but supportive of Bradwin's desire to further his education toward a degree from Queen's University—a B.A., the same qualification as Alfred had. But now, after long days and nights of travel, work, and study, Bradwin had completed his graduate thesis a few months previous and was now known in the list of association staff as Edmund W. Bradwin, B.A., M.A.—all accomplished utilizing extension education. This was a meaningful accomplishment for his time but more significantly, certainly to Alfred's mind, it meant Bradwin was now more academically qualified than his boss, who was noted on the association letterhead as Alfred Fitzpatrick, B.A. Now in the fall of 1914, Bradwin, the man Alfred had mentored, had been accepted to the Ph.D. program at Columbia University. It may have been building up for years, but now jealousy and envy, apparently beneath the surface of an amicable relationship, bubbled up in this accusatory exchange between employer and employee that Bradwin recounted in his twelve-page letter.

Aside from this letter, there is no mention in the archival documents of further tensions. Alfred, in his ever active and one could say ever preoccupied fashion, likely moved on to his next project. As for Bradwin, he was a calm and measured man who outwardly kept his emotions in check. Perhaps by committing the conflict to paper, he and Alfred were able to reconcile both for the good of their working relationship and the future of the association. Still, the letter survived.

In 1913, Canada had welcomed the largest number of immigrants in its history. Four hundred thousand new immigrants arrived in Canada that year—a total that superseded the previous year's incoming population by twenty-five thousand. Of the numbers that arrived the year before, almost one-third, some 120,000, came to Ontario and some 40 percent of those arrived in Toronto. Many of these took the train from Montreal and arrived in Toronto at Union Station—most homeless and some helpless. The vast majority were of British origin, supplementing, according to the census of 1911, the 86 percent British population that had preceded them to Toronto. At the same time, the proportion of the non–British population was growing. After all, Toronto was 90 percent British in 1906, and now it was 86 percent. Between the official census of 1901 and 1911, the three largest ethnic groups in the city had increased. The Eastern European Jews were the largest with a six-fold increase to eighteen thousand, the Germans numbered nine thousand, and the Italians increased from one thousand to four thousand. By 1913, Toronto's population had more than doubled to well over four hundred thousand compared to the turn of the century census of 1901 when it stood at just over two hundred thousand.

This rapid increase placed an enormous strain on the city's infrastructure, particularly transportation and housing. A headline in the May 13, 1913, issue of the *Globe* newspaper, for example, read "Immigrants in Toronto Need Better Housing." The same day the *Mail* noted a similar need: "Hostel to Shelter Immigrant Girls." The federal minister of public works, Robert Rogers, at a meeting in Toronto, assured a large, diverse delegation representing the board of trade, the trade and labour council, church ministers, and the YMCA that a permanent structure would be raised near Union Station on Front Street for the newly arrived immigrants. The situation was alleviated somewhat by a number of these new immigrants, especially the young men, being quickly persuaded to sign a contract with labour contractors and just as quickly herded into a rough passenger car or box car and taken north by train into Ontario's interior to the mines in Cobalt or Timmins or the secluded lumber camps of Whitefish, Parry Sound, or Blind River. The majority, however, remained in Toronto and immediately set out to find a meal, a room, and a job. Many, due to class and ethnic differences that inhibited their chances of jobs or housing, ended up in "The Ward."

The Ward, Toronto's largest inner city slum, was in an area bounded by Queen Street to the south, Yonge to the east, College to the north, and University Avenue to the west. This rectangle of downtown property and poverty also included Toronto's City Hall, Osgoode Hall Law School, and Canada's largest retailer and mail order department store, the T. Eaton Company. In a rapidly growing Toronto where the influx of wealth from Northern Ontario industries had led to higher prices for food, housing, and basic services, The Ward offered very cheap labour in a central location. The Ward was but a short walk from Union Station—past Government House, home of the Lieutenant-Governor, on the left, and on the right the "Mother Church" of the many Presbyterians of Toronto and across Canada, St. Andrew's Presbyterian Church.

To live in The Ward was not usually a choice but a necessity and not a very pleasant one for those trapped by language, culture, and prejudice. Allan Levine in his *Toronto: Biography of a City* quotes Reverend H. S. Magee's article in the *Christian Guardian* of 1911: "Here is the festering sore of our city life. The lanes, alleyways, and backyards are strewn with refuse, houses behind houses, and in the yards between unsightly piles of ramshackle, out-houses that are supposed to provide sanitary conveniences." And William Lyon Mackenzie King, future prime minister of Canada and faithful attendee of St. Andrew's Presbyterian Church, wrote in his diary, "What a story of Hell!"

His comment would not have surprised young investigative reporter C. S. Clark, who had called the neighbourhood the criminal underbelly of Toronto. His book, published in 1898, was sarcastically titled *Of Toronto the Good.* In his survey of sin, Clark wrote that "The whole city is an immense house of ill fame."

Before 1914, the newspapers of Toronto featured The Ward frequently with headlines like "Shocking Conditions in Foreign Quarter" (*Globe*, 1913); "Slums must go says Mayor Geary" (*Mail*, 1913); and "Thousands live in Toronto at 22 cents per day per head" (*Star Weekly*, 1912). They urged action by the city fathers, but neither the

The Ward was Toronto's largest inner city slum. Here it is pictured off of Elizabeth Street, with City Hall in the background looming over the houses. (CITY OF TORONTO ARCHIVES/WILLIAM JAMES FONDS/323A)

employment bureau nor the welfare office were forthcoming. Usually most of the support for such communities was provided by the various religious organizations in the city who were prepared to work in what one writer called a "pushcart world" where merchandise like clothing, food, and other necessities was sold from two or four wheel carts pushed by the sellers throughout The Ward. In 1913, the Carmelite Order of Nuns of the Roman Catholic Church was established to "work among foreigners." Many had language skills to communicate with the Polish,

German, and Slavic populations. The synagogue reached out to the Jewish community, while the Greek Orthodox Church assisted those of their faith.

For Alfred Fitzpatrick, who had been in Toronto for half a dozen years, The Ward might have seemed like a natural extension of the atrocious social conditions that he was addressing outside the urban areas. Why not therefore ally himself with other social gospel workers like the YMCA and the Presbyterian Church and perhaps work with them?

The Young Men's Christian Association of Canada was founded in Montreal in 1851 with the goal of bringing about the "improvement of the spiritual and mental condition of young men." By the late 1880s, the YMCA had established an education program for all immigrants as well as an active women's auxiliary to serve the humanitarian needs of the growing female immigrant population. In Winnipeg, both outreach programs assisted new immigrants as they arrived in the Canadian immigration sheds before moving west. The education component consisted, for the most part, of singing, prayer, scripture reading, and exhortation. This was around the time that Alfred was president of the "Y Association" while in his final year of his B.A. at Queen's, so he was no doubt familiar with the Winnipeg initiative. There was also discussion by the YMCA leadership about expanding their program to men in lumber camps, but little work was undertaken. In 1900, "the Y" was providing accommodation for railway workers in Montreal, and the Toronto YMCA minute books of 1886 to 1927 recounted an ongoing educational effort for the urban population. In April 1905, twenty-nine education classes were held with one hundred and fifty attending. Within two years this number had climbed to over eight hundred per month. It should be noted that Bible classes were held separately and were not increasing in number, unlike literacy classes.

A. MacLean teaching a reading class in Powell River, British Columbia, in 1910.
(LIBRARY AND ARCHIVES CANADA/FRONTIER COLLEGE FONDS/C-070699)

When Alfred was busy getting the Reading Camp Association's office established in Toronto, the Y had organized "A Foreigners' Class for the Study of English," and it was offering its "heartiest approval" to all efforts in "teaching English to New Canadians." By 1912, the Toronto West End Y Association had its largest program. There were 114 foreigners in class, and by the next year over 300 students per month were enrolled. However, just like the Reading Camp Association, numbers declined during the war as young volunteer instructors were joining the army. Also like the association, the Y was sending books and magazines to the soldiers in the trenches as well as organizing lecture tours. By 1917, the Y had begun to play a primary role in the University of Toronto extension courses being taught by the Khaki University in France and England (see more on the Khaki University below). The Y provided both organizational and financial support for the university.

Not surprisingly, Alfred's association could not compete with either the University of Toronto or the YMCA, and a few times in his correspondence Alfred spoke of the Y being admirably suited to take on the educational work of the Reading Camp Association, but nothing ever came of this notion.

The alternative choice for Alfred, noted earlier, would have been the Presbyterian Church—the most obvious parish being St. Andrew's of Toronto. St. Andrew's was erected at the corner of King and Simcoe Streets in 1876. This area, also bounded by Bay Street and the Lake Ontario waterfront, was considered by Stuart C. Parker in his *Book of St. Andrew's* (1930) as the most prestigious part of the city, where "most of the people of substance lived," not a few of whom had contributed substantially to the founding and ongoing operations of Queen's University. The new church, which seated one thousand parishioners, reflected the wealth of its surroundings and was designed with Romanesque architecture, carved woodwork, and granite pillars imported from Aberdeen, Scotland. It was certainly the largest and wealthiest of the eight Presbyterian churches in Toronto. From 1900 to 1930, Presbyterianism would expand exponentially from eight to thirty churches in that city, with total budgets growing from $76,000 to $400,000. Financially then, the Presbyterian churches were in an excellent position to support the Reading Camp Association. And St. Andrew's in particular was in the cockpit of power. Government House was just across the road, Upper Canada College was kitty-corner, and a hotel stood on the fourth corner. These four corners of the King and Simcoe intersection were known by the locals as Legislation, Education, Salvation, and Damnation. Remember, this is "Toronto the Good!"

Not long after its opening, St. Andrew's organized a night school for the young men (ages twelve to twenty-four) of the district, some of whom were from The Ward. There were eight classes teaching basic literacy and numeracy skills. The surge in non-British immigration in the early twentieth century had radically changed the demography of Toronto and The Ward, and some leaders within the church believed St. Andrew's had a central role to play in the assimilation of these new immigrants. This role included conversion to the Christian faith. Schools and colleges were all very well, but the first duty of the Church was to spread the gospel. Indeed, some felt that in order to assimilate, one had first to Christianize.

The focus of the Church was on the slums of the larger cities. In 1907, a committee of the Presbyterian churches of Toronto was established to "Work Among the Foreigners in the City," namely Greeks, Syrians, Bulgarians, and Jews. A year later a proposal was accepted to meet immigrants coming into the city and assist them as necessary with their welfare and settlement. Most of the churches in Metropolitan Toronto were involved in this effort; ministers and members of their congregation would walk to Union Station to meet the incoming trains. Perhaps some even carried banners like the one hanging recently at the entrance of the Canadian Presbyterian Museum in the basement of St. John's Presbyterian Church, Toronto. On the six-foot by three-foot white canvas banner was inscribed in red letters: "Canada: The Melting Pot of Nations: Population (1915) 8,000,000, Immigration 3,000,000." It added that immigrants were arriving in Canada at a rate of six hundred per week, with one in ten foreigners arriving in Toronto and either staying there or moving on to other parts of Canada.

So where does Alfred Fitzpatrick fit in all of this? Association secretary Jessie Lucas spoke of Alfred attending St. Andrew's, but true to his nature, he sat in the church gallery. She added, "He was not one who seemed to show an interest in the usual conventional work of the church." As he used to say to her, "Never wear your religion on your coat sleeve." However, Alfred did have himself listed in the Presbyterian record as a clergyman W.C. (without charge) in Toronto from 1907 to 1910, which was when he had first moved to the city.

Perhaps this was in case he was unemployed and an opening occurred in one of the city churches. He was also listed as attending one of the "Work Among Foreigners" committee meetings in 1908, but his name does not appear in any subsequent meetings. However, his connection to St. Andrew's is still evident. At the 1910 Reading Camp Association board meeting, the treasurer listed was D. M. Robertson. Robertson was a very active member of St. Andrew's Church who had lobbied and fundraised for the formation of the Forty-Eighth Highlanders—a famous regiment that was founded and paid for by St. Andrew's in 1891. As mentioned earlier, another member of the church was William Lyon Mackenzie King, future prime minister of Canada, to whom Alfred would look for political assistance in the 1920s.

Given Alfred's active fundraising efforts and his many contacts through Queen's and Principal Grant, St. Andrew's was likely aware of his work. In 1913, the Presbyterian Church had offered to take over the responsibilities of the frontier camps, but Alfred's written response was that "it cannot be carried on successfully by any religious denomination" as it was a task for the provincial department of education. He believed that St. Andrew's was not equipped to work in the frontier camps given its urban focus and also because the priority of the Church was primarily to proselytize for Christianity, while his was to proselytize for literacy. At the beginning of his journey in the 1890s, Alfred had wished to forge strong links between his religious heritage and his efforts at social reform. Now he believed that his educational reforms were really a task for secular society and the various provincial departments of education across Canada—not the Church.

Alfred, then, did not become involved with the immigrants or slums of Toronto or any other city for religious and organizational reasons. His constituency lay well beyond the city limits of a changing Canada. Nevertheless, he did approach a secular ally—the University of Toronto.

Buried in the "Announcement" section of the November 24, 1915, edition of *Varsity*, the undergraduate newspaper at the University of Toronto, was the following: "Former instructors and other students will be interested to know that the Reading Camp Association, formerly of 43 Victoria Street, is now occupying offices at 42 and 44A University College just below the Varsity offices."

In deep financial difficulty, the association had written to University of Toronto President Robert Falconer the month before requesting space for their office. Falconer had responded positively, and the association moved its office to the campus.

Robert Falconer was no stranger to Fitzpatrick. Fitzpatrick often sought out Pictou Academy alumni, and Falconer's father, Reverend Alexander Falconer, attended the academy and became a Presbyterian minister in Prince Edward Island, where Robert was born in 1867. Robert too became a Presbyterian minister and a well-published theological scholar. He received his Doctor of Divinity in 1906 and a year later was appointed President of the University of Toronto. A keen supporter of the work of the YMCA in the inner city, in 1911 Falconer instituted the University Settlement House in The Ward, at the corner of Adelaide and Peter Streets, to serve the needs of the immigrants living there. With a small staff and student volunteers, the Settlement House tried to deal with the "Problems of the City" with English classes, baby clinics, free dispensary, and assistance to women. Falconer himself was the chair of the board. Also, in response to pressures for the university to teach extension courses, in 1910 Falconer toured the US Midwest, especially Wisconsin, and was impressed by their extension programs. Fitzpatrick, of course, had already surveyed these university programs a decade earlier before establishing his association. By 1914, a broad range of service (i.e., non-credit) courses were introduced at the University of Toronto but were interrupted by the war.

Robert Falconer was president of the University of Toronto from 1907 to 1932.
(UNIVERSITY OF TORONTO ARCHIVES)

In Fitzpatrick's mind, the literacy, health, and social welfare challenges of a growing Toronto were being met by the churches, the YMCA, and the university. Therefore, he remained focused on what he had been doing all along in the areas of the country where these challenges were not being met. And, of course, he required financial support. Fundraising was not Alfred's strength, but it was certainly Falconer's.

In 1910, Falconer had approached the Massey Foundation for financial support, and well over $300,000 was granted to build Hart House, a structure of Gothic design that would be a focal point of student life on campus. Fitzpatrick's response was in *The University in Overalls*, published in 1920: "Instead of one, let there be hundreds of Hart Houses, built of peeled logs, for the comfort and entertainment and co-education of young men and women, in lumbering, mining, construction, and land-clearing camps." Fitzpatrick rarely missed an opportunity to compare the lack of support for the association with the largesse offered to other educational institutions. He believed his young men and women were just as deserving as the students on the university campus. This opinion might not have endeared him to President Falconer.

It is not clear what the relationship between Falconer and Fitzpatrick was when the association office moved onto the U of T campus in 1915. Two years previous, Fitzpatrick wrote to Falconer requesting letters of introduction to some financial contacts that he wished to approach. Falconer responded that he did not know them well enough to request funds "nor have I met Mr. [Andrew] Carnegie." In that same year, Fitzpatrick wrote to suggest a closer relationship between the work of the association and the university. Falconer replied that he could not be of assistance due to the university's commitment to the University Settlement House. In his book, Fitzpatrick would complain that in 1910 the men working in the woods, forests, and mines of the province created a revenue of almost \$3 million—one-third of the total revenue of the Ontario government—and that the "University in Queen's Park" received half a million dollars. Furthermore, "If 5,000 students can be so well provided for—what of the men of Ontario who spend so much of their time in camps." This and other criticisms of Falconer and University of Toronto would be levelled in greater abundance later. For now, the Reading Camp Association (RCA) in 1915 had its office on the university campus where it would remain until late 1917.

The six years between 1913 and 1919 witnessed a profound shift in what the RCA saw as its responsibility to the campmen. It was a time when the association renamed itself "The Frontier College" and undertook an important change in its message and therefore its audience. In the period leading up to the First World War, Alfred Fitzpatrick had realized his core audience was not just those who wanted to read, but also those, like the newly arrived immigrants, who needed assistance to learn the basics of the language before reading could even begin. In addition, during the war, patriotism around king and country was reinforced by the association in all the Canadian workplaces where instructors were sent. Knowledge about the war was shared with the campmen, and they were encouraged to "join up."

With the end of the war and the Paris Peace Treaty of 1919, the "banner of revolution"—Bolshevism—was being hoisted across Europe and would soon have its impact on North America. Consequently, it was no longer enough for the immigrants to be literate and patriotic; they must also be imbued with knowledge of the country and its values—values that included history, geography, politics, and literature. With his newly titled "college" in 1918,

Alfred was beginning to focus on something more than a "certificate of attendance" for its many thousands of students. True to its name, the Frontier College he envisioned would offer college level extension courses across Canada's frontiers, a program that would allow anyone to achieve a degree accreditation without ever attending a university. A detailed comparison of the association's annual reports during this period provides clear evidence of these constant revisions to its mission and how they were shaped.

In 1912, for the first time, the title of the annual report squarely stated the new reality of the communities the association was serving. Titled "The Immigrant," it was the longest report up to that time. Richly illustrated, the report included a montage of some seventy photographs with explanatory captions, which visually documented the work of the association. The activities of the fifty-five instructors for that year were detailed, interspersed with quotes by Maria Montessori, Leo Tolstoy, and Thomas Carlyle. The RCA's budget had increased from $15,000 to $26,000, an amount that still included loans from Alfred. His essay at the end of the report addressed the issue of prejudice against the immigrant and in that context suggested a solution to Toronto's "slum problem," specifically referring to the inner city area called The Ward. That solution was to highlight the benefits of frontier life, make it more attractive to the immigrants when they first arrived by providing education in the camps as well as assistance in securing a quarter section of land to farm. Education would be "an engine for social betterment," he wrote, quoting Thomas Carlyle. In his report, he also expounded on one of his favourite themes, the way in which Canadian society had "dishonoured work" and left it for the European "navvy" to do. According to this yearly report of the association, its mission was a financial and social success. Things could only get better.

The following year, the association boasted of having seventy-five camp teachers, and the budget was now $31,000. The 1913 annual report was entitled "Frontier College" and for the first time included a two-page spread of portraits of many of the instructors. The title suggests that a change was about to come. With many positive comments about the new immigrants to Canada, Alfred then proposed a new task for the association: not just teaching literacy, but also "Canadianizing the foreigner" by making them aware of their duties as citizens of Canada. Also, Alfred prophetically stated that "The task of the educationalist for the next ten years will be to devise ways and means of taking the school and college to the frontiersmen.... We must go to them; they will not come to us." The outbreak of the First World War the next year would interrupt this evolution for a decade.

With the effects of the war beginning to show, the annual report in 1914 was a pale imitation of its former self. It was entitled "Frontier Camp Schools" and contained the sum total of eight pages, which included the treasurer's report for the year. Bradwin, now on leave and studying for his Ph.D. at Columbia, criticized it as the "economy report" due to its size and the fact that it contained only four photographs. He portrayed it in his rather picturesque biblical language as being "as lean as Pharaoh's spine after seven years of want." He obviously believed that its publication did not portray the work in a favourable light, nor would it help with the fundraising.

For the first time since the association was founded, there was no annual general meeting in 1914. Alfred had no choice. The budget for the year was down to $22,000, a drop of 30 percent, with liabilities of $7,500 in loans. Alfred was under pressure in regards to the survival of the association. He mentioned in the report that when the war broke out, several supporters had made representations to him stating that "the work" should be suspended, for many men of university age were now joining the Canadian armed forces. The recruitment of instructors had fallen by at least 20 percent since the previous year.

In addition, hundreds of men from the frontier camps had enlisted. Alfred, however, decided that it would be "a short lived and dangerous policy" to cease the work for even a brief period. "It means," he concluded, "so much to the future of our country." With the whole of Canada on war footing, "the task of Canadianizing the foreigners within our shores" had become more urgent in order to ensure the well-being and security of the country and to "mould the diverse elements into a harmonious national life."

Apparently, Alfred heeded Bradwin's critical advice as regards to formatting and content in the next annual report. Entitled "Settlement Camps: A Cure for Slum Conditions," Alfred's twenty-eight-page essay in the 1915 report criticized the slums of major cities like Toronto and Winnipeg and offered the slum dwellers the choice of "hopeless hovels versus the great outdoors." He encouraged churches and rural municipalities as well as philanthropists to sponsor or "grubstake" those trapped in the city slums and thus allow them to go to the Canadian north and begin new townships. At a time of national suspicion of those in the slums, he urged "Do not deport the foreigners—put them on land." He promised that the Reading Camp Association would assist with education and social support. In this way, Alfred wrote, "our motto, 'No hyphenated Canadians' may become a reality, not a dream."

As the war entered its third year, the federal government's call for volunteers became more and more insistent, and some 30 percent of the instructors in the 1916 intake for the association decided to enlist. To address the association's needs, Alfred even travelled to the United States, not yet at war, and recruited six American students from the University of Chicago and Harvard to be instructors. In this, the first year of the RCA in the United States, most of them volunteered to work in the state of Washington. In addition, ten American university students were sent to Canadian locations as instructors during the war.

The AGM on March 17, 1916, was held at the association's head office, now at 44A University College, Toronto. The board acknowledged that "the year just ended has been perhaps the hardest the Association has had." The minutes show that it was certainly the longest meeting the board had ever held. There was a call to curtail all unnecessary expenses but also to recognize the place of the association in the postwar "era of reconstruction" and be ready to handle extensive work. Still, given the financial situation, the association had to survive the war before it could even begin "reconstruction."

The association reports from 1916 to the end of the war increasingly emphasized its wartime role as its patriotic duty, along with fulfilling its stated mission and, not incidentally though unstated, maintaining its benefactor base, a crucial part of its survival. Alfred would frequently attempt to tap his circle of wealthy friends by appealing to their vanity in order to raise money, especially in the association's difficult years of 1916 and 1917. For example, he wrote to an old acquaintance from his early days, Thomas G. Shaughnessy, now First Baron Shaughnessy, president of the CPR and also an old friend of George Monro Grant. In a letter written in 1916 with a follow up in 1917, Alfred asked if Shaughnessy would lead a campaign to raise $250 each from ten "prominent" Canadians—Shaughnessy, of course, being one of them, in Alfred's estimation. Shaughnessy had been providing an annual CPR pass for Alfred and ongoing financial support to the association since 1900. But in this instance, the response was a firm no, with no reason given.

In the 1916 report, Alfred noted that although donations had decreased in 1915, it was only $670 less than the previous year. The Association was able to "stay afloat" due to the financial generosity of long-time philanthropic supporter and millionaire Joseph Flavelle, who, through the Bank of Toronto, gave a guarantee of financial support to the Reading Camp Association on a year-to-year basis.

He also offered loans with no interest. Alfred was very grateful and noted the contrast between Flavelle and "the certain number of wealthy men who hedge themselves about with quantities of unavailabilities and we are unable to get past their secretaries." Later, throughout the 1920s, Flavelle donated at least $250 a year and said to Fitzpatrick, "You do good work and always put to shame those of us who are mere onlookers."

In addition to Flavelle's support, eight of the nine provincial governments were "on board" financially in 1915 and 1916 with the following amounts:

- Ontario: $2,000
- Manitoba: $500
- Saskatchewan: $400
- Alberta: $300
- British Columbia: $300
- Quebec: $300
- Nova Scotia: $150
- New Brunswick: $100

As there were rarely any instructors in Prince Edward Island, the provincial government never provided funding to the association.

Instructors were keeping the men in the various camps well informed with war maps and newspapers. One instructor had succeeded in convincing eighteen labourers to enlist. Alfred's wartime reports also included a list of the association's instructors overseas and noted that some were even involved in a "small way" as instructors with the Khaki University.

The University of Vimy Ridge, renamed the Khaki University, had been established in England by the Canadian military and the YMCA in 1917. It would serve for the duration of the war as an educational extension program at temporary colleges in central England, offering secondary and post-secondary studies. Serving as its first president was Henry Marshall Tory, president of the University of Alberta (1908–28), who was on leave from the university in order to serve with the Canadian army in England. Given his obvious academic influence, he gained the support of Canadian universities to accept the prerequisite courses the Khaki University taught. These courses were recognized by the Canadian government, and professors were sent to England to teach them. In addition, the Khaki University taught basic English literacy and numeracy skills. By war's end, over fifty thousand Canadian soldiers had received certificates from the Khaki University of Canada.

In the 1916 report, Alfred established the Reading Camp Association's connection to the war effort overseas by highlighting the work of a four-year association instructor, Sgt. S. A. Fasken, who was serving in 224th Forestry Corps in Scotland, where he had established a social and educational centre at every woods camp. Alfred remarked with some pride, "he is a soldier, logger, and instructor." Also, J. E. Gray acted in a similar capacity with the 198th Battalion. In truth, the association played a minimal role in the adult education of the Canadian soldiers in Europe although the annual report for 1916 highlighted that over fifty former association instructors were in active service overseas. Still, Alfred would draw two important conclusions from the creation of the Khaki University that would assist him after the war. The first was that the fundraising campaign of the YMCA, after it became involved with the university extension program, had been highly success-ful—from \$300,000 in 1916 to over \$3 million in 1918. Second, of greater interest to Alfred, was that the Canadian government had legislated into existence a university extension program when it allowed the university level courses taught at Khaki University to be recognized by universities across Canada. Soon after the war ended, Alfred would seek the same legislative recognition from the federal government for his Frontier College. He also hoped that such a degree-granting institution would attract the same level of public funding that the YMCA had received.

The 1916 report was titled "University Settlement on the Frontier," and it urged that homestead camps be established for those who wished to leave the city. The Reading Camp Association would then send a college man to work and teach in each homestead. In 1917, Canada's Soldier Settlement Act was passed by the federal government (and revised in 1919). It was intended to make grants and loans available to demobilized soldiers after the war. When Alfred published *The University in Overalls* in 1920, he included a chapter entitled "Frontier Settlement and Unemployment," which outlined a homestead policy that would lessen unemployment, depopulate the urban slums, and assist the returning soldiers by establishing "colonization by townships," especially in Northern Ontario. The "soldier settlement" was attempted but was soon discouraged by, as one bitter settler put it, "seven months of snow, two months of rain and the remainder mosquitoes and black flies." In the early 1920s, Ontario would actually enact a program of "settlement camps" or "homesteads" that would become part of Frontier College's responsibilities, as is outlined in Chapter 7.

Alfred continued to lobby for a decentralization of the education system, such that the school and the college would be brought to the camp and the homestead. This, of course, returned Alfred to his initial plea of so many years previously to allow for education to be provided to the people "whenever and wherever they are gathered together." The Khaki University that was established in Europe for Canadian soldiers stood as a successful model of that tenet.

The minutes of the 1917 AGM are missing, but fortunately those of the 1918 AGM survive. This meeting was pivotal to the future of the association. It was now in better shape financially, and much of the discussion revolved around what direction it would take after the war. For the first time, a reporter from the

Toronto *Mail and Empire* newspaper was present. She would recount the discussions in full in the next day's edition. Fiscally, contributions had increased as the war stimulated the Canadian economy, and the organization's debt, which had accumulated during the early years of the war, was reduced. The Ontario government's grant was due in a few days, and this would almost balance the budget.

The year previously, in 1917, a committee had been struck to formulate a new constitution for what was to be called Frontier College. The committee, composed of Fitzpatrick, Bradwin, and board member (and former instructor) Ray Dearle, presented the new constitution and it was adopted unanimously. The new board reflected the new electoral reality of the province. In 1917, women won the right to vote in Ontario provincial elections. In recognition of this and with Alfred's enthusiastic approval, four prominent Toronto women were added to the board. This brought the total number of new women members on the college board to eight, from six different provinces. The college was also working closely with national women's organizations like the Woman's Christian Temperance Union, the Women's Citizen League, and the National Council of Women with whom the college sought a more formal affiliation. Their cooperation with the college was in order to advocate for three major issues that they shared. These were:

1. that the Ontario government recognize the right of men to have schools in the camps;
2. that there be better sanitation in the camps; and
3. that naturalization and higher education standards for new citizens be compulsory.

The issues of naturalization and citizenship were becoming important and were beginning to be analyzed in some depth. James Thomas Milton Anderson, an inspector of schools in Yorkton,

A woman visits a railroad maintenance camp in British Columbia, circa 1912.
(LIBRARY AND ARCHIVES CANADA/FRONTIER COLLEGE FONDS/C-046167)

Saskatchewan, published *The Education of the New-Canadian: A Treatise on Canada's Greatest Educational Problem* in 1918, and in it he emphasized the need to assimilate the newcomer. He believed this must be done more systematically, as at that time, the foreigner, after five years, could apply to be naturalized, was given the vote, and although he did not know any English or French, "over his shoulders the toga of Canadian citizenship is thrown." Anderson, however, saw the "New-Canadians" as the children of these foreigners, and they should have priority. As for the adults in urban and rural areas, he wrote, they could be served by the not-for-profit organizations. Clearly, the issues of assimilation and the "alien question" were on the minds of many Canadians and on the new board's mind as well.

The two issues—literacy and citizenship—would certainly occupy the time and energy of the brand new Frontier College and its instructors in the years to come. For now, however, the title of the annual report for 1919—"The Instructor and the Red"—made it abundantly clear where its immediate priority rested.

These wartime reports and board minutes of the association delineated the difficult financial and staffing conditions of the time, but they can also be seen in hindsight as building blocks for a new and very different mission for Alfred's Reading Camp Association, now known as Frontier College.

In addition to the many difficulties being faced in the head office, Alfred continued his itinerant journeys to the villages, mines, and bush camps to further the goals of the college. Although there were fewer instructors during the war, they were still located in almost every province as well as in Europe, as shown by their efforts in 1917 with the Forestry Corps in Scotland.

One of Alfred's surviving notebooks reflected on the jumble of tents, shacks, and log buildings at the junction of the Fraser and Nechako Rivers, now a suburb of Prince George, BC. R. L. Lovitt, the instructor who worked on the river scow, had set up his reading tent in a camp of two hundred men. When nobody came on the first night, Lovitt took pencils, scribblers, and a phonograph (a very popular feature) to the Italian bunkhouse and got acquainted with the men there. As part of his class, Lovitt encouraged men to remain in Canada and settle on the land.

During this period, Fitzpatrick still travelled with his knapsack of books, although there were fewer books during the war due to the libraries sending them to the tens of thousands of soldiers in the military camps of both Canada and Europe. He would also pack a number of "comfort bags" for the workers, supplied to the college by the Woman's Christian Temperance Union. These included buttons, needles, thread, and other items not obtainable in the camps. On his visit to Donald McDougall, who was working at the Mond Nickel Co. at Levack, forty kilometres west of Sudbury, Alfred delivered copies of *Popular Mechanics, Popular Electricity, Punch*, and *Canadian Pictorial*. "Illustrations always appreciated," he wrote, then added, "[W]hen the church and school come along, we should move on," as they could do that work.

The other item that Alfred would carry with him was money. Often on his trips, he was doling out money to instructors who had very little or buying them breakfasts if the camp was not far from a town. Alfred himself was constantly borrowing money from banks or individuals including, at one time, a hotel elevator boy (five dollars) and even his secretary Pauline Smith (one hundred dollars). He had a reputation for always repaying such loans, but often the lender had to wait. (The elevator boy was repaid the next day.) It must have been very frustrating for him, and although he didn't complain often, in a 1916 letter to Miss Smith from a CNR railcar, after giving her instructions as to whom certain cheques were to be sent he added, "I have beggared myself for years paying out money for outfits that I have never charged the Association with. I once had a better house than Mr. Dickey [General Secretary of RCA office] has. I let it go and everything else. I'm not going to do it anymore!"

Such proclamations, rarely expressed in writing, did not last long and were never carried out, as can be seen by the amount of money that Alfred continued to lend the association over the years.

The association in Toronto had received a stream of correspondence from their frontier placements. Some instructors wrote as many as fifty letters a month describing their work and social experiences both positive and negative and revealing both discouragement and accomplishment. For example, William Diamond, a Jewish Master of Arts student from the University of Chicago, was posted to the Northern Fish Company, Eagle Island, Manitoba, where there were eighty men, the majority being Galicians (Ukrainians and Poles) with some English men and a few Germans. School was four nights a week, and twenty-five to thirty attended, mostly foreigners. He taught English, arithmetic, and Canadian history, and found the short tales of Tolstoy very popular. Sunday afternoon was reserved for assisting the men with their writing.

From the CPR rail camp in Glacier, BC, Thomas Garratt described his week in detail with some pedagogy included. Saturday night was concert, dance, and gramophone music night until after ten o' clock with seventy in the room and many more outside. There were also music recitations, debates, and speeches. A sample program mentioned a solo of the Swedish National Anthem, well-known popular songs, the "Soldiers' Chorus" from Gounod's opera *Faust*, and on this occasion, an "Address by Fitzpatrick." Garratt noted: "Our former estimate of the frontiersman as a brainless fellow caring for nothing but coarse dances and 'booze' needs revision. The life of solitude leads him to crave for fun…I have never seen men too tired to be entertained."

But there were others who were discouraged and frustrated. One such young man was John W. MacKenzie, an arts student from McGill University, who vented his frustration to Bradwin in a letter written in early 1914. In it, MacKenzie, who was working as a navvy labourer-teacher with the CPR construction in Broadview, Saskatchewan, complained, "I don't think I have succeeded at all," as none of the fellows in his bunk car were interested. They "just grunted and said no more." What students he did have had all quit the class the previous week because of "my trouble in getting men to learn English." He expressed his conviction that he had not earned his twenty dollars a month extra from the Reading Camp Association and would not accept it even if offered. He ended his letter with a plea to Bradwin for a few specific instructions on how to build up his classes and to "please give me suggestions I can act upon with effect."

There is no direct response in the records to MacKenzie's appeal, but it is highly probable that Bradwin would have responded along the lines of his diary entry, which is undated but likely written in the early 1920s: "The problems of teaching English to the foreigner adult demand a different method of teaching. We must take into consideration the national characteristics as well as the home life and daily work of the members. Then seek to relate the lesson to their experience…. [L]et the instructor inform himself of the national customs and peculiarities, etc. of the people he is teaching."

This comment represents a profound pedagogical observation for the early twentieth century—an observation that directed the instructor to teach a subject based on what the student's knowledge and experience was and then discover what the student wished to know.

Still the contribution to the war effort continued in Canada. J. H. Hooper was an instructor to the POWs at the internment camp at Spirit Lake via Cochrane, Ontario, between 1915 and 1917. In August 1916, he wrote the following to the association office: "Everything is going along good except nearly all the prisoners have been released." So much for a captive audience! As for the Canadian military bases, Alfred had dispatched an instructor to Camp Borden to establish a reading tent and conduct classes among the Canadian Russians who had volunteered for overseas service and were now in the 198th Battalion.

"On tour," Fitzpatrick made good use of his time on the long train rides. As we've seen, he was a prolific writer whose material appeared in a variety of publications, including the *Globe* and the *Star*, Toronto's two major newspapers.

As the work of the Reading Camp Association and the name Fitzpatrick became more widely recognized, Alfred was published in a variety of media. In his "Notes" file is a manuscript titled "The Swing Team Boss." This four-page article was published in *World's Work* in 1914. The year before, "Canadianizing the Immigrant: A Picture of a Real, Sensible Missionary Work that is Going on in the Lumber, Railway, and Mining Camps of this Country Without Reference to the Church or Formal Religion" was published in the *Canadian Courier*, a Canadian Pacific Railway monthly newsletter in newspaper format. In these and many such other articles in company publications, Alfred emphasized the kind of work the Reading Camp Association carried out, using examples from across Canada. Photographs illustrated the reading tent and cabin classrooms as well as the various instructors who worked on the Grand Trunk Pacific Railroad at Mile 288, British Columbia, or with the gang on the Fraser River scow, or the "Cant-Hook Brigade" in the Georgian Bay Lumber Company getting a lesson on the digestive system. He often remarked that these instructors were not just teachers, but they also must have skills in the work the men around them were doing where "the standard of excellence in a camp is not culture but physical strength combined with experience in camp work." He would frequently add his standard criticism about an education system that did not train boys to be better craftsmen and thus made them unwilling to do any kind of work. The subtitle of his article spoke of "real, sensible missionary work" but "without reference to the church or formal religion." With this juxtaposition of "missionary" and no "church or formal religion," the title illustrates Alfred's personal struggle between secular needs and religious goals.

The Reading Camp Association had moved well beyond that struggle by the second decade of the century, although it was still supported by some churches and church groups. In this *World's Work* article and several others, Alfred always urged the various provincial departments of education to become involved in not just sharing with Canada's frontier camps and homesteads the benefits of primary and secondary education, but also in sharing the benefits of a university education—reinforcing his appeal for some form of extension education beyond the secondary level.

Overall, Alfred's articles in the popular media were descriptive of the work being done by the Reading Camp Association but were also a challenge to the government and society at large to participate in what he believed was an important endeavour with important results. In his article "Outnavvying the Navvies" in the *Canadian Magazine* (May 1916), he described an American, W. E. Givens, who was an instructor laying steel with two hundred navvies on the CPR in Saskatchewan. Using Givens's work as an example, Alfred concluded that if the immigrant is to become a citizen, he should not remain "estranged, misunderstood, often despised, and therefore politically and socially dangerous."

In addition to his mainstream essays, Fitzpatrick also sought academic outlets for his work. Not surprisingly, perhaps, one of his preferred academic journals was the *Queen's Quarterly*. Founded in 1893 by his mentor, George M. Grant, the quarterly included articles by Grant as well as many of the professors who had taught Alfred or whom he had admired, like John Watson, O. D. Skelton, and Adam Shortt. It frequently published articles on immigration, the need for training new citizens, or the "Asiatic Problem." Alfred's contribution in the *Quarterly* in 1913 was titled "Education on the Frontier." In it, he charged that the university had neglected to teach their young students the dignity of labour, and thus higher education had become the monopoly of cities. Again, in emphasizing extension programs, Alfred claimed that "the scene of men's labor is the proper place for their education." In less than a decade, Alfred would directly challenge university students and professors to engage in educating both "head and hand" within and without the cloistered halls of academia.

Alfred's writings were not always just about "the work." After a trip to Chicago's city slums in 1912, Alfred wrote to the association secretary, Frances McMechan, informing her that he was writing a story based on the darker side of life and the grave dangers that lurk in the streets of every large city for "young and inexperienced girls from the country." He asked how such a woman was able to fathom "who is clean and who is sincere." This encapsulates Alfred's attitude to the corruption of the city and reaffirms for him the rightness of his mission to the campmen. Another story of his was "The Men Without Homes," about building railroads in the west. Here he referenced the ethnic discrimination against the Chinese worker "who used to figure largely in construction camps, but they are now in disrepute due to 'white men only' rule." His ever-active mind was frequently on his fiction writings rather than his administrative responsibilities. In 1911, he noted that he had been so worried about finances that he had not been able to give a name to his new manuscript on frontier life in the United States and Canada; the possible titles were either *The Gates of Hell* or *God's Frontiersman.* Perhaps Alfred hoped to duplicate the financial success of his friend and fellow Presbyterian, Reverend C. W. Gordon, also known as bestselling author Ralph Connor. Whichever title he chose, Alfred's novel was not published. Much of his fiction, his notes, and first or second drafts never found their way into print and have disappeared from the records. Nevertheless, his non-fiction writings—articles in *Queen's Quarterly* and the *Canadian Magazine,* as well as newspaper editorials, letters to the editor, and opinion pieces—kept his fervent mind engaged. Some of the themes he raised found their way into his book *The University in Overalls,* which is examined in the next chapter.

Finally, Alfred wrote occasional pieces about his travels. One that is particularly notable is an account of his trip to Nova Scotia in December 1917, where he witnessed the effects of the largest

man-made explosion up to that time and one that would be superseded only by the atomic bomb some three decades later.

Just before midnight on December 5, 1917, Alfred boarded the
late-night train from Sydney to Halifax, Nova Scotia. While in
Cape Breton, he likely visited instructor John Burke, a medical
student of Dalhousie University who was spending his third year
working for the Dominion Coal Company in New Aberdeen as
a timekeeper. At night John taught Italian and Ukrainian immigrants who worked in the coal mines. Alfred's good friend, Frontier
College board member Reverend C. W. Gordon, who was described
in the Halifax dailies as "Minister-Author-Soldier," was scheduled
to give a lecture about his bestselling Ralph Connor novels the
next evening in Halifax, and Alfred may have wanted to attend
and discuss the work of the Reading Camp Association with him.
Gordon, no doubt, had many contacts and friends that could be
lobbied for financial and public support.

After a short stopover in Truro, Alfred boarded the Number 10
along with over three hundred people, and the train headed south-
east to Halifax, over one hundred kilometres away. It was scheduled
to arrive in Halifax at 8:55 A.M. that morning, December 6.

Meanwhile, in Halifax, the Norwegian supply ship *Imo* had
slipped its moorings just after seven o'clock that morning and prepared to leave Halifax Harbour, which was sheltering over one
hundred warships and supply ships in the Bedford Basin just north
of the city. "The Narrows," a water passage like the neck of a rum
bottle, connected the basin to the upper harbour and the Atlantic
Ocean. The Narrows was crowded with ships, boats, and tugs—a
nautical obstacle course that the *Imo* would have to weave its way
through in order to steam on to New York and from there take
much-needed supplies to German-occupied Belgium. The French
munitions ship *Mont-Blanc* had just entered the Narrows, having
arrived in Halifax to join a convoy sailing to Europe in support of

John Burke (seated) with a pupil at Dominion Coal, New Aberdeen, Cape Breton, Nova Scotia, circa 1910. **(LIBRARY AND ARCHIVES CANADA/FRONTIER COLLEGE FONDS/PA-142929)**

the war effort. On board was what one writer called "A devil's brew of cargo." The *Mont-Blanc* had loaded its munitions in New York, consisting of 250 tons of the very volatile benzol, which was stored on deck, and 60 tons of gun cotton, 2,400 tons of picric acid, and 250 tons of TNT in the hold.

The *Imo*, in its effort to leave the harbour, sideswiped the *Mont-Blanc* at 8:46 A.M. in the narrowest part of the harbour, and sparks from the collision ignited the benzol on deck. The resulting fire quickly spread to the gun cotton, picric acid, and TNT. Firefighters and ship crew members battled the blaze, but at precisely 9:04 A.M., the detonation occurred—an explosion that was equivalent to eighty-three million ounces of gunpowder or three kilotons of explosives. (The bomb dropped on Hiroshima was the equivalent of fifteen kilotons.)

The earth-shaking shock was immediate and was felt as far away as Sydney, Cape Breton, four hundred kilometres away. The explosion was followed by an enormous fifty-foot tsunami that rolled over part of the city. The result for Halifax was absolute devastation.

Minutes before the explosion, telegrapher Vince Coleman's last message had sped through the copper lines to nearby Rockingham Station, six kilometres from the Halifax terminal and situated on the west side of Bedford Basin. It then coursed on to Truro, alerting all small stations along the way to halt incoming trains to Halifax. Conductor J. C. Gillespie on the Number 10 train was held up by the dispatcher at Rockingham, and he announced to the passengers that there would be a delay. Alfred's account picks up the narrative: "[W]hile sitting at the Pullman window looking out on the magnificent old harbour with its hundred ships lying in the sunshine, suddenly I seemed to be lifted into the air. The window crashed in. I thought a bomb had struck the train…. [W]e saw a dense cloud full of colour rise from the harbour and concluded a bomb or magazine had exploded…on or near the water."

The train then slowly moved forward toward Halifax, and Alfred began to view the ghastly impact of the explosion. "I saw a woman rushing about outside her house, wringing her hands and crying. We saw that the windows in her house were gone, as was the case of other houses...many of the houses in ruins." The overhead bridge near the train station was burning, and men and women walked around with bleeding hands and faces. Gillespie quickly turned the train into a hospital. Blankets and pillows were appropriated, bandages were made from sheets and pillowcases, and the berth beds were pulled down for "the mangled and half naked victims." The general manager of the Dominion Atlantic Railway, George Graham, arrived and he ran the train backwards to Rockingham where he called Truro to inform them, Canada, and the world about what had happened in Halifax. Some two hundred wounded and dying were put on the train to Truro, accompanied by Alfred who made calls to "all the doctors and nurses I could."

A week later, Alfred returned to Toronto. Upon arrival, he gave his graphic description of a devastated city to a *Globe* reporter, and it was published quite soon after. Two weeks later, on December 28, the *Pictou Advocate Weekly* advertised a film by Pathé filmmakers on the Halifax Explosion called *The Halifax Disaster*. It was a 1,000-foot film shot twenty-four hours after the explosion and would be shown on January 4, 1918. The paper also included the account by Alfred that had appeared in the *Globe* with the new title: "Former Millsville Man Saw the Explosion."

There is no mention in the college records by Alfred or anyone else of the explosion and his role except for a brief comment by Jessie Lucas in a later interview. Whether he realized the close call he had experienced or the name of the man, Vince Coleman, who saved him and three hundred others is not known. If the 8:55 train had continued to Halifax, it would have been crushed when the roof of the north end train station collapsed from the explosion. As it was, in this city of fifty thousand, sixteen hundred men, women, and children died instantaneously—many were never found. The final death toll was almost two thousand, with nine thousand injured and many blinded by the shattered windows of their homes blowing inward. Twenty-five thousand (50 percent of the population) were rendered homeless, and a large area of the city was demolished. The First World War's lightning flash of death and destruction had come to Canada.

As a postscript, Vince Coleman, who was killed in the explosion, is well remembered in Halifax and beyond. His recovered belongings, including the telegraph key that tapped out that fateful message, are now on display in the Maritime Museum of the Atlantic in Halifax, and his heroism has been commemorated in the most watched "Heritage Minute" ever produced. A new ferry that now shuttles across Halifax Harbour several times a day bears the name *Vincent Coleman* with his name spelled out beneath in Morse code.

This chapter opened with a vignette that focused on the conflict between two men. An appreciation of the relationship between Alfred Fitzpatrick and Edmund Bradwin is fundamental to any understanding of the history of the Reading Camp Association that became Frontier College. These two men led the association/college for over fifty years (1900–1954), and in that time together—between 1904 and 1933—there were no doubt many disagreements in addition to the one already outlined. However, only a handful of such disagreements arise in the documents that might indicate the personal and professional tensions between them. Fortuitously, it would appear that the war years served to consolidate their trust and respect for each other. At the same time, their vision for the association and their own personal goals as to what they wished to accomplish increasingly diverged.

There were many instances of the ways in which they complemented one another. Alfred was the "visionary," the one who was repulsed by social injustice and wanted it corrected, the one who was persistent enough and persuasive enough to go out and find support for what to many was an ill-conceived venture, that of taking literacy to the Canadian backwoods. He would now attempt to mould this extension education program into a degree-granting national university.

Bradwin, for his part, was the "enabler," whose passion for the task would see him organize and train the literacy labourer-teachers and maintain the tenuous, far-reaching threads of contact with the workers and the work locations across Canada. At the same time, Bradwin also wanted to complete his education so that he would better understand how best to further the work of the association and have a safety net of education in case it failed. After the First World War ended, the visionary and the enabler took different paths within Frontier College that would culminate in a bitter parting of ways in 1933. For now, though, in 1919, they were inextricably linked.

By January 1915, Bradwin had begun the coursework toward his doctorate at Columbia University in New York. Alfred had in effect given him a paid leave of absence. The association contributed a weekly stipend of twelve dollars to Bradwin's expenses despite the verbal altercation with Alfred barely three months before. While Bradwin was in New York, there was a continuous exchange between himself and Alfred with regard to a variety of issues and problems facing the association, as well as Bradwin's financial situation and how he was faring in his studies. Bradwin's letters were full of questions about and advice to instructors. For example, he wrote that Instructor Gilbert was no good, "always grunting with some kind of ache or pain" and that Instructor Parker was too young and unsuitable because he was "a coddled kid who can't inspire men." He urged Fitzpatrick to ensure that he would only take on instructors that would differentiate themselves from the camp followers: "the usual beggars who plague the camp—whether priests, preachers on a one-night stand, Sisters for Catholic picnics, et al." These were often Alfred's sentiments, although perhaps expressed more eloquently.

Regarding his studies, Bradwin observed that he had done more writing at Queen's than was required at Columbia. His now yellowed and dog-eared copy of Marx and Engels's *Communist Manifesto* for his course in Marxian socialism has survived, and in Bradwin's handwriting are trenchant marginal notes both critical and complimentary on every page. Nevertheless, neither Bradwin, and certainly not Fitzpatrick, would ever be mistaken for Marxists.

As for New York City, Bradwin enjoyed the historic sites and scenery, making observations that Alfred would no doubt have agreed with. He praised the architectural beauty and immensity of the new Anglican cathedral, St. John the Divine, which could seat two thousand parishioners, but he noted that it cost $12 million to build and "to me it is a crime to tie up millions like that." Bradwin believed that money would have been better spent assisting men in the work camps. As we've seen, Alfred had always been sharply critical of the vast amounts of money spent by churches. In the annual report of 1910, there is a two-page spread of photographs positioned to face each other. One page contains views of six large churches in Toronto, including an interior view of the pews of his own church—St. Andrew's. On the opposite page is an interior view of the crowded, clothes-strewn, confined space of a bunkhouse. The first is captioned "Where the people of Toronto worship" and the second "Where the frontier toilers worship."

In May 1915, Bradwin returned to his home in Wingham to look after his mother. As he was no longer a paid employee of the association, Alfred appointed him as one of the directors of the association's board in order to draw upon his expertise and his counsel. Bradwin likely accepted the appointment with some trepidation. Some two years previously, he had reported in a careful handwritten letter to Alfred on the many complaints of the low wages in the work camps. His acid comment on the owners? "They are the type to make rich men...like our own H. L. Lovering, who can then go around and be a good fatherly man at Methodist meetings." H. L. Lovering was chair of the Reading Camp Association board of which Bradwin was now a member. Fortunately Bradwin was not obligated to attend meetings.

While home in Wingham, Bradwin began to work on his dissertation, but he also spent a considerable amount of time preparing a booklet on teaching: *English for New Canadians*. Alfred had contracted him to prepare it for print. As early as 1913, Bradwin had begun distributing to the instructors what he called "group words for foreigners." Now he had an opportunity to edit a print copy. His booklet was completed in 1917, and copies were given to all instructors as they travelled to the camps. In this handbook, Bradwin also added national ideals for Canada, Canadian government and history, and what he felt were the principles and duties of Canadian citizenship. Most of it—both the language and civic history materials—would find its way into Alfred's *Handbook for New Canadians* published in 1919.

In Bradwin's absence from the office (1915–17), Alfred continued his travel to camps, managing the "administrivia" of the Toronto office with the assistance of a capable staff and tending to the never-ending rounds of fundraising. Raising money for non-profit organizations is not an easy task even in the best of times, let alone during a world war. In addition, as a war measure, the Canadian government introduced the income tax act. Now competition for donations was fierce. In a country where government social benefits were non-existent, there were almost 150 charities in Toronto alone looking to the city and provincial coffers for assistance, including Dr. Barnardo's Home for Boys, Prisoner's Aid Association, Ontario Society for Reformation of Inebriates, and, of course, the many usual requests from hospitals, orphanages, and universities.

Neither Fitzpatrick nor Bradwin liked this aspect of the work—to lobby and "to beg" for support for an obviously needy cause. But it could not be avoided. Since its very beginnings, this was and would continue to be a requirement for the association (later the college) to flourish. Nevertheless, they succeeded and in addition, the skills that each of them brought to the organization ensured its long-term success. As secretary Jessie Lucas observed, "Mr. Fitzpatrick had the idea," but it would never have succeeded if it hadn't been for Dr. Bradwin. "So, I always feel there were two founders," and one should never be mentioned without the other.

The Reading Camp Association would emerge from the First World War intact, with a new name, Frontier College, and a new purpose. It would not only continue the basic literacy program for the camps, but also make a much greater effort to instill nationalism, or Canadianism as it was called, in a diverse population. In addition, new goals would be formulated that would take the association far beyond the education in the camps. Now the objective was to provide extension courses at a university level to all who wished to graduate with a bachelor or master of arts degree. It was this last objective that would almost destroy the newly named Frontier College in the decade to come.

CHAPTER 6

ESTABLISHING A NATIONAL COLLEGE 1918–1922

JESSIE LUCAS

WELL, THE PLACE CERTAINLY NEEDED A CLEANUP. JESSIE LUCAS *was not impressed. The Frontier College office was Suite 1323–24 in the Bank of Hamilton Building, 62 Yonge Street at the corner of King, formerly the Traders Bank Building. Impressive address! However, it was really only one room made into two by a partition separating a front and back office. The back room had some sunlight through a large window, but the view was obscured by a fire escape. This was the principal's office, and Jessie's as well if she took the job. But she was having her doubts. "It was dark and dingy... the most Dickensian set-up imaginable—part office, part store room, and part shipping room" with dust in every nook and cranny. And it was untidy. The principal, Alfred Fitzpatrick, admitted to making the rather unstable shelves. Jessie noted "he was no carpenter," and there were "a couple of pairs of trousers hanging behind the roll-top desk."*

This was not what Jessie imagined a college might be. The entry in the City Directory had listed The Frontier College in large capitals together with the principal's name and degree: B.A. Born in 1894, Jessie had graduated with her Bachelor of Arts from the University of Toronto in 1918, and when the Great

War ended and the soldiers began to return home, there were fewer and fewer jobs available for young women. Consequently, she took a business program, hoping it would help her gain an administrative position. The advertisement for a secretary at Frontier College was appealing. Jessie liked what she read about the college's work, and a friend assured her that if the college board included the well-known businessman James Playfair, prominent in shipping, lumbering, and manufacturing circles, then it must be all right. In addition, on that self-same thirteenth floor of the bank building was the office of the Lovering Lumber Company, and Jessie noted that another prominent and prosperous businessman, H. L. Lovering, was chair of the Frontier College board.

Principal Fitzpatrick, when she met him at her interview, struck her as very tall and quite thin, almost gaunt. He wore a high collar and yet "his neck would protrude from his collar." He was very kind but very serious and "not very fluent." She later noted that he always tried to measure her and others he interacted with by his remarks and with his eyes. She wrote, "he had the most penetrating gaze of anyone I have met. Very deep blue eyes and very...well, almost piercing. ...[Y]ou just felt as if he was looking right through your soul. You just felt too that you had to measure up."

At the end of the interview, Alfred gave Jessie a copy of the recently published Handbook for New Canadians *and a couple of pamphlets and asked her to consider the job. Jessie liked the idea of Frontier College, but she didn't make her decision right away. A month later, not having heard back from her, Alfred telephoned and asked for her decision. She responded that the salary was fine, twelve dollars a week, the normal starting salary, and the hours were fine, but she had decided not to take the job. Alfred asked why and she responded, "the place is too untidy." Alfred laughed and said, "I think we can fix it up [and] I think we can satisfy you."*

In order to make the office more presentable, he sent her off to Underwood Typewriters to pick out a new desk and moved it into the partitioned back office— the area with the window. Jessie began work in September 1920. She enjoyed the work to no end. "It was just a challenge and it just appealed to me very, very much.... [T]he whole atmosphere of the place was of a very high caliber."

Jessie Lucas would spend the next forty-three years at Frontier College, outlasting both Fitzpatrick, who retired in 1933, and Bradwin, who stepped down in 1954. She would serve as secretary, bursar, registrar, treasurer, and archivist. In 1954, in his last address to the Frontier College board, shortly before his death, Bradwin urged the board to appoint Jessie as acting principal due to her "intimate knowledge of the work." The board turned down his recommendation. Jessie retired in 1963 and died in 1996 at 102 years of age.

In response to the First World War, Canada had successfully recruited tens of thousands of young men and women and sent them to the bloody battlefields of Europe. It became clear that explaining the causes and purposes of the war was essential in order to mobilize the rest of Canada industrially, physically, and mentally for the struggle, and to win it. Educational extension programs became an important aspect of this mobilization, and the university and college graduates who were Frontier College instructors did much of this "explaining." But as the war ended, it also became clear that the basic educational needs of the country still had to be addressed.

In 1918, the Workers' Educational Association, modelled on the WEA in England, had its Canadian inception in Toronto at a meeting of university and labour representatives. Its purpose was to bring higher education to farmers and unionized industrial workers. This was not to be vocational or elementary education but adult education on such subjects as economics, history, and current events. The lectures and seminars were geographically limited to the urban centres of Ontario like Toronto, Kingston, and Hamilton. By 1923, the Ontario WEA was conducting thirty-three classes with one thousand students, usually offered by the universities of the province, especially U of T, Queen's, and McMaster.

In other parts of the country, the University of British Columbia was offering extension lectures in different communities as well as short and long courses. Alberta had started a well-organized travelling library system, and Dr. Walter Murray, president of the University of Saskatchewan, in his annual report for 1912–1913 had already written of the need for extension courses, travelling libraries, and correspondence courses, not just in agrarian practices but in the humanities as well. In Fitzpatrick's home province of Nova Scotia, there was another "adult education visionary"

Jessie Lucas was secretary and registrar of Frontier College from 1920 to 1963. (PRIVATE COLLECTION OF JESSIE LUCAS)

who, like Fitzpatrick, stood outside the educational and, for that matter, the religious establishment. Father Jimmy Tompkins was an agitational presence who believed that in addition to preaching about change, the Roman Catholic Church actually had to enact it. Tompkins was a leader of other reform-minded priests who wanted to assist the poor and the worker—farmers, fishermen, and miners—by instituting a "social Catholicism." To reach this goal, in the early 1920s Tompkins called for education for all ages. Perhaps due to Tompkins's prodding, in 1921 the People's School was begun at St. Francis Xavier College (now University) in Antigonish, Nova Scotia.

Writing in a descriptive booklet published by the Nova Scotia Department of Agriculture entitled *The People's School* (1922), Dr. Moses Coady, a member of the teaching staff at St. Francis Xavier and colleague of Tompkins, observed "the time is ripe for a vigorous program of adult education in this country." As with Fitzpatrick's mission with the labourer-teachers in the work camps, Coady added that the goal was to find out what people wanted and to provide it—to bring "the great majority who stand outside and must remain outside the walls of our College" into the university and provide a useful education to the fishermen and farmers about their problems and possible solutions. What would become known as the Antigonish Movement had begun with this commitment to adult education. By 1928, St. Francis Xavier College had established an extension department, with Coady as the first director, with the task of utilizing adult education to combat social and economic problems in rural communities.

Nevertheless, none of these university-led initiatives was making any effort to address the needs of immigrant workers. So there was a place for Frontier College.

With the war over, Alfred became consumed by his efforts to incorporate Frontier College and have it recognized as a Dominion institution. There was still, however, the day-to-day administrative duties of the Toronto office and the enabling of the work in the distant camps. Unfortunately, with war's end his chief "enabler," Ed Bradwin, had resumed his Ph.D. studies at Columbia University in New York. For the next four years, once he had established the labourer-teachers in their camps, Bradwin attended the spring semester at Columbia and enrolled in courses about labour union organizations and industrial history, and a number of reading courses. Frontier College still listed him as Director of Instructors and assisted him financially when the need arose.

By May 1922, Bradwin had passed his oral examinations at Columbia and had his first major article published on the subject of his thesis, "The Challenge of the Migratory Worker," a paper he had presented in Buffalo in 1921 to the International Association of Public Employment Services. In it he provided background on the very original work of Frontier College and also wrote of his own first-hand experience with the far-flung camps of Canada to which the labourer-teacher was sent. Much of this information on labour would appear in his doctoral thesis as well as his subsequent book, *The Bunkhouse Man*, which was based on his thesis.

In 1918 there were 3,700 camps in Canada with migratory workers, and 1,500 of them were in Ontario, each with an average of some sixty men. Bradwin made the point that any traveller going to Northern Ontario by railroad might think they were traversing the empty tree-shadowed spaces of an uninhabited area when, in actual fact, there were thousands of men working on or near the rail line. Well over two hundred thousand men lived for a large portion of the year in a Canadian bunkhouse, and some 40 percent of them were in Northern Ontario.

There had been changes in the composition of the labour force during and after the war. Foreign-born workers (or "bohunks" as they were derisively called) were the majority in the camps before the war, but many had gone back to Europe or had been replaced by returning Canadian soldiers. In a survey of one hundred winter camps in the area around the Great Lakes, just 25 percent of the men were foreign-born, 60 percent were English-speaking Canadians, and 15 percent were French Canadians. Still, some 80 percent of the railway extra gangs, which consisted of men living in various locations along the rail lines to repair the tracks, was foreign-born workers who were also seasonal workers. Most of these workers were given little rec-ognition by organized unions, and even the OBU (One Big Union) seldom made it to Northern Ontario. The Canadian government had established labour bureaus in 1918, but much of their work was in the industrial sector. Therefore, as Alfred had envisioned, the task of basic literacy for the many and higher education for the few was one that Frontier College must attempt to carry out.

The title of the annual report for 1920 was "The University and the Frontier" with the inside cover noting the objectives as "Welfare – Instruction – Canadianization – Leadership." That was certainly work enough to keep the Frontier College office on Yonge Street busy. In addition, with the forthcoming struggle to push incorpora-tion of the college through Parliament, the office was, as Fitzpatrick often said, "unspeakably busy." With Bradwin away part of the year for his studies, the office comprised one other staff member (R. W. Collins), the new secretary (Jessie Lucas), and Alfred himself. In Bradwin's absence, Jessie assumed more and more responsibility for the men in the field.

It was during this time that job appointments for university-educated women were made. Alfred had sent out an almost Biblical newspaper advertisement for the college in early 1919. Utilizing a quote from the German philosopher and educationalist Friedrich Froebel (1782–1852), it read:

WANTED

Graduates and undergraduates to engage in manual labor during the day and teach evenings. Will you not obey Froebel's call? "Come let us live with our students," combat Bolshevik ideas at their source, demonstrate that you too belong to the working classes, and thus find your own life by losing it.

Good wages.

This call for graduates and undergraduates to live and work with their students did not differentiate between men and women. As noted earlier, the first Reading Camp Association instructor was Mrs. Alex Scott in 1900, so Alfred was very open to the idea of hiring women. Bradwin, on the other hand, was always opposed to "sending women out" to be labourer-teachers, basically because he felt they would require greater supervision and support. Alfred for his part believed that women could cope with any hardship. As he wrote in *The University in Overalls* in 1920, if conditions in the various work camps such as cleanliness, sanitation, and safety were unfit for women, then the camps were also unfit for men. Perhaps, with Bradwin away, there was an opportunity to try again. Consequently, three women were sent out as Frontier College instructors in 1920. The last time a woman had been an instructor was in 1903, when Miss B. M. Laverie served in a railway camp of the Temiskaming and Northern Railway. Now, Marjorie Wickwire, B.A., and Miriam Chisholm, B.A., both from Acadia University, were sent to work at a fish processing plant in Bear River, Nova Scotia, with many other women on the assembly line, gutting fish. The third woman, Isabel Mackey (M.A., University of Toronto) was an education and welfare worker with the women around Stalwart, Saskatchewan, during the grain harvesting in July and August. Alfred had equipped her with a three-foot by four-foot rubber blackboard, arithmetic books, Ontario Readers, a CNR map of Eastern Canada, and of course the ubiquitous *Handbook for New Canadians*. Alfred's brother John and his family owned a farm outside of the community of Stalwart, and Mackey stayed with them. Her task, as she recounted in an interview with historian Marjorie Zavitz (deposited in Library and Archives Canada in the mid 1970s) was to "work up" the community spirit "because a lot of these people were not Anglo-Saxons and I think to encourage them in meeting together." Teaching reading was an important part of this. She added, "I really worked hard…

[when] the thrashers came. I had them to feed and they came early in the morning.... Had to make the most of their days, and I didn't have many hours in bed, but I did the best I could."

A year later, in 1921, Mackey was working with the women at the Connors Brothers sardine canning and packing factory in Black's Harbour, New Brunswick, which employed 150 women and 200 men. "I worked in the canning factory whenever the fish were available. I worked with the women. I wasn't the poorest packer but I wasn't the best, [as] the women...had years of experience." Alfred was so grateful for her performance in New Brunswick and Saskatchewan that in December 1921 he sent her a barrel of apples and a personalized card with "Hearty Christmas Greeting and Best Wishes." Isabel Mackey would later serve as a member of the Frontier College board of governors.

Alfred was open to any and all methods that enabled the college to more effectively do its job. There is scattered evidence in the Frontier College files of the variety of, at times, outlandish initiatives by which Alfred sought to assist the college. Jessie Lucas draws a wonderful word-picture of when his "innovative mind" was seized by an idea, which, she remembers, was not an infrequent occurrence. She recounts vividly that his hair would seem to stand out from his head and his blue eyes would sparkle with electric excitement. Many of Alfred's ideas and initiatives were recorded in his own personal filing system—a scribbler that he always carried with him.

A now yellowed and faded Empire Scribbler from the T. Eaton Co. in Toronto made a useful clippings book and research source for Alfred. Dating from 1919, it included clippings of information that Alfred, a voracious reader, often used for his essays, editorials, and talks. For example, when he was pursuing "Canadianization" for the camps, a clipping outlined plans for a conference called by the United States Department of Interior on "making Americans." In this regard, the Carnegie Foundation in New York had contributed five million dollars in 1919 to carry out an "Americanization" study. Research from the war had shown that 25 percent of America's draft army were unable to read a newspaper or write a letter. Obviously, literacy and nationalization were inextricably linked, and Fitzpatrick was no doubt pleased to read that the United States was beginning to undertake the same analysis that he had already been doing in Canada. In later years, Alfred would successfully apply to the Carnegie Foundation for similar support.

To maintain his clippings book with current material, the college was registered with the Canadian Press clipping service, which forwarded any mention of college activities and interests to the Frontier office. One example was "The Immigrants and Canada," an article published in 1919 that noted the state must be responsible for providing the immigrant with an opportunity to acquire an education in English. This reinforced Alfred's opinion as did the 1921 article "A Problem of Settlement," which examined the efforts of Northern Ontario and Western Canada in promoting settlement.

No doubt this attention to popular media would have stimulated Alfred's mind in other directions as well. In the National Archives file labelled "Inventions" is a submission to the Patent Office, Washington, for a clothes dryer and clothes hanger. This was a wire device to support clothes hung on a radiator, kitchen tank, or heater. In its description, Fitzpatrick wrote: "It often happens that women overtax themselves on washing and ironing days. This invention will enable a busy mother to do her washing piecemeal as opportunity affords, drying articles, not requiring bleaching, hardily [*sic*] without going outside in severe weather." Fitzpatrick may well have been thinking of his mother. This invention would have no doubt been useful to Mary when she raised her eleven children. Whether there would have been room in their farmhouse for this somewhat complicated wire device is another matter.

His other inventions were closely related to a life on the road and staying in places like bunkhouses and boxcars that did not have all the amenities. His combination, one-piece comb and razor was one such item. This was patented in Canada for an eighteen-year period in 1920. A more outlandish one was the rubber suit for taking a bath. It looked like a diving suit and was a loose rubber, neck-to-toe suit that could be worn with an orifice at the shoulder so water and soap could be poured in. Thus the person could bathe "privately" in public.

In 1923, Alfred registered at the trademark office in Ottawa the name Fruit Cereal Company Ottawa. He had already been manufacturing and distributing cereal samples in stamped boxes for a year or so. By 1924, he was in touch with the James Mills Orchards Company in Hamilton City, California. Mills had acquired 8,500 acres in Northern California and specialized in the production of dried fruit. Alfred was requesting dried pears "at a good price" for his new cereal, called "Fruit Cereal," that he was putting on the market, with profits to benefit the college. Mills responded in less than a week that he could not do it at present but would in future "if sent more information." No information was sent.

Alfred always stated that any money earned from his inventions would go to the college, but lacking both capital and the attention required for follow-up, his concepts and inventions were doomed to failure. (As the saying goes, don't give up your day job, Alfred.) Consequently he had to continue the activity he despised most— asking for money. Perhaps he thought a more modern approach was necessary to achieve financial stability for the college.

To Alfred, the visual image was always an important component of promotion. He often engaged local professional photographers to take photos of labourer-teachers and their environment, but with the war over, Alfred felt the "message" had to move to a more contemporary medium. The Canadian film industry was just beginning, and Alfred saw film as a new method by which he could publicize the college. The location chosen for a Frontier College film could not have been more grandiose: Niagara Falls.

In late summer of 1920, Alfred noted he had a Mr. Wolf of the Pathéscope of Canada film company "looking for film sites." The new United Farmers Party of Ontario had come to power in 1919 on the basis of its promise to provide cheap electrical power to the province utilizing the Niagara Falls, 130 kilometres from Toronto. Two hydroelectric generating stations were to be built at the Falls, and Frontier College would post labourer-teachers to a number of the locations in 1920 and 1921. This seemed to be an obvious location for the film because it was both near the city of Toronto and a project that might win even more favour with the already supportive Ontario government. Within the year, Mr. Wolf had made a two-reel, sixteen-millimetre film of the college's work on the construction at Niagara Falls. The film was then shown at Massey Hall, local cinemas like the Allen Theatre in Toronto, and various churches as an awareness raising and fundraising activity. But as Alfred travelled on a Toronto streetcar to a showing, he left one of the reels on the seat, and over the years the other half of the film also went missing. There was only one copy. As Jessie Lucas explained, "Mr. Fitzpatrick lost everything...he was that kind of person." The only visual evidence that there ever was a film are a half-dozen outtake photographs in the Library and Archives Canada of the labourer-teachers working and teaching at the Niagara Falls location. The college had to return once more to the ever dependable glass lantern slide showings. It would be another three decades before the National Film Board of Canada made its 1954 film *Frontier College*, which focused on President Ed Bradwin and the work of the college in the early 1950s.

When Alfred began his efforts to correct the living conditions and illiteracy in the work camps, he had flirted briefly with the idea of working with the labour unions. However, there were no unions established in the Northern Ontario camps at this time, so in order to gain access to the migratory workers, Alfred sought out company owners and mill managers to assist him. Elsewhere, in the first decade of the twentieth century, the International Workers of the World (IWW), a US-based union, was attempting to represent the rights of migratory workers and organize them in order that they could express their specific grievances. IWW became active in the mining and railway camps of Western Canada, especially British Columbia. By 1912, the IWW was involved in the Canadian Northern Railway strike and also undertook union activities in the isolated railway camps of the Grand Trunk Pacific. The provincial authorities were quick to respond with strike-breakers, intimidation, and ultimately jail for over 250 "wobblies," as they were called. By late summer 1912, the strikes were over.

Meanwhile, political and social developments had affected European economies negatively, and this economic slump crossed the Atlantic. Thus, leading up to the First World War there was widespread unemployment in Western Canada in the resource and transportation industries, and workers were much less susceptible to calls to protest their working conditions as doing so could lead to job insecurity. The social and economic tensions between workers and owners were in abeyance for much of the war, until the "Bolshevik" cry for revolution echoed across the Atlantic with war's end.

The Reading Camp Association, newly christened Frontier College in 1917, had survived the war, but could it survive the ideological conflict that followed? The revolution that had removed Russian troops from the muddy trenches and rutted battlefields of Europe had now spread to an unstable Germany, the rest of Europe, and beyond. Bolshevism was on the rise, and Canadians watched with mounting apprehension what was taking place in Europe and feared for themselves. In Canada, 1919 brought upheaval— unemployment, industrial unrest, rising prices, the Spanish flu that killed almost fifty million worldwide, and now the red scare in an increasingly unsafe world.

Having successfully avoided any entanglements with unions, Alfred, and therefore Frontier College, was now faced with a new rival and a new dilemma. Since the beginnings of the college, Alfred had, for the most part, ensured the men in the camps were subject only to the call of literacy and "clean living," not the call of religion, but now there was a far different call—to strike for social change with potentially violent consequences. The IWW had established the spectre of industrial unrest in the face of appalling labour conditions and low wages in 1912, and now with the threat of the red menace—Bolshevism—this spectre was back. What exactly would and could the college do when the demands of capital impacted so severely on the welfare of the worker? In this regard, it was caught between the obvious social and economic needs of the worker and the risk of facilitating the work of what would be labelled a radical "red" union that might cause violence. Just what aspect of the labourer's life could the college serve and still survive as an organization?

In his introduction to the annual report for 1919, entitled "The Instructor and the Red," Alfred voiced his opposition to the efforts of the IWW and what he considered radicals who were "carefully schooling willing converts in the camps," provoking discontent with strikes, and distributing "fiery" pamphlets about "perverted forms of socialism." Alfred's solution for counteracting this schooling was what Frontier College had offered for twenty years, namely literacy and learning. He then went on to criticize both church and state for not having "cultivated the ground" much earlier with education, literacy, and citizenship. In these revolutionary times, the government should support the college's instructors to the extent that every settlement, camp, and industrial plant would take on the character of learning institutions like schools and colleges. In his view such action would contain the unrest.

Given the labour analysis that Bradwin was undertaking based on his extensive experience in the camps, the college was well prepared. Still, when the instructors in unsettled camps wrote of strikes, firings, and layoffs, they felt caught in the middle. The workers may have felt that although the instructor worked shoulder to shoulder with them, he was still not one of them. Perhaps the labourer-teacher was a government agent. Alternatively, if the labourer-teacher showed too much consideration or sympathy for the men he worked with, the bosses might view him suspiciously as a possible "red" union backer; the reading room might even be used for union assemblies.

By 1919 the college was under great pressure by its business, government, and public partners to explain exactly what it was doing and why. The college, therefore, increasingly emphasized its role in providing instruction in "literacy and Canadianization." This in turn led to the publication by the college of the three-hundred-page *Handbook for New Canadians*, which was in effect a guide to the instructors.

In addition, the college told the labourer-teachers to avoid taking sides with either workers or management—in other words, to keep their heads down. As Jessie Lucas recalls, the instructor was told quite plainly by Bradwin and Fitzpatrick "to keep his tongue between his teeth and not criticize the company" and "was supposed never to take sides." A few did get involved in the labour unrest, but most stayed away from criticizing management. They were there at the sufferance of the company to convey Canadian values and teach basic English. One step beyond that would lead to the instructor being told to leave the camp, and once expelled, any college instructor would not be allowed to return to that camp.

Given their isolated locations, the labour camps where the college had focused its activities were well beyond the reach of the unions based in urban areas, so the college was rarely forced to make a choice between its goals and those of the unions. Not surprisingly, neither Fitzpatrick nor Bradwin were supportive of any "radical" orientation. Alfred had always been a social gospel liberal, albeit somewhat paternalistic, who wished to bring about change from inside the system. At the same time, he recognized how little he knew about the union movement and set out to educate himself accordingly. Around 1920 or '21, he met Tom Moore, president of the Trades and Labour Congress. Moore became a supporter of the college, helped it to raise funds, and was an advisor to Alfred on all union matters. By 1922, he had become the first union leader to sit on the college board, and his presence, no doubt, assisted Alfred in lobbying Ottawa to recognize the college's national aspirations. In the 1922 annual report, Tom is quoted as saying, "The work of the Frontier College has always appealed to me as one of great value."

Both the Canadian government and the Canadian economy would affect the issues in the camps. Returning servicemen were given employment priority, and this meant there was less need for immigrant labour and many were thrown out of work. At the same time, the country experienced a postwar recession. For its part, the Canadian government under Prime Minister Robert Borden enacted, through orders-in-council, the Anti-Loafing Act of 1918, which meant any immigrants without jobs could be deported.

A year later, Section 41 of the Immigration Act gave authorities the power to deport any immigrants considered "dangerous aliens." Between 1919 and 1925, 75 percent of the deportations from the country were for "criminality" and "being a public charge." No immigrant would want to risk this. In 1922, in the face of a new postwar reality, any possibility of the organization of the camp workers for radical ends had been snuffed out. The college in its annual report for that year reflected this new reality, as there was no mention of Bolsheviks or Reds.

As we've seen, the Reading Camp Association had been involved in Canadianizing new (and old) Canadians since its earliest days. The Canadian nationalism aspect of its work was somewhat abstract. The central focus was on literacy as taught by a labourer-teacher who would serve as an exemplary representation of the values of a "good Canadian." Even as the numbers of foreign workers increased with the swell of new immigrants to Canada, the literacy curriculum changed very little. However, with the First World War, love of country became a priority, and a new college approach, in addition to literacy, had to be explored. It was no longer enough to provide books, newspapers, and magazines to isolated camps for leisure reading. The reading tents, bunkhouses, and boxcars must be centres for civics classes with a comprehensive curriculum for all. To achieve this, the college introduced a standardized teaching approach for labourer-teachers.

In 1919, a "textbook" to counteract the Bolshevik menace and foster national values was published by Ryerson Press in Toronto with Alfred Fitzpatrick's name on its spine. He was acknowledged on the title page as Alfred Fitzpatrick, B.A., Principal of Frontier College, and on the overleaf was a listing of the many booklets he had written over the years. This new three-hundred-page book, the aforementioned and appropriately titled *Handbook for New Canadians*, had been in the making for fifteen years and contained substantial input from Ed Bradwin, especially given his earlier work creating English-as-an-additional-language booklets.

The first section of the handbook included lesson plans and grading guides for the instructor, photographs, and 130 short lessons in paragraph form. Many of these lessons were site specific, not about some urban setting in a child's vocabulary but related to the reader's environment with titles like "Logging," "The Sawmill," "The Bunkhouse," "At the Mine," and "The Coal Wagon"—work and activities in which these men were actually engaged and that were part of their everyday reality. The last fifty pages of the book were vocabularies of much used "stock words," translated from English into Italian, French, Swedish, Ukrainian, Russian, and Yiddish. These listings were to assist the labourer-teacher in his communication with the other workers. From the perspective of the college, English was an essential skill to more easily integrate the newcomer into Canadian society, but acknowledgement of the students' first language was important as well to establish contact. The remainder of the handbook represented the completion of an education that would "make them efficient, healthy, self-respecting citizens." It consisted of another 150 pages of information on Canadian geography, government, and history, from the "discovery" up to the current prime minister, Robert Borden. Perhaps of most value to some workers was the forty-page section on how to obtain Canadian naturalization, which was presented in considerable detail with the "demand that every man who comes to Canada become a citizen."

Thus, the handbook was not just written for camp pedagogy, but also as a primer directed at the Canadian government to make adequate provisions for the assimilation of the population. For its part, the government demanded that new citizens have a knowledge of English or French, but it made no effort to teach them. From the point of view of the college, in order to be eligible for Canadian citizenship after the required five-year period had passed, the applicant should have a language exam in French or English as well as an examination of their knowledge of Canada in general. Only in this way would a "New Canadian" be accepted. Rather than the Canadian government simply mailing a certificate of citizenship, the book suggested that the naturalization ceremony should be a celebration for the immigrant, perhaps on Dominion Day, July first each year.

This compendium of material was clearly a joint venture between Fitzpatrick and Bradwin. How much of the handbook is Bradwin's contribution cannot be known, but given his experience he presumably played a substantial role. As for Alfred, perhaps he viewed Bradwin as a research assistant gathering and editing the material as part of his job. Although he does not list Bradwin as co-author, Fitzpatrick does dedicate the *Handbook for New Canadians* "To E. W. Bradwin, M.A., My Colleague And Friend, Who Has Given So Many Years Of His Life As An Instructor And Canadianizer In Bunkhouses And Camps Of Canada."

Three thousand copies of the handbook were printed, and from 1919 on, it would be issued to every labourer-teacher going to the camps. True to Reading Camp Association policy from its very beginnings, any textbook could not stand alone. The handbook's Introduction stated clearly: "These outlines must be supplemented by the wholesome contact of an instructor interested in the foreigner," in other words, a labourer-teacher who worked with them in the daytime and taught them at night. Given the plethora of copies, many were also distributed to friends, politicians, and any from whom the college sought support. Despite positive reviews from the *Canadian Mining Journal* and the *Pulp and Paper Magazine*, the handbook did not fly off the shelves, and in the end sales did not cover the printing costs. But the *Handbook for New Canadians* did serve as a practical, hands-on application of Alfred's philosophy of adult education, which would be published the next year under the title *The University in Overalls: A Plea for Part-time Study.*

The Quebec press called Alfred's book *L'Université en Salopettes*, and in the July 1921 issue of *Le Semeur: Organe de l'Association Catholique de la Jeunesse Canadian-Français,* Eugene Dubois reviewed it very positively. This was just one of the many book reviews that greeted *The University in Overalls* after it was released in late 1920. Again, as with the *Handbook for New Canadians*, it was written with the careful blue pencil editing of Ed Bradwin whose photograph, all six-foot-three, two hundred and twenty-five pounds of him, appeared on the fly-leaf of the cover. In the photo a much younger Bradwin is completely kitted for camp, in workshirt, breeches, and high-laced leather boots—the epitome of the labourer-teacher. In his preface, Alfred thanks Ed in particular for his help and many practical suggestions based on his first-hand knowledge of frontier conditions. The organization of the volume certainly manifests Bradwin's editorial expertise.

The University in Overalls was a long time coming. Its gestation period of some twenty years could be signposted by Alfred's yearly booklets that were usually included with the annual reports of the college. The book is a clearly articulated compilation of what had occupied Alfred's thinking over the years, since his first exposure to the work camp conditions in the early 1890s. Simply put, it was, as stated in the preface, "intended as an appeal for increased efforts toward extending the university to all. It is vital that higher education be brought to the masses.... Classes must be held, not only in the schools and universities, but in the shops, on the works, in the camps and fields and settlements of the frontier." *The University in Overalls* represented Alfred's practical and philosophical rationale for how to do just that.

Aside from J. J. (Jimmy) Tompkins's soon-to-be published *Knowledge for the People* (1921) and Fitzpatrick's own *Handbook for New Canadians* (1919), there was still very little literature on or interest in adult education, especially by Canadian universities. As noted, the WEA in Toronto offered lectures to union employees and farmers but always in an urban setting and with a typical classroom pedagogy. This initiative did not include the workers—either new immigrants or non-immigrants—who lived and worked in the secluded camps of Canada's vastness. It was into this void that Alfred, outspoken as ever, flung *The University in Overalls: A Plea for Part-time Study* in 1920.

In this time of social ferment for labour, ethnocultural groups, and women in a rapidly changing Canada, Alfred offered his many criticisms of the present situation and a reasoned blueprint for the future. Based on his experience, Alfred presented his four guidelines for literacy, guidelines that the college had adhered to since its beginnings:

CONTACT: The personal association between instructor and student.
RELEVANCE: Learning what the needs and interests of the men were.
RAPPORT: Sharing both work and leisure time with the men.
CONTENT: Teaching what the men thought necessary to learn.

He went on to provide a brief historical overview of the college then proceeded to lambaste a number of what he identified as long-standing shibboleths within Canadian society as to labour, class, and education. He criticized the wealthy class for their financial vanity, pointing out how easy it is to find a "generous millionaire who is willing to donate a public library bearing his name in some small town" but not willing to spend a dime to support social change in work camps. The large endowments for universities by wealthy men provided for the few, yet their own workers in camps and mills were in substandard living and housing conditions. From Alfred's perspective, these workers needed social justice.

As for universities, his opinion was that they would not "stoop down and fraternize with the workers" and that "It was high time that we dropped the egoism and middle-ages idea that education can only be had in a separation from the world." He wrote, "Higher education should never have become the monopoly of the cities." He then commented that the university's biggest failing was with their students, who should have been taught, by participation if possible, to respect both mental as well as manual work. Any undergraduate who is physically fit should undertake part-time manual work before receiving a degree. Alfred also suggested that professors should do manual work as well as teach in camps, settlements, and factories. And, of course, he returned to his plea that there must be extramural courses everywhere. He also stressed that the work of the miner, the lumberman, and the navvy was not unskilled, and therefore these workers should not be considered either uneducated or uneducatable. He wrote that "to know how to handle a peavy, break a jam of logs or drive a spike accurately or fall a tree perfectly, is Education."

Many of Alfred's exhortations in *The University in Overalls* were clearly not attainable. Still, a number of his reflections were prescient and have taken decades to be appreciated, like the need for citizenship training as well as a naturalization ceremony, a recognition that the ideal state must "educate all the people not a chosen few," and how higher education has systematically depopulated rural communities. He emphasized the need for more women in the many settlements of the north, that they should be given their own land on exactly the same terms as men, and that single women should have homesteads of their own. Alfred had already sent out three women as labourer-teachers in 1920, and he made it clear that "It is high time that women should be introduced to all camps and works. For those who say these sites are no fit place for women, it is self evident that any place on land or sea that is unfit for women is equally unfit for men."

Finally, Alfred wrote in favour of harvesting the great resources of nature but stressed that they should be used "not to make the few rich, but to make the many wise." Jessie Lucas remembered how Alfred complained about the wastage of timber by the various lumber operations in Canada. This was not a financial consideration but an environmental one that reflects today's values. "We must teach them not only how to cut trees without destroying the forest, how to stump and till the land scientifically, and how to catch fish in the proper seasons without threatening their extermination—in other words, show them how to wrest a living from Nature without becoming her slave or destroyer."

Alfred Fitzpatrick had finally written his opus. Now, to get it read. Ryerson Press had told Fitzpatrick in early 1920 that the cost of overall production of the book would be less if he looked after publicity and sent out review copies himself: "it is better to have it handled altogether from your end, so you will know what is happening." Alfred, master promoter that he was, agreed, and over the next year hundreds of copies were dispatched for review, for political lobbying, and as gifts with the hope that a positive response would be received and then utilized to publicize the book further and also raise the profile of the college.

Alfred dispatched an advance copy of the book to his brother J.W. at his farm in New Liskeard shortly after he received his full shipment of copies from Ryerson Press. J.W. soon responded, complimenting Alfred on the book and adding an encouraging comment, which he underlined: "I want to say that you have made out an absolute case in favour of your movement, for such as it is, and the work before you now is to get the book read by the right people and there is no fear of your movement. You have your propaganda in good shape. Get it read." He included six dollars for three copies, "as a donation." No doubt Alfred hoped this would not be the only sale of the three thousand copies that had been printed. Mobilizing the Frontier College staff, he began to send out numerous copies of his "propaganda" in January 1921.

The newspaper reviews soon began to come in, and most were positive. As Alfred had hoped, they were about the college as well as the book. In the headline for its review, the *Sun* in New York called it "A Peripatetic University" and in the review itself called it "a novel college important to Canadianization." According to the review for the *Syracuse Post-Standard*, Frontier College "brought mental refreshment and nourishment to thousands in the backwoods.... We wonder why we in America have heard so little of it." The *Oakland Tribune* declared the college represented "educational extension with a vengeance." The *Hebrew Journal* printed a positive review in Hebrew, and the *Aberdeen Free Press* wrote glowingly of the college.

Of course Alfred's Canadian audience was the one he sought to influence, and in this regard virtually every newspaper—large or small, daily or weekly—received a copy of *The University in Overalls*; the *Mail and Empire* (Toronto), *La Presse* (Montreal), the *Hamilton Spectator*, and the *Edmonton Journal* as well as the *Napanee Express* and the *Eganville Leader* were all on the review mailing list. Reverend C. W. Gordon, Alfred's longtime friend, mentor, and Canadian literary icon under his pseudonym Ralph Connor, wrote that the book "blazed its own trail. It invites investigation, courts criticism, and challenges contradiction." Probably the most influential review of Alfred's opinions appeared in the *Star Weekly* (Toronto), a longtime advocate for Fitzpatrick and Frontier College. Under the headline "Varsity Must Become Less of Monastery" in the January 22, 1921, issue, the *Weekly* stated that the university's extramural courses did not go far enough and "higher education must be brought to the masses." But not all were positive and supportive of what Alfred envisioned for the college. In the *Winnipeg Free Press*, the reviewer observed that the universities were doing all they could and professors were working as never before. "I cannot see how these 2,000,000 workers can receive university instruction beyond lectures of the most elementary kind. Nor can I understand how a university could be so diluted. I advise readers to read the book for themselves." This critical perspective of Alfred's "visionary" concept would be heard from other quarters as well in the years to come.

And Alfred didn't stop at newspapers. Over the next year, copies were sent to the major literary figures of the day, like H. G. Wells, Rudyard Kipling, Arthur Conan Doyle, and Canadian novelist Mazo de la Roche. Canadian politicians—including Prime Minister William Lyon Mackenzie King—senators, government officials, and even the occupant of Number 10, Downing Street in London, Prime Minister David Lloyd George, received copies of the book.

While continuing to fulfill the college's original literacy purpose with the *Handbook for New Canadians*, Alfred had cultivated the political ground well with a new name (Frontier College); a new direction, as outlined in *The University in Overalls*; and a full-blown publicity campaign across Canada and beyond. The college even had a new crest created in 1922. It was an original painting by J. E. H. MacDonald of Canada's Group of Seven. Its circular frame included a quote by nineteenth-century philosopher Ralph Waldo Emerson paraphrased to read "I would not have the labourer sacrificed for the result. Let there be worse cotton and better men." In addition was a college shield with the imprint of Seneca's "Vita Sine Literis Mors Est" (Life without literature is death). Both were succinct and clear, work and literacy together. In Alfred's mind, the Parliament of Canada didn't stand a chance in his single-minded quest for educational reform and social justice. But before his quest for a degree-granting institution took its next steps, Alfred needed to be better qualified in the face of academic opposition that he was convinced would arise because he didn't possess a graduate degree.

Like many other universities in nineteenth-century Canada, McMaster University had been founded as a church-based institution, as were Acadia (Baptist), Laval (Roman Catholic), and Alfred's alma mater, Queen's (Presbyterian). The Toronto Baptist College was founded in 1881 by the Baptist Convention of Ontario and Quebec. With an endowment of $900,000 from the late senator William McMaster, first president of the Canadian Bank of Commerce, in 1882 it became McMaster University. This new independent institution of higher learning was centred around McMaster Hall on Bloor Street West, not far from the University of Toronto. Initially, it was like the others already mentioned, a sectarian undergraduate university for Baptist clergy training and for the most part, students who were Baptist adherents.

As noted, Alfred had first enrolled at McMaster in 1908–09, but the busy office work of the Reading Camp Association and his frequent travels did not allow him to attend classes. With the end of the war and the new directions of Frontier College, it had become clear to Alfred that to legitimize his college and, not incidentally, his position as principal, he needed much stronger academic credentials. His loyal "lieutenant" Bradwin had both a bachelor's and a master's degree and was enrolled in the doctoral program at Columbia University. There were few principals of degree-granting universities that had only a bachelor's degree.

Alfred had long since given up any thought of a divinity degree. His focus over the previous two decades was in the fields of adult education and literacy, and his frequent articles and annual report booklets were more reflective of an interest in the relatively recent field of sociology than of religion. The two books he had published, *Handbook for New Canadians* and *The University in Overalls*, were not religious, faith-based publications. Neither was the national degree-granting college qualification he sought from the Canadian government. Also his many commitments would hardly give him time to attend and focus on a graduate program at any university. Nevertheless, by November 1921, Alfred applied to the master's program at McMaster University in Toronto. He had engaged in several discussions with the chancellor and president, Abraham L. McCrimmon, a noted scholar of sociology, author of *The Woman Movement* (1915), and chair of the political economy and sociology departments at McMaster.

Alfred registered for Sociology I and Sociology II, and it seems his activism and previous publications were taken into account by McMaster University as equivalent to graduate courses and would therefore count toward a master's degree. He worked closely with McCrimmon, and by late January 1922 was prepared to write his exams on the topics of education and social problems.

For the McMaster University convocation in May 1922, Alfred Fitzpatrick, B.A., of Toronto is listed in the program as receiving his Master of Arts in Sociology. It is doubtful if Alfred even attended convocation, as he was likely in Ottawa lobbying Parliament for the passage of the Frontier College federal charter. Ironically, that same month, Alfred received a letter from Queen's University, specifically O. D. Skelton, former chair of the political science department and now dean of arts (1919–1924). Skelton wrote to express his regret that Alfred would not accept the honorary degree that his alma mater had offered him in recognition of his life's work. Indeed, the university had wished to honour Alfred with a Doctor of Divinity (D.D.) degree due to the impact he had made on education extension programs for the men in work camps and for Alfred's thirty years of tireless devotion to his work. This degree would have also recognized the "fresh ground that had been broken in Christian and social service" by Alfred with his educational outreach. Alfred had declined the honour. With approval from the federal government pending, a D.D. (Queen's) after his name would have carried considerable academic clout; however, it may also have led to Frontier College being considered a religious institution, which Alfred had made every effort to avoid over the previous two decades. True to his non-sectarian approach to the work, he rejected the honorary degree not only due to its religious associations, but also, as he replied to Skelton, on the grounds that "his work lay amongst all races and creeds and he could not conscientiously accept the honour." So it would have to remain "Alfred Fitzpatrick, B.A., M.A., Principal" on the college letterhead.

With his earned academic credentials in hand, Alfred then took up the contentious struggle to win his battle with Ottawa over incorporation.

The *Star Weekly* (Toronto) of September 27, 1919, had two headlines on page eleven. The first was "The Unsolved Riddle of Social Justice" and was a long article by Stephen Leacock, author and professor of political economy at McGill University, concerning the dream of socialists to change the world but without violence— violence which in his view was precisely what Bolshevism wanted to achieve. His conclusion was in the article's subheading: "Only One Thing Wrong With The Dream of the Socialist. It Won't Work." Next to the Leacock article was one by a man who would no doubt have agreed with Leacock—Alfred Fitzpatrick, who was, like Leacock, an advocate of social reform without socialism.

With his photograph at the top of the page, Alfred's article, although not directly attributed to him, was self-explanatory: "Frontier College Is Making Foreigners Into Canadians." It is no accident that these articles are on the same page, for in his article Leacock called Alfred a "pioneer of social justice." Alfred's article provided a short introduction to the history of the Reading Camp Association and then informed the reader that the newly named Frontier College had been granted a charter by the Ontario government. This charter would allow the college to reach the very edges of Ontario's "civilization" with higher education—with no fees, with no buildings but tents and log huts, and with a staff of university-educated young men and women. The college also urged Canadian universities to establish extramural courses so the college "staff" could complete their degrees while working and teaching in the isolated camps. In this way, Alfred was encouraging Canadian universities to offer to all an extension program of their own.

When the board of governors passed the Frontier College constitution in April 1918, the bylaws gave Alfred carte blanche to do what he wished with what was effectively his creation. Within a year he had conveyed his cause with his considerable lobbying skills to the Ontario government. The government then passed under the Ontario Companies Act "An Act to Incorporate the Frontier College," which recognized the college as "a teaching organization in the same sense as any other College." However, the Ontario government did not recognize the college as having a university charter, nor would it be qualified to award degrees. Therefore, it was not eligible for the same funding support that Ontario universities received. Nevertheless, through the department of education, the government was supportive of the educational component of the college's work in rural Ontario. This support may have been due to the fact that an upstart agrarian, populist party had come to power in the province.

Formed in Toronto in 1914 as a farmer's educational, social, and political organization, by 1918 the United Farmers of Ontario (UFO) had become a political force that represented rural Ontario. With the First World War winding down, the people of Ontario, unhappy with rampant inflation and job losses and dissatisfied with both of the long established parties—Liberal and Conservative—elected the untested UFO to power. Despite receiving fewer votes than the old-line parties, the UFO was able to gain a plurality of seats, and together with the Independent Labour Party, this coalition of reform rural-urban labour-farmers governed Ontario until 1923 under Premier Ernest Drury. It was an unusual coalition, which Drury's successor as premier, Conservative leader Howard Ferguson, labelled condescendingly as "intellectual and political freaks."

The major planks of the UFO platform included the abolition of political patronage, nationalization of banking, a minimum wage for women, and an expansion of cheap electrical power (hydro) by the utilization of Niagara Falls, which would become by 1921 the world's largest electrical power system. In addition, the UFO sought better educational opportunities for non–urban Ontario. Reflective of its attitude to these possibilities and also in line with the goals of Frontier College was the headline for the front page editorial in the UFO party newspaper, *The Farmer's Sun*, of December 1921, which read "Taking the University to the People." It concluded with the observation that if the people in rural Ontario could not come to the university, then the university must go to them. It championed "the gospel of higher education…to the people in the outlying parts of the Province." Consequently, with Premier Drury's support, the provincial grants for Frontier College climbed from $2,500 in 1919 to $14,500 in 1923—the largest amount ever—at a time when only one other province, British Columbia, supported the activities of the college.

Still, the resistance of the bureaucrats within the government of Ontario was made crystal clear in 1920 when Ontario's Royal Commission on University Financing refused to even give the college a hearing due to the objections of University of Toronto President Robert Falconer. Falconer was generally in favour of the adult teaching and tutoring that Frontier College was doing. He had, in fact, given his institution's support to establishing the Workers' Educational Association in Toronto in 1918. As noted, the WEA was urban based and taught industrial workers and farmers to be "good citizens." Although somewhat similar to the Canadianization curriculum of Frontier College, its pedagogical approach was classroom based, did not include literacy training, and did not provide a labourer-teacher who would be with their students at work and in their spare time. Therefore, although Falconer supported the concept of the adult learning provided by the college by making available an office space on the U of T campus during the war, he was unalterably opposed to it attaining degree-granting status. This resistance foreshadowed the attitudes of the Ontario government and the Canadian government as well as the Ontario universities, especially the University of Toronto, over the next decade.

Alfred wanted his college to have degree-granting authorization; however, there were few ways that he could achieve this goal. As education, under the British North America Act, was a provincial responsibility, even if Ontario acceded to his proposal, he would then have to go through a bureaucratic struggle with each of the other provinces where the college's men and women were serving. In 1920, they were in eight of the nine provinces, with a total of fifty-four labourer-teachers, 40 percent in Ontario and the rest scattered across the country. It may have been possible in most provinces to gain recognition, but it would take much too long, and clearly the financial resources were not always adequate to fund such perseverance. But there was an alternative.

To Alfred, the constituency for the college was not in one province, but nationwide. Second, the primary goals of the college were two-fold: to promote literacy among New Canadians and to teach the values and responsibilities of Canadian citizenship to the foreigners, essentially the immigrants, in the camps. If Alfred made his case for support on the basis of education, he would be pleading with provincial governments; however, immigrants were the beneficiaries of Frontier College classes, and immigration was a federal responsibility. So, Alfred decided he should make his case in Ottawa, with the federal government. He felt Ottawa would be ready to consider his proposal given the Winnipeg labour strike of 1919 and the ongoing fear of Bolshevik "agitators." Furthermore, the Canadian government was not prepared to set up its own citizenship program, so the Frontier College proposal would be a godsend. Alfred then decided to pursue degree-granting status as well, per-haps bearing in mind the example of the establishment of the Khaki University by the Canadian government during the Great War.

Jessie Lucas remembers:

[T]hat idea came to Mr. Fitzpatrick very soon after I went to Frontier. I went in September of 1920 and I would say it would be about six months later that he came in one day and said, "What do you think of Frontier College trying to get degree conferring power so that an opportunity could be given to everybody no matter where he or she is located." I was aghast, because here we were in a little two by four office and very sparsely furnished, and we were having difficulty, financially, always, and I thought, "Well, that's rather a big undertaking when we have so little." But Mr. Fitzpatrick was very serious…in fact he was obsessed with the idea…and read everything he could about early days of certain universities [including] Booker T. Washington on his work at Tuskegee Institute.

For his part, Bradwin, who was always supportive of Alfred's initiatives, questioned whether this could ever succeed given the nature of Ontario's resistance. Still, he felt that there was a real possibility of federal government aid. His sole condition was that the labourer-teacher camp work not be sacrificed to the university concept. Alfred assured Bradwin that his stipulation would be observed and then proceeded with his strategy.

As noted, Alfred was a tireless letter writer. His letter campaign elicited countless supportive letters from businessmen, educators, and former labourer-teachers as well as civil servants and politicians in Ottawa. By the middle of 1921, he had convinced the leader of the Liberal opposition, William Lyon Mackenzie King, to assist him in a fundraising campaign for the college. During the succeeding months they corresponded frequently, and King committed to raising the issue of support for the college with his party. On December 6, 1921, the Liberals won the federal election with the support of the Progressive Party who, like the UFO party, had been supported by the farmers of Ontario as well as those in the Canadian West. Just as the UFO had sustained the college in Ontario, Alfred now looked to the new government in Ottawa to do the same. He would not be disappointed.

At the board meeting of February 15, 1922, a committee of four was appointed, chaired by Alfred, to consider the advisability of applying for a charter and degree conferring power for Frontier College. Interestingly, William Lawson Grant, son of Alfred's mentor, George M. Grant and Principal of Upper Canada College, was a member of this committee. A petition to the House of Commons was drawn up and signed on March 4, 1922, by two prominent members of the college executive, namely D. B. Hanna, vice-president of Frontier College and the first president of the Canadian National Railroad (1919–1922), and D. A. Dunlap, a Toronto-based mining official. The petition requested that Frontier College be incorporated so that it could provide men and women with university courses at their work or at home when, due to other commitments, they were unable to attend the centrally located universities. Two weeks later, a request was sent by the college to Charles Stewart, federal Minister of the Interior, outlining the work of the college over the previous two decades and requesting the government grant fifty thousand dollars to allow for 115 instructors to be employed, which would "help materially to solve the problem of naturalization." Alfred then followed up a week later with a letter to now Prime Minister Mackenzie King requesting his political support and the financial support of the government to assist the college in its task of Canadianizing the immigrant. Alfred, always the skilled lobbyist, even quoted King himself: "Industry and Nationality exist for the sake of Humanity, not Humanity for the sake of Industry and Nationality."

In the months to come, Alfred would mastermind a public campaign through the press on two fronts: in Ontario to gain financial support from the provincial government, and in Ottawa to receive the legitimacy of a Dominion charter from the federal government. For example, Alfred wrote to the *Ottawa Citizen* on April 19, 1922, and appealed to the newspaper to put pressure on the Ontario government to support the college "as it does other educational institutions." The same day there was an editorial in the always supportive *Toronto Daily Star* demanding that the Drury government make a grant to "this educational work in the northern camps." The month before, the daily *Mail and Empire* carried a notice of the Frontier College application to the Canadian government with the headline "Incorporation Sought for New University." Both the *Star* and the *Mail and Empire* were subject to a barrage of letters to the editor stating that the college should have more financial support.

Bill 68, "An Act to Incorporate the Frontier College," received first reading on May 2, 1922, the chief objective being "To promote the education and welfare of our Canadian frontiersmen and other working men and working women." Article 10 of the bill permitted the college to award degrees. Over the next eight weeks, Alfred was in either Ottawa or Toronto seeking, persuading, and likely beseeching all possible support from MPs. As well, he was meeting frequently with Prime Minister King who thought that some small amount might be taken from the immigration appropriation. Alfred was drawing on every personal connection and personal favour he ever had. For example, the Honourable George Gordon, Deputy Speaker of the House of Commons, was a board member of the Reading Camp Association and more recently Frontier College; Ira Mackay, professor of law and later dean of arts (1925–1934) at McGill University and a Pictou Academy graduate, provided Alfred with legal information as to the bill and bylaws; O. D. Skelton, dean of arts at Queen's University, did some helpful lobbying; and finally, the bill was introduced as a private member's bill by Charles Tanner, Conservative senator (1917–1946) of Pictou County, and E. (Ned) M. MacDonald, MP for Pictou County, who was part of the Liberal sweep of Nova Scotia. First elected in 1904, MacDonald was quite close to Prime Minister King. After the Liberal victory in 1921, he was appointed to the position of minister without portfolio, and in 1923 King promoted him to Minister of National Defence. With such prominent bipartisan support from his home constituency of Pictou County, Alfred had two powerful and persuasive allies. As might be expected, both Tanner and MacDonald were graduates of Pictou Academy.

Alfred knew he did not have the support of two other important Maritime acquaintances: Sir Robert Falconer, president of University of Toronto from Prince Edward Island, and H. M. Tory, president of the University of Alberta and first president of Khaki University, from Nova Scotia. On June 1, as the incorporation bill was about to be read for the third and final time, Alfred, now in Ottawa, was preparing to once more make his case to Falconer. He had spoken to him on the phone a few days previously about the college bill but typically felt he could make a better case by writing a letter. He reiterated the history of the college and cited examples of previous academic incorporations passed by Dominion statute, examples researched by professor Ira Mackay. These were Emmanuel College in Saskatchewan and Shandong College in China. Frontier College, Alfred wrote, was quite willing to co-operate and had asked members of the faculties of the five largest universities in Canada to assist: Manitoba, Toronto, McGill, Montreal, and Queen's. Four professors had already agreed to serve as members of the examining board. "This should be sufficient guarantee that the standard will be maintained." He continued that this educational opportunity was both for the instructor as well as the frontier worker. "Toronto University will never be able to overtake one-tenth of the work for it to do" in the frontier areas, and a national university like Frontier College devoted "to the interests of men so long neglected" could be sustained.

In closing, Alfred asked for Falconer's support "as Queen's has apparently already done" by withdrawing any protest. Alfred also noted that in their phone call, Falconer mentioned that he had approached Dr. Tory to join him in opposing the Frontier College; therefore, a copy of Alfred's letter would go to him and to the deputy minister of education in Ontario, A. H. U. Colquhoun.

Within a day, Falconer had responded and his opening sentence concisely summed up his disapproving perspective: "The controversy between us, in so far as there is one, in regard to the Frontier College narrows down to this, that the Dominion Government has no right to authorise any college to grant degrees." Falconer did not respond to the precedents that Alfred had cited and instead stated that he would still strongly oppose its power to grant degrees. He expressed his sympathy for "your work" and was in no way opposed to it but explained that he would have to take the matter up with other Canadian universities at their upcoming annual conference in Winnipeg on June 16, 1922. As to the legality of what was being requested, he closed somewhat intimidatingly: "It is...in your interest not to ask for privileges which would be contested."

With multiparty support, the bill passed its third and final reading less than a week later on June 8, 1922, and received royal assent on June 28. By then Alfred had already received a wire from Bradwin: "Sincerest Congratulations − Your biggest day yet for bringing education within reach of all. You alone are entitled to the accomplishment." However, even in the glow of triumph there were dark mutterings of what was to come. Even before it was passed, the Ontario minister of education had sent a telegram to the effect that "Ontario takes great exception to Dominion charter. Will protest immediately." Fitzpatrick was being warned that strong opposition was developing from both the education department's Minister Grant as well as University of Toronto President Robert Falconer. Two days after the bill was affirmed, Jessie Lucas, in a phone call from the deputy minister of education, A. H. U. Colquhoun, was told that "Fitzpatrick does not have precedents in this matter" and "Fitzpatrick is making a big mistake as Dominion government cannot grant what he is after."

Despite this, Alfred's two strongest allies were confident that the struggle was over. Bradwin wrote, "You will take the wind out of the sails of 'Farmer' Grant as well as out of Sir Robert before you are done with them." Alfred's legal expert, Ira Mackay, believed Robert Falconer would come around and "now that we have won...Toronto University, Alberta University and the Ontario Government will throw up the sponge." However, despite this optimism, these powerful opponents to the Frontier College charter would continue the struggle for another decade by political, legal, and, most importantly, financial means, and Fitzpatrick knew that he would have to "fight on until the war is over." He expressed his hope to Jessie Lucas the day after Bill 68 was passed that "our little institution will come into its own."

On his train trip from Ottawa back to Toronto after the political dust had settled somewhat, Alfred Fitzpatrick must have exulted in his success. After several years of lobbying politicians, cajoling the moneyed classes, and composing countless articles, editorials, and letters to the editor, Frontier College, in the full measure of its title, was a reality. It had by Bill 68 been awarded degree-granting status in all nine provinces of the country—indeed, it was the only institution in 1922 and for the foreseeable future to hold such a national educational outreach into the isolated work sites of the Canadian interior. Perhaps, Alfred may have mused, it was now conceivable that an immigrant worker could begin with literacy skills, a knowledge of Canadian history, politics, and geography, and eventually go on to receive a Bachelor of Arts, all through the efforts of the extension work of Frontier College. As the train sped to Toronto, Alfred must also have considered the objections that had been raised by some notable universities and Ontario's provincial department of education, but for now he had won. He was tired and wanted to escape the office and the city of Toronto.

After visiting his brother J.W. in Northern Ontario in July, by mid-August of 1922 Alfred was back home among his kin in Millsville, Nova Scotia. Going home had become an annual pilgrimage. So much had changed since he moved out of his community to attend Queen's University. He had departed almost four decades previously to pursue what seemed now to be a perpetually changing career. But he believed this would be his last change.

A year before, in late July 1921, he heard from his sister Jane that a terrible fire had swept through the structural core of the Millsville community. The blacksmith shop was gone. The two stores run by brothers Tom and Robert Young, as well as Tom's house and barn,

The sprawling fields of Millsville, circa 1900. **(PRIVATE COLLECTION OF GORDON YOUNG)**

were all consumed by the blaze. The village had been effectively gutted. The Fitzpatrick farm had not been affected, but it had aged greatly since Alfred had moved away in the 1880s. Each year he came home to the same place but not the same time in this changing community.

Likely Alfred thought frequently of the choices and the chances he had taken and not taken. As *The University in Overalls* was nearing publication, he sent another manuscript to Ryerson Press for their consideration. *Blue Nose in the Redwoods* was a novel about a Nova Scotian who became a Presbyterian minister and undertook missionary duties in the redwoods of California. It was never published, but it was clearly autobiographical. In the two years since that submission, the life of this "Blue Nose" had changed irrefutably.

Now, in August 1922, Alfred was sixty years old, and with his success barely two months ago he would have a very different account of his life to tell. Canada's Parliament had effectively named him principal of a university, just as his mentor and preceptor George Monro Grant had been for a quarter of a century at Queen's. In addition, Alfred had received his master's degree from McMaster University and had published two books over the past two years. In the 1914 book *Pictonians at Home and Abroad*, Reverend J. P. MacPhie called Pictou County the "Home of Educators as it produced more college Presidents than any other county in the country." In addition to the aforementioned Grant, the county had contributed seven university presidents to Canada, including William Dawson (McGill), Arthur Stanley Mackenzie (Dalhousie), and Daniel Gordon (Queen's). Alfred had no doubt read MacPhie's book and likely believed that he was now in that illustrious company.

And these were his roots. A struggling farm in a somewhat deserted village. He went for a car ride with family over the dusty, bumpy summer roads of the county. The road was recoated each year with gravel, utilizing local labour, and would not be paved for another ten years. Next year, in 1923, cars would have to be driven on the right side of the road instead of the left, conforming to the American standard. This change would come just in time, it was hoped, for the 150th anniversary of the arrival of the Highland Scots colonists in 1773 and also, somewhat optimistically, a flood of American tourists. Pictou County was changing in the face of many new challenges. There were already heated discussions in the town and county about merging the Presbyterian, Methodist, and Congregationalist churches to form the United Church of Canada. In a schismatic vote in December 1924, Pictou County voted in favour of such a union, as did Alfred's church in Millsville, by twenty-seven to five—a result that Alfred was pleased with. The religious discussions and vociferous disputes of these Scots settlers went on as they had for a century and a half, but it is clear that Alfred was no longer fully engaged in them.

In the town of Pictou, the academy still flourished, even though it had been destroyed by fire in 1895 and would be again in 1938. But it would be rebuilt each time, and in 1920 Academy Hall, a men's residence, was constructed. As for Alfred's old instructor, "Little Goosey" as the students had nicknamed him, Dr. A. H. MacKay, had long since left Pictou Academy and was enjoying an illustrious career as a scientist and as president of the Victoria School of Art and Design in Halifax and was soon to retire, in 1926, from his position as Superintendent of Education in Nova Scotia. MacKay had not forgotten Alfred; he faithfully donated $150 each year to Frontier College.

In his meditative moments on that summer visit in 1922, Alfred may have also considered the influence of his extended family. His parents, Alexander and Mary, had died over twenty years previously. None of his surviving brothers now lived in Millsville. Two were in California, one in Northern Ontario, one in Saskatchewan, and brother Thomas was with Alfred in Toronto. Two sisters, Jane and Mary Annie, lived in Millsville near the old homestead, and the youngest, Margaret, was now in New England. Jennie had passed away in 1877 at the age of thirty-four.

Most of the family believed that Alfred was still a "man of the cloth." A year or so before, J.W. had written from New Liskeard, Ontario, with a request that Alfred baptize a mutual friend's baby. Alfred responded, "I would rather not. I withdrew from the Ministry when I took up this work." Others, like his niece Annie in Korea, were more substantively critical of his work and his book, *The University in Overalls*. She wrote, "It is fine! But it does not speak of Jesus and his great salvation enough. It must be faith in Christ, and change of heart first—then good literature, baths, good food, etc."

This is not the first time he had heard this argument from his family and many others. There is no record of his response. Ever the diplomat, he likely didn't send one.

Barely two years previously, Alfred and Bradwin had talked about Edmund being Alfred's successor. Then a year later, in 1921, Alfred raised the possibility of his retirement with his brother J.W. in New Liskeard. Typically he expressed his dislike for the city in the following terms: "I have been praying for a long time that Heaven would not [punish] me for my sins in the form of compelling me to end my days in Toronto." He then went on to write of retiring with Thomas to a homestead in the north "to earn my bread and butter with a pair of snowshoes, fishing rod, an axe, and a box of matches. Tom and I could put up a respectable log house in a month." Possibly he saw society growing more complex around him and wished to retreat to a simplicity like the Millsville he remembered, where human needs were satisfied by basic self-sufficiency—sort of a Walden in New Liskeard, Northern Ontario.

What reminiscences flowed through the mind of Principal Alfred Fitzpatrick, B.A., M.A., in August 1922 cannot be known. Given the restless energy of the man, these memories would likely recede as his time at home ended. After all, he had a college to run now. All he needed was faculty and students—immediately.

CHAPTER 7

"FIGHT OF MY LIFE" FOR SURVIVAL 1922–1931

THOMAS FITZPATRICK

ALFRED WAS SINGLE WITH NO CHILDREN. WHEN HE FIRST TOOK over the care of his mentally-challenged brother, Thomas, Alfred was living in a farming area in Northern Ontario. They lived there for the first few years, then when the Reading Camp Association established its head office in Toronto during the first decade of the twentieth century, Alfred had to make changes. As he frequently travelled and was away for long periods of time, he arranged for Thomas to board and work at various farms outside Toronto in the summer where he would visit him when he could. During the winter, Thomas moved into the city and lived with Alfred, usually in a boarding house. At times, neither a farm nor a boarding house was easy to find. Many people did not wish to have Thomas around the house, due to his mental incapacity.

Both Bradwin and Jessie Lucas would assist Thomas when Alfred was travelling. He would write to Thomas almost every week with a promise of bringing him a five cent cigar on his return. The cigars were a bribe to wean Thomas off his chewing tobacco habit of which Alfred did not approve. In one letter, Alfred even offered to send him a carload of chewing gum and chocolates if Thomas would only cut out his chewing tobacco habit. In another, he asked Bradwin to buy Thomas fifty cigars and he would settle with him later. The two brothers obviously had a joking relationship. In 1922, Thomas was admitted to the hospital with an injury to his face. Alfred, in a letter to Jessie, wrote, "Tell Tom to stay in the Hospital until his face is perfectly well or he'll never get a wife."

Frequently, Alfred's letters to Thomas were about the farm labour he was doing. In 1919, he wrote, "I suppose you're busy with the threshing.

Edmund Bradwin (left), Thomas Fitzpatrick (centre), and Alfred Fitzpatrick (right) pose for a portrait in 1924. (LIBRARY AND ARCHIVES CANADA/FRONTIER COLLEGE FONDS/ PA-142931)

It is not very pleasant work. I wish I could relieve you for a day."

Whenever he reflected on his family's agrarian background in Millsville and his mission to the labouring men of Canada, Alfred often expressed his feelings of guilt about not having done more physical work in his youth. He summarized this succinctly in his dedication to Thomas at the beginning of *The University in Overalls* (1920): "To my brother Tom who did too much manual labor while I did too little."

Four years after the book was published, in May 1924, Thomas suffered a stroke; he died in August of the same year. He was buried in Mount Pleasant Cemetery in Toronto. Jessie Lucas remembered Ed Bradwin saying, "It's the biggest thing Alfred Fitzpatrick ever did in his life was to take care of Tom."

The 1920s and '30s was a period of economic boom and bust in Canada. In Ontario, as with the first decade of the twentieth century, this was an era of sustained growth. The "boom" was very dependent on primary products. Wood, minerals, and foodstuffs were in high demand, and consequently there was a mad rush to construct transportation systems—rail and roads—to convey goods to market. The boom had little impact on immigrant workers, who stood on the bottom rungs of the wage hierarchy. Many faced layoffs, wage reductions, and unemployment. These workers were not adequately represented by the unions, who were having their own difficulties. Anti-unionism and industrial paternalism led to a decline in influence of some unions. For example, the OBU (One Big Union) had plummeted from 50,000 paid members in 1929 to 1,600 who paid their dues in 1932.

With the UFO under Premier Drury voted out of office in 1923, the incoming Conservative premier, Howard Ferguson, adopted a policy of limited government intervention. This meant "unfettered private enterprise" with grudging assistance to those in need. The familiar refrain in Ontario was that the northern part of the province existed to serve the south, and in this regard all natural resources were viewed in terms of their productive capacity for revenue generation.

With Alfred increasingly busy establishing a curriculum and finding faculty and students, it became necessary for Bradwin to assume more and more responsibility for the labourer-teachers and their training and dispersal. He and Alfred still continued to tour the camps, and although he would often defer to Alfred to make the final decision as to who was hired or fired, Bradwin still kept a tight leash on those who were in the field, seeing them through their discouragements and triumphs in the camps and classrooms. By 1926, over fifty labourer-teachers were assigned to camps across the country, with the bulk of them, some 70 percent, in Ontario. Others, like Benjamin Spock, were sent west.

Spock, later to become a renowned pediatrician who wrote the bestselling *Book of Baby and Child Care* (1946), worked on the CPR in the summer of 1926 with "Joe Contini's extra gang #2," which consisted of some forty men working out of Shelley, Manitoba. A graduate of Yale University, Spock had lined up a cushy summer job as a tutor-companion to a "rich boy" with the promise of a lot of time off and a car to drive. His mother was not impressed that he chose to be "a soft-living parasite." In his words, she had endowed him with a conscience, and so not long after, he was with Frontier College and working on the Canadian Pacific Railway. The work gang, for the most part, was composed of Galicians from eastern Poland. The Galicians were migrant labour rail gang workers in the summer, wheat harvesters in the fall, and lumbermen in the winter. Most of them believed they had enough of a vocabulary and manual expertise to do those jobs, and when they had earned enough they would return to Europe. They felt no need to learn English. They first came to Spock's classes perhaps out of curiosity or politeness. But soon he was teaching a rapidly diminishing number, and eventually they stopped coming.

Spock wrote to Bradwin that he was a complete failure as a teacher. In his response, Bradwin expressed that he was well aware of this shifting migrant population and encouraged Spock to not just focus on the classroom activities but to try to affect their education in other ways, perhaps as he laboured with them. He pointed out that this experience was a personal test for Spock as well, unintentionally echoing Spock's mother's words. Spock's later memory in the 1950s was that he didn't teach anything, but at least he learned something about "straightening track, laying track, sleeping on a wooden shelf, getting along without toilet facilities, washing clothes in a creek, [and] resoling my shoes." At the same time his field report showed that he taught thirty-seven classes of English and geography with a total attendance of 309 students. Perhaps when he returned home after the long, hot summer his mother would no longer view him as a "soft-living parasite."

Early in the 1920s, it was becoming increasingly important to wealthy funders that the effectiveness of an organization be measured qualitatively as well as quantitatively. Therefore, Bradwin made a substantial change in the reporting system of the labourer-teacher, making it more descriptive as well as statistical. His graduate training at Columbia University in political economy and sociology prompted Bradwin to collect statistics assiduously on the instructors and the camps. Thus, there were monthly reports that included student names, nationality, age, grade, attendance, and remarks as well as the topics taught, e.g., stock words, spelling, and civics. The Frontier College annual report for 1922 contained several samples of these instructor reports as well as acknowledgements of material assistance (books, magazines, etc.) and a list of donors, much like previous reports had done. In addition, Bradwin had begun to include individual pages recording each instructor's situation, including their photograph, location, ethnic composition of the camp, and comments from the foreman, the Frontier College supervisor, and the instructor himself. For example, H. E. D. Ashford (Mount Allison University) was located in Dauphin, Manitoba, on the Canadian National Railway (CNR) as a track layer. Over 60 percent of his camp was of Slavic origin. The railway foreman wrote, "one of the best six men on my gang"; the Frontier College supervisor wrote, "his classes attentive and interested"; and Ashford himself wrote, "I never knew anything about working conditions for the average day labourer until this summer...they are well below what they should be." There was also a page of handwritten notes of appreciation from the men of the work gang: "The instructor of the Frontier College... has helped me much to learn English," signed Birger Melberg, and John Mastukuk wrote, "I like to learn."

Monthly class attendance at various railway, hydro, and lumber camps in 1922 ranged from five hundred to nine hundred students. The majority of the "foreign-born men" were either Italian or Ukrainian. The ethnic composition of all camps in 1922 showed that the Slavic population was among the largest (31 percent), followed by French-Canadians (17 percent), Italians (13 percent), and a few "Orientals" (1 percent). The remaining 38 percent was made up of other groups, including American, Scandinavian, and English-speaking Canadians. Across Canada at this time (1922–1926), well over 70 percent of the seasonal camp workers were foreign, and of the two hundred thousand workers, Frontier College labourer-teachers were in touch with 8 percent of them. The end of this 1922 report featured a page of several quotes from "Press and Public," leading with that of the novelist H. G. Wells: "It is the most interesting piece of educational work I have read about for some time," a quote that was featured prominently, for obvious reasons, on several of the college's reports and brochures.

As the decade progressed, the annual reports of the camp work became longer and much more detailed. Increasingly, donors, contributing businesses, and provincial government bureaucracies sought greater accountability, especially statistics. The Dominion Bureau of Statistics had been created in 1918, and by 1924 its Education Statistics Branch was including extracts of Frontier College reports in its annual report for Canada. These statistics, often arranged in

Workers of different nationalities at Kennedy and McDonald's railway camp, New Brunswick, circa 1912. **(LIBRARY AND ARCHIVES CANADA/FRONTIER COLLEGE FONDS/A139833)**

pie or bar graphs, also provided comparative data for the college itself as it planned the next year's activities.

Education statistics were not the only area of qualitative and quantitative data that was of interest to the Canadian government. With government apprehensions about radicalism, Bolshevism, and socialism, some of which were expressed through unionized labour like OBU and the IWW, the RCMP had stepped up its surveillance and intelligence gathering in factories and primary resource industries at a national level. The RCMP's first intelligence officer, Colonel Charles F. Hamilton, was appointed in 1922. He was a graduate of Queen's University, and as a fellow alumnus Alfred saw an opportunity for Frontier College to solicit funding from the federal government.

Always the networker, Alfred had received support from Hamilton in his approach to the federal Department of Immigration and Colonization for funding in early 1922. With Hamilton now in charge of the Intelligence Office, Alfred sought him out again to widen his financial sources for his new, cash-strapped college by seeking monetary support from the RCMP. In 1924, as the RCMP was closely associated with the federal Immigration and Colonization Department and therefore immigrant labourers in the camps, Alfred requested funds from the RCMP to support the work of the labourer-teachers as they dealt with the "radical elements" of the camps. Alfred believed they, the labourer-teachers, "supplemented the efforts of your own splendid organization."

Alfred perceived this potential largesse as a means to assist his instructors and promote Canadianization of "New Canadians." With increased accountability as represented by the new reporting system devised by Bradwin, the college's potential donors could see its activities as an antidote to socialism. In this way, the labourer-teachers showed that the work and education tasks they carried out were the best precautions against radical organizers. From the perspective of the RCMP, however, this was a means by which to maintain a surveillance system of the "radical agitators" in the bush camps.

There is little to no evidence to suggest that any collaboration between the RCMP and Frontier College was actually effected. No official funding was provided to Frontier College by the RCMP nor any other federal agency until the early 1930s.

Bradwin's correspondence with Alfred usually reflected the day-to-day operations of the college both in the home office and in the field. However at times there were the "confidential" reports in which he bared his soul to Alfred about his own discouragements as he "railed," rode, and walked from camp to camp. In July of 1928, he visited the labourer-teacher Frank Wishart, who was working on the extra gang in Northern Manitoba on the Hudson Bay Railway, a branch line of the CNR. Bradwin wrote a furious letter to Alfred as to the conditions in the rail camp. Wishart and his gang were working fourteen to seventeen hours a day with overtime, and therefore he did not have the time or energy to hold classes. "I simply don't know how Wishart can stand fourteen hours with a shovel under a bone-head of a Scotchman—McNabb—who is sticking it to Wishart.... [S]hovel work on an extra gang after eleven hours is cruelty." Using this as an example, Bradwin said that when fundraising, the college should emphasize how much work the instructor does in addition to the teaching. He then went on to express his opposition to any overtime work when men were receiving only thirty cents an hour for a full day's work. He roundly criticized rival railway presidents Sir Henry Thornton of the CNR and Sir Edward Beatty of the CPR as to the treatment of these men "who can and will be treated like dogs." He blamed both the CNR and the CPR for the condition of labour in Western Canada. Traditionally, both railways had been donors to the college with financial assistance and railway passes. In the previous year, 1927, the two railways had donated a total of $3,000. This was a welcome donation, as the Conservative Ontario government under Premier Howard Ferguson was threatening to cut the Ontario grant of $7,500 completely, which would mean a 25–30 percent reduction in the college budget. As was usually the case, Bradwin would leave any public protests about these matters to Principal Fitzpatrick.

Bradwin concluded his letter with the following vivid description in a cri de coeur about the conditions in the camps: "I think at times I am too balanced, and too Conservative by nature to ever be a Red, but if anyone had followed my heels for the past 3 weeks, sleeping on boards, eating slugs that would test any hungry man, and above all flopping among men whose sweaty bodies exude offensively—as they sprawl snoring heavily and exhausted by undue physical effort—one can scarce accept favours from his own flesh and blood. Poor hardworking men are seemingly ignored the common decencies."

A day later Bradwin was in Brandon, Manitoba, where he was somewhat rejuvenated by his visit to Instructor John Drake on the CNR extra gang. Drake was quite accomplished, with an attentive class of sixteen, but Bradwin's experience with the Hudson Bay Railway still nagged at him. Drake was doing well because there was "No overtime!!" "Where men are given reasonable hours we can get them to class [but nothing] can get men out to class after 12, 13, and 14 hours heavy work—let alone 17 hours on shovel gangs." Bradwin's Columbia University dissertation was published the same year, 1928, and was a reasoned analysis that addressed just such difficult conditions for the workers.

Ed Bradwin had pursued his doctoral research and written his dissertation as he carried out his many obligations as supervisor of camps for Frontier College. This included twenty-two thousand miles of travel each year visiting countless camps across Canada— a country he called "a land of camps!"—Bradwin's dissertation was a critique of the conditions in the camps of Canada in the two decades leading up to the First World War. It was more sociology than economics as, in Bradwin's view, the subject matter of economics should not be figures and percentages but men and women and what is done to them. His analysis was not as an observer but an engaged participant, not theoretical but practical. He criticized government, church, press, and educators. Specifically, the low wages, living conditions, and job hazards in the camps; the neglected responsibilities for seasonal workers by unions; the contract labour system and poor health care in the camps; and the fact that the universities had turned their backs on the problems of these Canadians. To Bradwin, it was a national necessity that "no body of illiterate adults whether on the frontier or crowded in the city be left without a reasonable means to improve themselves."

As previously mentioned, the published version of Bradwin's dissertation, *The Bunkhouse Man: Life and Labour in the Northern Work Camps* (1928), was very positively received by the press and academic journals like the *Journal of Sociology*. It provided a careful academic analysis, which served to legitimize much of what Alfred had written about in various of his publications, including *The University in Overalls* some eight years earlier.

For his part, Alfred was very supportive of Bradwin's research in the 1920s, which he publicized quickly and widely with photos and news stories. He congratulated Bradwin warmly on his success but also recognized the utilitarian value to the college of his efforts. In a letter to Jessie Lucas, Alfred wrote, "The Frontier College will get more publicity out of that thesis than he'll get in dollars." Bradwin, he continued, "is working for the instructors, working for the Frontier College." Alfred was quite aware that this publication would raise the profile of the college, assist in fundraising, and provide academic authority and prestige to the functions of the college. *The Bunkhouse Man, The University in Overalls,* and *Handbook for New Canadians* are a trilogy of books written by those closest to the activities of Frontier College in its first quarter century of existence.

In *The University in Overalls,* Alfred had written a full chapter on frontier settlement and homesteading with particular reference to Northern Ontario and what he called the "Great clay belt," an area well-suited for farming that stretched north and west from the head of Lake Temiskaming, encompassing the communities of Cobalt and Cochrane. In addition to the work camps, Alfred also outlined a role for Frontier College in the communities that would be shaped by settlement in the north, and he was already actively seeking just such a role. In early 1914, before the First World War broke out, the Ontario Minister of Lands, Forests, and Mines had granted Frontier College permission to experiment with a homesteading plan in one of the townships, Kapuskasing, with the objective being to establish a community of "home-seekers." Alfred believed that it would be difficult to convince individuals and families to homestead without the support of community centres, which he also saw as "community educational camps." In his view these would be attractive to the urban unemployed, the immigrant cohort, and would include ethnic group settlement. He even suggested that penitentiaries be moved to the clay lands of the north and become community centres, the inmates being well equipped to clear the land. And of course, part-time study would be available to all.

Alfred was very critical of the Dominion Lands Act of 1872, which allowed any male over twenty-one or the sole head of a family, either male or female, to pay a registration fee of ten dollars and receive 160 acres of homesteading land, but excluded women from acquiring these homesteads if they were not the sole head of a family. In the early twentieth century, women's organizations and the press protested this exclusion but with little result. In 1918, the war was over and women had not only won the vote, but had also supported the war effort at home and in the factories. It is clear that Alfred saw an independent place for women in the homesteads. He wrote that the single woman must have the same rights and privileges as a man and should be present on the land. Referring to the war, Alfred wrote, "It would be a sin against womankind were her heroism and self-sacrifice forgotten and unrewarded. There never was a time where public opinion was in a more plastic, more receptive state. Women have demonstrated their right to share in moulding public opinion. They should also seize the opportunity and demand an equal share of land."

The war had clearly interrupted Ontario's homesteading plans and Canada's search for and reception of new immigrants. However, with the end of the war, tens of thousands of soldiers were now homeward bound from Europe, eager to take up their old jobs or search for new ones. Both men and women were looking for work. Some twenty-five thousand of the returning soldiers applied to the soldier settlement program that the Canadian government had instituted for support. Many were provided with loans to purchase land, equipment, and livestock. With the low price of land in Northern Ontario, less than fifty cents an acre, many bought land, usually ten acres, with the intention to settle or farm or maybe, if they were really fortunate, get a "lucky strike" in the mineral rich north as others had done. Alfred believed his suggestion for a "community education camp" would appeal to the soldier settlers in addition to immigrants, the unemployed, and women. Many of the returning soldiers, however, did not remain in Northern Ontario due to the difficult farming conditions, which usually led to ever increasing debt.

Governments and philanthropic organizations were also promoting northern settlement. In 1919, the Ontario government was building "colonization roads" and branch roads to the north. Among others, the Western Canada Colonization Association was founded in 1921 to promote settlement of the Prairies. That same year, the British Immigration and Colonization Association was founded to attract British boys between the ages of fourteen and eighteen to Canada to become farmers. Sir John Middlemore's Children's Emigration Homes, Dr. Barnardo's Home Children, and several others served as conduits for young, cheap labour from Britain to come to Canada, leading one federal immigration superintendent at a 1923 child welfare conference to state critically, "We have laid ourselves open to the charge of nation-building on the backs of children."

Nevertheless, Alfred recognized an opportunity in these diverse developments to further his settlement and homesteading goals. On December 20, 1920, the *Star Weekly* (Toronto) under the bold, black title "Settle the Bushland. Solve Unemployment," featured an interview with Alfred in which he stated his firm opposition to individual isolated settlement and espoused community camps in an eight-mile-square township with 160 acre lots, much like a commune. He went on to note that this would be more appealing to the unemployed of the urban areas and thus would clear some of Toronto's slums. In early 1921, his address to the annual general meeting of the Ontario Education Association, entitled "Homesteading by Proxy," urged better planning for land clearing in "New Ontario." Virtually foreshadowing the Canadian government's relief camps of the next decade, Alfred urged that "Canada for all time abandon the foolish policy of homesteading her bush clay lands by individuals working separately against unequal barriers. Rather let her undertake now a permanent land clearing policy by using gangs of unemployed men, living in community camps, supplied with every facility for education and entertainment—the movies not excepted." Clearly there was a role here for Frontier College. Alfred concluded his address with a plea, saying that support for this initiative must come from philanthropists, universities, businesses, and governments. Land clearing and draining in preparation for future settlement must be "a great permanent public policy."

Indeed, with the release in 1920 of *The University in Overalls* and its references to homesteading, Alfred began to receive a number of requests from individuals who wished to take up a free grant of land or buy acreage in Northern Ontario for farming and market gardening.

True to form, when he was passionately seized by an idea, Alfred sought to cast his message as widely as possible. In September 1921, a circular letter was sent out to the mayors and the newspaper editors of Ontario that spoke of the need to homestead the north, expand land grants from 10 to 160 acres, cultivate the land, and in this way "help warm it up." The current grant of ten acres each was not enough to take out the enemy: "the summer frost." Also that year, Alfred negotiated with Premier Drury about a "Frontier township" in the clay belt that would give homesteads to women on the same terms as men.

After degree-granting status was awarded to the college in 1922, Alfred saw an active role for his undergraduate labourer-teachers to combine manual labour with serving the homesteading community in terms of education and medical support: they would assist adults but also teach the children of the settlers until such time as there were enough to warrant a school. A note to this effect was sent out with the 1925–26 academic calendar of the college and the offer of a one hundred dollar scholarship.

Alfred knew Bradwin was not enthusiastic about the homestead concept. Nevertheless Edmund was reconciled to it as he had been to so many other projects that Alfred had suggested in the past. Alfred even proposed that Idington in Algoma District would make a good headquarters for the college. Bradwin's reaction to this proposal is not known. By 1927, Alfred was ordering chickens, boards for construction, roofing, windows, and plows, and in addition, his brother John had moved from Saskatchewan to supervise the settler farmers in Edlund, northwest of Timmins, Ontario. Nevertheless, with inexperienced settlers, an arduous climate, and lack of financial support, it was becoming increasingly difficult to keep potential settlers there. So once more Alfred turned to the press to plead his case.

In a *Hamilton Spectator* interview for an article entitled "Aid For Home-steading" that appeared May 25, 1928, Alfred urged the cities to solve their unemployment problems by establishing a "grubstake" of eight hundred dollars for those prepared to settle the north, saying it was only fair that the city dwellers "living in comfort and profiting by the exertions of the pioneers on the frontiers, should make a contribution." A month later in the *Calgary Herald*, Alfred expressed his annoyance that Dominion and provincial governments had not supported the "benighted settlers" as there were still no schools, no sanitation, no doctors, and acres of undrained muskeg nearby. He decried the capitalist and educated classes who would do "anything for the worker except get off his back." As for the churches, they would enthuse over a foreigner who was in his own country, but when he came to Canada "a stranger within our gates," he was "left in the ditch" and "passed by on the other side." Perhaps somewhat hyperbolical, but with its "good Samaritan" reference, it does show that even after over thirty years of his "mission," Alfred's crusading light had not been diminished by disappointment or a lack of support.

That year, 1928, Prime Minister Mackenzie King set up the Select Committee on Agriculture and Colonization. At the same time, there was still apprehension about the Communist menace, and several hundred political deportations were carried out. With the onset of the global economic depression, fewer and fewer new immigrants were arriving and some were even moving back to Europe. There was no private or public money for Frontier College homesteading. The deficit of the college had grown from $7,200 in 1924 to $29,300 in 1930. Alfred's concepts of homesteading became largely defunct.

Still, there were labourer-teachers who benefitted the settlers' communities in the north with their knowledge and their devotion to service. One such was Dr. Margaret Strang, who was twenty-eight years old and, as she writes in her letter of application, "in perfect health as far as I know." She had just graduated from the University of Western Ontario medical school in the spring of 1929. In her letter she emphasized her capabilities, saying she had always been accustomed to hard work "and I want more." Originally from a farming family in Southern Ontario, she wrote, "I can handle a team or hoe a corn patch or take off an apple crop better than I can sew or keep house.... I can handle a carpenter's tools sufficiently to make shelfs [sic] and cupboards, a dinner wagon or a passable cedar chest." By mid-July of 1929, Dr. Strang was in the small homesteading settlement of Edlund, Northern Ontario, 140 kilometres west of Cochrane on the main CNR line near Kapuskasing. Edlund was

Dr. Margaret Strang travelled between communities on horseback. Photo taken circa 1929. (PRIVATE COLLECTION OF JAMES MORRISON)

one of five townships set aside in this area by the Ontario government in the early 1920s for homesteading. However, as the decade progressed, the initial enthusiasm for farm settlements on the fringes of the Canadian Shield waned, largely due to the climate, long winters, and isolation. With the deepening of the Depression, both the settlement "homesteading" program of the Ontario government and the small community of Edlund ceased to exist by 1932.

Still, Dr. Strang lived and worked in the Frontier College log cabin centre in 1929, teaching a class of seven children two days a week with the bulk of her time spent on horseback visiting the settlers, riding her horse King to attend to their medical needs. With whatever time she had left she worked on the college farm run by Alfred's brother John. Her final report in 1930 noted that she was a favourite among the settlers and she had "won her way into the hearts of both the children and parents."

Even the somewhat chauvinistic Bradwin, who didn't think women should be sent to the north, must have been impressed by Dr. Strang.

Alfred, as principal of his "university in overalls," considered it his responsibility to be a public activist, like his mentor George Grant, so he reacted frequently to issues of the day. As noted earlier, Alfred demonstrated that he was an environmentalist at a time when the harvesting of Canada's natural resources was rampant. He was a great admirer of the influential Canadian conservationist Jack Miner who was considered by many to be the "father" of North American conservation in the twentieth century. In a *Mail and Empire* article entitled "More Power to Jack Miner," Alfred lauded his bird sanctuaries that despite the "pleasure seeking hunters" would save birds for generations to come. He mourned the loss of the buffalo, wild turkey, and white pine that were little more than a memory for which "civilization on this continent stands condemned." He was deeply critical of the lumbering industry. In his view, they had to take responsibility for conserving, reforesting, and utilizing their production. He exhorted them to "Conserve our natural resources by applying science to your tasks."

In 1928, Alfred responded to a letter to the editor in the Halifax *Evening Mail* in which George Lloyd, an Anglican bishop in Lloydminster, Saskatchewan, proposed a Quota Act that would allow only British immigrants to enter Canada, not the Eastern Europeans whom he characterized as "dirty, ignorant, garlic-smelling and undesirable continentalists." Alfred rebutted this proposition, saying Canada should be "a young nation professing belief in the doctrine of human brotherhood," especially in a land that could support "two hundred million." Alfred felt all nationalities should be welcome. He added a swipe at the churches and urged each of them to give up "the mad race for extension and supremacy, drop denomination rivalry and find its own soul."

As if Alfred's homesteading efforts, public pronouncements, and the day-to-day responsibilities of the college were not enough, he now had to recruit an unpaid faculty, develop appropriate university courses, and convince students to apply to this very uncertain venture—a national university. He began with the faculty as soon as he left Millsville in August 1922. Within two weeks, Alfred had "rounded up" Professor Henry Munro at Dalhousie University and had "chased Dr. Stewart to Cape Breton and landed him between Truro and Stewiacke." Dr. H. L. Stewart, George Munro Professor of Philosophy at Dalhousie, was to be the philosophy/ psychology examiner. All of the universities in the Maritimes were approached, then Alfred continued west to visit McGill, Laval, and the Universities of Toronto and Manitoba. He asked Columbia University and the University of Chicago to teach courses in sociology. He also planned to raise funding to establish an endowment for five academic chairs over the next five years. "Must be good men so we don't give impression standards will be lowered."

There would be no cheap degrees. Bradwin supportively suggested that the college initiate academic studies in the labour field every fifteen to twenty months.

The Frontier College board was so pleased with Alfred's ambition, drive, and success that in 1923 they elected him Principal/Vice Chancellor and raised his salary from $3,500 to $5,000 (including expenses). Since the beginning, Alfred had donated much of his salary to the college to keep it afloat. The early financial records are sporadic, but in 1912, for example, Alfred was to receive an annual salary of $1,500; however, the records reflect that the college owed him $5,000, which he had loaned to the college over the previous years. In 1925, some $1,500 of his salary increase went back to the college. And in 1929, as the college faced severe financial difficulties, Alfred refused to accept 60 percent of his salary, which had been lowered to $4,000. Not surprisingly he had seemingly endless financial problems with the Dominion Tax Office.

Alfred felt so confident with his success in obtaining Canada's only national degree program in the arts that he decided to return to the Ottawa "academic trough" once more, in this instance with a bill to allow for professional training in medicine, forestry, and mining—all relevant subjects for the college's work on the frontier. But this time the universities were prepared. In a letter to Alfred in 1922, Bradwin warned that although Ontario and other provinces had been "caught napping" by Alfred's successful political lobbying of the Canadian government, which led to the recognition of Frontier College as a national university, the universities would not be napping a year later.

In 1922, the National Conference of Canadian Universities (NCCU), founded in 1916, had briefly discussed the Frontier College application to Parliament for degree-granting status. Despite the lobbying of Robert Falconer (University of Toronto) and H. M. Tory (University of Alberta) against the college charter, the NCCU was not concerned; it believed the federal government would not approve such a venture. Now, one year later, at its April meeting in Toronto with Falconer and Tory joined by the concerned principals of Queen's and McGill, the association finally perceived what they saw as a clear threat to the integrity of Canada's institutions of higher learning. This bill had to be opposed. With a petition to Parliament delivered personally by Falconer, the NCCU pointed out that Frontier College was not equipped with laboratory or hospital facilities to deliver a professional degree program to Canadians. The second argument, this one from the Ontario government, was that the British North America Act of 1867 clearly stated that education was a provincial responsibility, although this provincial right had never been tested in court by either federal or provincial governments.

It quickly became obvious that Alfred, in his innate enthusiasm, had overplayed his hand. Now he realized that this opposition by both provincial and academic authorities would jeopardize his charter of 1922. He decided to withdraw his application to Parliament to avoid losing not only this addition to the college mandate, but also the mandate itself. In turn, the Ontario government did not pursue a challenge to the constitutional legitimacy of the charter—yet. For the next half dozen years their struggle with the college would be waged as a financial one, not a legal one.

But that was to come. For now the college needed a blue ribbon list of eminent academics to serve on the examining board. Alfred was concerned about prestige, so to show the college was a valid and well-qualified institution, only senior academics, including deans or heads of departments, were recruited. Within two years he had thirty academics from Canada and three from the United States. Of these, nineteen were full professors and eleven had received honorary degrees from Canadian universities. They included Maritime poet Charles G. D. Roberts; Dominion Archivist of French Canada Gustave Lanctôt;

and even Ed Bradwin himself as an examiner in economic and political science. As one writer put it, Alfred wanted a "genuinely national enterprise" with due consideration for Canada's regional differences in addition to those of religion (Protestant and Catholic) and language (French and English). As noted, the college board was national, including representation from Nova Scotia to British Columbia with politicians like the Honourable E. M. MacDonald; labour leader Tom Moore; novelist Ralph Connor (Reverend C. W. Gordon); the "gold king of Canada" J. P. Bickell, a former labourer-teacher and now president of McIntyre Mines; and Mrs. P. E. Doolittle, national president of the IODE (Imperial Order Daughters of the Empire). By 1924, this board had authorized Alfred to publish the first academic calendar for Frontier College.

As mentioned earlier, the 1920s in Canada was a period of increasing outreach by Canadian universities. University of Toronto's Workers' Educational Association, established during the war, had two thousand enrolled in its extension courses with branches in Ottawa (established in 1919), Hamilton (1920), and London (1922) that had attracted urban workers and farmers. The University of Alberta instituted a highly regarded travelling library system. The university's president, H. M. Tory, who had played a decisive role in blocking the ambitions of Frontier College, was quoted in 1923 as saying, "what you've got to do is find a way to take the University to the people." From his perspective, although he supported its literacy work, what the college was now proposing would not be the path to a degree of any value.

In addition, the University of British Columbia offered extension lectures to different communities, while Saskatchewan employed fifty school teachers in the 1920s to teach at least a year in non-English-speaking districts. As noted, the "People's School" at St. Francis Xavier University in Nova Scotia had started in 1921 for farmers and fishermen, and the university began its extension program, the Antigonish Movement, in 1928. All were well regarded adult education initiatives that many Canadian universities had not offered a decade previously. But none of them extended basic literacy to the isolated camps of Canada nor allowed Canadians the opportunity to attain a nationally recognized degree anywhere in Canada without attending one lecture at a university.

The first academic calendar, for the 1925–26 "First Session," appeared in early 1925. It was organized as an eighty-page booklet in the standard academic calendar format with lists of courses, professors, instructors, regulations, and fees. In his introduction, Alfred began with Friedrich Froebel's classic admonition to "come let us live with our students" and the familiar Frontier College rejoinder that instructors "both live and work with their pupils." He explained that the goal of this college was to provide a comprehensive education of the body and mind up to and including a university degree. He decried the fact that Canadian universities did not recognize that practical life experience is a form of education, something that is standard practice today in admitting mature students and has been for the past half century. Alfred accused the universities of overlooking the needs of "farm, camp, shop and homestead." Frontier College was not only different, but would make a difference.

Alfred then went on to describe the program of study, drawing on the example of extramural students set by the University of London. The members of the examining board, largely unpaid, did not teach but would send out synopses of their lectures related to the course the student had applied for, and the labourer-teacher instructors—now mostly university graduates—would tutor the student so they could proceed through the necessary courses and eventually earn a degree. With B.A.s, honours, and master's degrees being offered, there was a wide range of subjects, from English, sociology, and physics to horticulture, forestry, and animal husbandry.

As with Alfred's two previous books, the academic calendar was distributed widely. Copies were sent to thirty-one newspapers from coast to coast in all provinces with a request for a review and an editorial. The *Globe* was one of many that complied; their September 23, 1925, issue noted that the college's program "combines scholarship, altruism and *manual* labour," and it encouraged big business, universities, and service clubs to be more active in supporting the college. Subsequent academic calendars (1927–29 and 1929–31) received the same publicity campaign. As registrar and bursar, Jessie Lucas was a vital part of this effort. It is safe to say that without her loyal commitment to the college, these administrative obligations would not have been realized.

Meanwhile, Bradwin was still not persuaded that the degree program was necessary, despite his admiration for Alfred's success. He reiterated his view that the primary obligation of the college was to the men in the camps and complained frequently. In 1928, he wrote a disgruntled letter to Alfred, concluding with "Why do you people waste precious time in summer on that calendar?" He estimated that 30–40 percent of the college staff time was on the charter. Although loyal to a fault, as time passed it was obvious that Bradwin was progressively more exasperated by the direction the college had taken. By the late 1920s, he feared for its existence.

Much of that fear was based on the precarious financial situation the college found itself in. Alfred's fundraising efforts had kept the institution afloat for a quarter of a century, but this degree-granting addition to the college's responsibilities had upped the ante. Alfred turned once more to his cousin A. P. Willis in Montreal, for whom Alfred had sold pianos in 1900. In 1924, Willis left two thousand dollars for a scholarship in his name that if matched, the interest would be used to support deserving students. A year later, while in New York to address the Canadian Club, Alfred approached the Carnegie Foundation for assistance. He received five thousand dollars. The effort to maintain the current donors and also to attract new ones was ongoing.

On top of that stressor, during this time Alfred was still plagued by his own money issues. In 1924, he persuaded Jessie Lucas to contact his landlady. "Please phone Miss Brock and tell her that if she possesses her soul in patience the rent will be forthcoming sometime next week."

Now representing a national organization, Alfred approached every provincial government in the country with the exception of Prince Edward Island. At one time or other during the 1920s, each province contributed, with Ontario's yearly grant of $7,500 being the largest. If any donations were forthcoming it was worth a celebration. On one such occasion, Alfred wrote, "That is very great news and did me more good than six visits to the movies." It is clear, however, that not all Alfred's presentations were successful. Of his 1923 meeting in Halifax with the new premier of Nova Scotia, George Armstrong, he wrote, "He was very cordial but says N.S. Dept. of Education is harder up than Frontier College. I had to let him off." Nova Scotia provided no grant that year.

The largest part of the college budget between 1921 and 1929, some 25 percent of it, came from the Ontario government. With the defeat of Premier Drury and the UFO in the election of 1923, there was a new government led by Conservative leader G. Howard Ferguson who would also serve as Minister of Education. He promptly cut the Ontario grant in half. This drastic reduction marked the beginning of a financial life-or-death struggle between the college and the Ontario government with the root cause, not surprisingly, being the degree-granting status of the college. It was a struggle the college could not win.

Ferguson and Robert Falconer, president of the University of Toronto, communicated frequently about higher education in the province, with Ferguson entirely supportive of Falconer's objections to the new status of Frontier College.

During his term of office (1923–30), Premier Ferguson, in alliance with Quebec Premier Louis-Alexandre Taschereau (1920–36), sought to delineate and demand provincial rights in the Canadian federation, with education being an important one. And there were other issues on which Ferguson and Fitzpatrick were not in agreement. Unlike Alfred, the premier did not hold conservationist Jack Miner in high regard and offered little aid or concern for conservation of natural resources; there was very little replanting of trees in Northern Ontario during his tenure. As Minister of Lands, Forests, and Mines, Ferguson had assisted in breaching the Crown Timber Act in the interests of the paper industry. In social policy, "Foxie Fergie," as he was called, opposed plans for the federal introduction of old age pensions and was hostile to labour and immigration, with the exception of juvenile immigration from Britain.

Finally, unlike the progressive individual programs of the college, Ferguson believed the "average fellow likes to be dictated to and controlled." And as for what the college and similar organizations hoped to accomplish, he once remarked, "Doesn't a lot of this uplift stuff that's talked about nowadays make you tired?" Clearly, it was not the most propitious time for Alfred Fitzpatrick to be seeking financial support from the Ontario government for his academic aspirations.

Over the next five years, despite Alfred's constant request that the Ontario government increase their grant to $10,000 for rising costs, Ferguson and his government held steady at $7,500. Alfred had hoped the national recognition for the college would lead to greater financial support from the province, but more extensive fundraising became the norm and Alfred was once more submerged in "the hell and the heat" of begging for money. Even lobbying by prominent board members and former labourer-teachers like

J. P. Bickell had little effect. In January 1927, as Bickell was preparing
to board the *Aquitania* in New York, he wired Ferguson, asking him
to deal generously with Frontier College as it has raised "standards
of citizenship." Ferguson's courteous noncommittal response a few
hours later? "Mrs. Ferguson joins me in wishing you a delightful
voyage."

As the decade passed, the minutes of the board of governors
of the college are replete with references to fundraising. In 1924,
Alfred was placed in charge of a campaign to enlist the support
of service clubs like Kiwanis and Rotary, and two years later his
close personal friend, Reverend Dr. Robert Johnston, a Presbyterian
minister in St. Catharines, Ontario, was asked by the college board
of governors to carry out a financial campaign. A year later, in 1927,
a finance committee was established to assist Principal Fitzpatrick
in fundraising. But financial support for the college continued to
decline. The annual deficit of $281 in 1923 soared to $7,188 in 1930.
The accumulated deficit in that same time period climbed from
$7,374 to $27,966. In 1927, due to its straitened financial circumstances, Frontier College moved from its office at 67 Yonge Street
to a less expensive space at 26 Queen Street East, several blocks
north. Salaries were abated by 20 percent and travel decreased.
Then in 1929, just as the world plunged into an economic depression, Ferguson's Ontario government cut funding to the college
completely.

Despite the difficulties, the college had continued in its two-
pronged educational effort to provide basic literacy to isolated
camps as well as offer an opportunity to anyone seeking a degree
anywhere or anytime. At the 1929 AGM, Bradwin's "report on
the field" for 1928 noted that 62 Canadian and American university graduates served in the camps as "Guide, philosopher and
friend"; 1,559 adult workers enrolled in actual study; and 17,000
men attended general discussions on topics of current interest.

At the same meeting, registrar and bursar Jessie Lucas, in her overview of the university phase of the college, stated that since the college had received its Dominion charter, 121 people had applied for studies and 17 had actually enrolled. Of these, nine had written examinations, and three had obtained a Bachelor of Arts degree with one Master of Arts awarded to Reverend Thomas B. Moody, principal of Stanstead College, in Stanstead, Quebec. Practically all those men who applied had left university without a degree and now studied on their own while working full-time. Jessie concluded that "Frontier College has thus filled a need in our educational systems."

The National Conference of Canadian Universities agreed. At their annual meeting in 1930, which Bradwin attended, the college charter was discussed and the conference decided not to oppose the work of the college, partly owing to the reaction of "the people of Canada" toward any effort to thwart the college's activities. No doubt the universities were also aware of the college's financial situation and might have concluded it was just a matter of time.

The Ontario government was another matter entirely. Premier Ferguson, a promoter of provincial rights, which included education, did not wish to take the college to court on the matter due to the negative publicity this would attract. Also, there was the danger that a public legal judgment might validate the recognition of a degree-granting Frontier College by the federal government. Cutting all funding was the easiest way out, followed by simply weathering any public protest. In response, the college suspended its university program in 1929 until the issue could be resolved, perhaps by Ferguson being voted out of office. However, in 1930, even with Ferguson's departure from office and Conservative George Henry becoming premier, the exclusion of Frontier College from provincial grants continued.

It was clear to the board and Bradwin that changes had to be made, but in this "fight of my life" as Fitzpatrick characterized it, he was as unyielding as ever—the college must continue its work. However, his tenacity was about to be severely tested by the thirtieth annual meeting of the college, on May 22, 1931. After three decades it had come down to a question of survival for the college itself.

CHAPTER 8

FINAL YEARS OF ADVOCACY 1931–1936

26 QUEEN STREET EAST, TORONTO

JESSIE LUCAS LOOKED AT HER WATCH THEN GLANCED OUT THE window of the second-floor boardroom of Frontier College on the corner of Queen and Yonge. There was a city sewer construction crew working beneath the window, and she hoped the noise wouldn't disturb the annual general meeting. Perhaps the workers would quit early. It was just after four o'clock on a Friday afternoon, May 22, 1931, as she prepared the room for the momentous meeting. She arranged the chairs around the boardroom table, and at each location she placed a writing pad, pencil, glass of water, and the rather short agenda. Principal Fitzpatrick had always been a stickler for a properly laid boardroom table. She had also arrived early so she could compose herself and organize her thoughts for the meeting some twenty minutes away. She hoped her work at this point was not a matter of "rearranging the deckchairs on the Titanic," as the popular expression went.

For Jessie Lucas the two protagonists in the struggle ahead were clear. She had worked closely with both of them since her arrival in the office a decade before. In her view these two men—Alfred Fitzpatrick and Edmund Bradwin—had "ministered" the college for almost thirty years in a comple-mentary relationship, not always agreeing but always prepared to overlook any frictions that might affect the interests of the college. But the changing circumstances of the college in terms of its mission and its money had made them antagonists, and Jessie knew the upcoming board meeting would be a struggle for paramountcy.

As she sat in the boardroom, Jessie may have seen the future of the college as a Hobson's choice of either diminution or demise. Diminution of the college activities meant no degree-granting status in order to focus on the labourer-teacher tradition. Demise would be the financial failure of the college as it tried to continue on its current path and both administer Alfred's degree-granting program and fulfill Bradwin's labourer-teacher commitment. Fully aware of these dangerous undercurrents, Jessie straightened a notepad and pencil on the board table, sighed deeply, then turned to welcome the nine board members as they arrived. It was four thirty and the meeting was about to begin.

Alfred Fitzpatrick, founder of Frontier College, had frequently consulted with Jessie as to the various decisions and crucial choices that faced the college in order for it to stay alive. As was his custom, he committed many of his thoughts to paper. He would then share them with Jessie, the college registrar and bursar, and seek her advice.

The previous year, in July of 1930, he had sat down with two sheets of unlined paper before him and in his large clear script thought through on paper the "Following Alternatives that confront us." He listed four, which he asked Jessie to consider:

1. Continue as is, which means debts would accumulate.
2. Compromise without surrendering the charter.
3. Solve the financial situation with a $250,000 donation, which would pay off debt in ten years.
4. Lobby one hundred businessmen through Henry Thornton (president of CNR) in a campaign to wipe off debt.

Clearly Alfred appreciated the quandary he faced. His solutions were to compromise on some things but always keep the charter as it was with its degree-granting clause for the college. As a last resort, he could do what he had done so many times before—go to the press and seek public financial and political assistance. The question was, what would a compromise look like? He no doubt recalled the sage advice mentor George Grant had given him so many years before to not count on the government but to turn to the public for support—something Alfred had consistently done. But times had changed. The "public" itself was in dire straits, caught in the vice-like grip of a global financial depression. A press campaign for support would not likely be heard over the roar of the voices of the unemployed and the homeless. One voice within his own office had also spoken out. Edmund Bradwin, Alfred's long-standing lieutenant, was now unalterably opposed to the maintenance of the Frontier College degree clause, given the risk of the college having to close its doors.

The Frontier College offices were not large. Moving from the previous Yonge Street location to a smaller space had been a step down, but staff squeezed in. In such a confined space, there was no personal privacy, and virtually every discussion the principal or anybody had was overheard by the staff: Bradwin, R. W. Collins, and Jessie Lucas. Confidentiality in such a situation was impossible.

Jessie remembered the loud voices coming from Alfred's tiny office space on a Thursday afternoon some eight weeks before the May 1931 AGM. The tension between Bradwin and Fitzpatrick had been building for months. Their disagreement was over the charter, and the financial and administrative impact it was having on the college. The taciturn Bradwin had tried to contain his frustration with the lack of support for the young men and women in their work sites across Canada. He was in Fitzpatrick's office advising him, in no uncertain terms, that with the withdrawal of grant support by the

Ontario government, Alfred's cause was hopeless. Jessie heard Alfred slam his desk with his fist and shout, "You'll resign, or I'll resign!" Ed responded in a clear, low voice of controlled anger: "Mr. Fitzpatrick, I'll not resign. You may dismiss me, but I'll come into my office every day until I am dismissed." Incensed, Alfred grabbed his coat and stormed out of his office. Without saying another word to anyone, Ed left as well. The next day neither was speaking to the other.

Jessie advised Ed to take some time off. He wrote of walking the Toronto streets for the whole of April wondering what his options were. He believed Alfred had treated him "like a yellow dog or one of the untouchables of his friend Gandhi." The one thing that had been successful for the college and that he believed he was responsible for was being taken from him. He wrote about it to Reverend Robert Johnston, chair of the college board, but his response was noncommittal. Johnston said "he was pained and distressed at this rupture." But what could Bradwin expect? Johnston, like so many others on the board, were "handpicked friends of Alfred." To Ed, the matter was simple. All he was asking was that the board make a decision about its financial position and what programs the college would support. Indeed, the crucial question for Ed was: who was running the college, Alfred or the board?

Bradwin had outlined his frustrations in a thirteen-page, handwritten account of his position to staff member Collins on May 9, 1931, some two weeks before the board meeting of May 22. This meeting would decide his future, Alfred's fate, and the existence of Frontier College.

The substantial pressure on Frontier College to revoke its degree-granting status had, for the previous two years, continued to build. At the 1929 meeting between the Ontario premier,

Howard Ferguson, and chair of the college board, Reverend Robert Johnston, the premier was assured that no new students would be accepted in the program until a negotiated settlement could be reached. Provincial grants were not forthcoming in either 1929 or 1930. In February 1931, the new premier, George Henry, wrote to Fitzpatrick and reiterated the government's position that no further grants would be given until the college "definitely and unequivocally agree[d] not to use the powers set out in the Charter from the Parliament of Canada." This essentially meant the repeal of section 10 of the charter, which had sanctioned the college's degree-granting authority in the first place. The point was driven home by the Ontario government when the April 1931 provincial budget marked the third year in a row that no financial support was made available to Frontier College. Thus, as the college's annual general meeting began on May 22, the shadow of the Ontario government's legal and financial power loomed over the table. Fortunately, Jessie Lucas's twenty-page handwritten minutes of the meeting were saved. Likely by her.

On paper, the board was listed as twenty-four members representing nine provinces, but only nine members were present at this meeting. After a "brief and inspiring" report from Bradwin about the importance of the labourer-teachers in "fashioning new Canadians" and the report from Jessie Lucas, registrar and bursar, on the university aspect of the work, the board began to discuss the quandary the college was in.

After noting the Ontario government had shown antagonism toward the college "as an incipient university," the board began a heated discussion about the sustainability of the college in this situation. As with Alfred's "alternatives" from the year before, a number of solutions were discussed, including affiliation with an established university. Another suggestion was that no degrees would be awarded until the validity of section 10 was tested.

Widely respected judge Joseph Wearing, a labourer-teacher in 1905–06 and then a staff member—a man whom Fitzpatrick greatly admired—spoke first and at length. He provided a most persuasive perspective. He had travelled to Ottawa with Alfred in 1922 and enthusiastically assisted him in obtaining the charter. Theoretically, he remarked, "equality of opportunity in education was absolutely a good thing." However, even though it was ahead of its time, he now believed that the college had made a great mistake. By sticking with the charter, it had created animosity with other universities and effectively "snapped its fingers at the Provincial Government." Wearing supported the elementary and secondary education the college provided, as the Ontario government said it did, but he now believed Frontier College should not be in the field of higher education at all. From Alfred's perspective, the loss of this longtime ally must have been devastating.

Alfred was then asked by the chair of the meeting, Reverend Johnston, if he wished to express his views on the matter. Alfred didn't have a set speech, but he had obviously thought about this matter deeply and also about what alternatives were available. His arguments came as no surprise to the board or to his staff—they had heard them before. First, the college must again inform Canadians through public presentations and publicity of the work of the college "in such a way that they would be with us in spite of the [Education] Department." He also pointed out that quarrelling with the universities was not new, that formerly, the University of Toronto "turned up its nose at education by correspondence" and was opposed to what Frontier College was trying to accomplish. He urged the board to hold on to the charter and in ten years the college would be on its feet financially; by that time, he was convinced, the province would increase the grant by a factor of ten, especially if the college still had the charter. As to giving up the higher education responsibility of the college, "I am opposed; I would resign, but I hate to do so and

Alfred Fitzpatrick in January 1929. (LIBRARY AND ARCHIVES CANADA/
FRONTIER COLLEGE FONDS/C-047539)

leave the work in its present financial condition." Joseph Wearing felt that the financial situation would not be solved by Fitzpatrick resigning. Bradwin, who had said little in the meeting, then stated that he had serious misgivings as to the future of the college as well and that a compromise with the Ontario government might ensure its survival.

In the end, a motion from Wearing that a committee of the board, including Principal Fitzpatrick, be struck to meet with Premier Henry with the objective of having the government continue the grants, even if it meant conceding to his wishes. In the discussion that followed it was agreed that the efforts of the labourer-teacher were large enough to absorb all the resources of the college. The vote was taken, and the motion carried with one vote against—Principal Fitzpatrick's.

This was a crushing defeat for Alfred in this most detailed discussion of the college mandate ever held by the board and recorded. In that list of alternatives Alfred had proposed to himself ten months previously, this action had not been one of them. The college would essentially be stripped of its power to award degrees. Would he go to the premier or to the public? He did as he was directed by the board, and the committee met with Premier Henry in July 1931. At this meeting, it was clear that the Ontario government sought to have section 10 of the charter—the power of the college to confer degrees—nullified. They requested that the college go to Ottawa and have section 10 repealed. In the months that followed, the college committee tried to present other options to protect the charter, but the premier refused to consider them. It all came down to a special meeting of the board on December 19, 1931.

In the months leading up to this crucial meeting, Alfred sought to find any possible way to maintain the status quo. Jessie Lucas remembered that salaries of staff were cut and Alfred would come around almost every day asking, "What could you manage with today?"

Still, even in the growing despair of the Depression, "he didn't for once think of dropping anybody from the staff." Always outlandishly innovative, Alfred suggested that perhaps as the college already had labourer-teachers working on the hydro canal in Southern Ontario, it could vacate its Toronto office and the staff could live communally with the labourer-teachers at Niagara Falls. Bradwin was appalled. He was newly married to Minnie Fessant, and he thundered, "I'm not going to have my wife making meals for the Frontier College." The unmarried Alfred's "wife" was obviously the college. Bradwin and Fitzpatrick had become increasingly estranged by the situation. It was clear to all except Alfred, it seemed, that the college could not carry on much longer.

Just before Christmas 1931, essentially the same members of the board as the May meeting sat around the board table. Jessie, in her usual role of secretary, remembered "Right from the first, the air was almost electric. There was so much at stake." As he had done previously, Wearing presented the situation. The college could not go on in its present condition in the face of the government's intransigence. He moved that the principal and Reverend Johnston request Ottawa to abrogate section 10 of the charter in accordance with Ontario's demands. The motion passed. Alfred refused to sign the appropriate forms and left the meeting. His old friend Reverend Johnston then persuaded him to return. Alfred did so and signed the papers. He then turned to the board and tendered his resignation and nominated Johnston to succeed him, despite the fact that Johnston knew nothing about the everyday workings of the college. Johnston pointed out that Bradwin had been Alfred's man in the field for three decades and refused the nomination. Alfred then—reluctantly—named Bradwin his successor.

Bradwin was stung by Alfred's initial rejection of him as the successor. According to Jessie, "big, proud, intellectual man that he was, [Bradwin] sobbed just a little and was unable to say anything."

There was a seemingly interminable silence. Then the board, in recognition of Alfred's commitment, moved to express its appreciation and confidence in him and hoped that he would continue as principal. The motion of appreciation was passed unanimously. No action was taken with reference to Alfred's resignation. Alfred's ten-year dream of providing an opportunity for anyone, anywhere to study for a degree was shattered. So too was Alfred. Jessie recalled, "I could see now that it was more than he could stand. He was no longer a part of it." Alfred remained on as principal but now primarily as a figurehead, for the sake of continuity. Bradwin, Lucas, and one other staff member, Charles Longmore, a former labourer-teacher, now did much of the work.

At the 1932 annual general meeting, some five months later, it was reported by Reverend Johnston "that Section 10 of the Frontier College Charter, that section which gave degree-conferring power, had been repealed by the Government of Canada." On April 27, 1932, Bill No. 53 was passed, amending the act and removing section 10.

The response by the Ontario government was immediate. Following the terms of their agreement with Frontier College, the Ontario grants for 1929, 1930, and 1931, amounting to $22,500, were paid in full, and with this payment the accumulated deficit for the college was now only $6,900. Alfred and Sir Joseph Flavelle, a wealthy, long-standing supporter, had already started a campaign to eliminate this overdraft.

The Ontario government had delivered its promised support of the college in spite of the global depression. This may have been due to the lobbying of Flavelle and others or the fact that an agreement had finally been reached by the college and the province after a long, fractious dispute. More likely, however, it was due to the funding policies of the federal government to the provinces. Fifteen million Canadians needed relief, and millions of dollars would have to be spent to stabilize the economy. Frontier College would receive some of these "survival benefits" from the federal and provincial largesse, much of it spent on infrastructure projects. However, this was small comfort to Alfred. He was discouraged and worn out by his long, losing struggle and decided that the 1933 annual general meeting would be his last as principal. The detailed minutes of the meeting record that somewhere between agenda items, Alfred quietly stood and in his soft voice mentioned that he would like to tender his resignation. He assured the meeting that he had no ill will toward anyone, that he would be only too glad to cooperate in the work in any way he could, but this was the third time for him to bring this matter before the board of governors and that he would prefer not to be tied down to the regular work of the college.

The board accepted his resignation this time and appointed him Principal Emeritus with a retirement allowance of $1,200 a year. Mrs. Craw, long-time board member, hoped that this would give him the opportunity to "regain something of his old time vigor." Alfred moved that Edmund Bradwin be the new principal immediately, and that formal installation be held in July, the thirty-third anniversary of the work. Carried unanimously. Alfred would not be there for that anniversary. He was heading back to Northern Ontario and this time he intended that it be permanent.

By June 1933 Alfred had moved in with his brother John who lived in the small village of Harty, Northern Ontario. Alfred was deeply indebted to John, as he had kept their farm and the Frontier College homestead settlement functioning successfully in Northern Ontario for almost ten years.

John Rae Fitzpatrick was born in Millsville in 1848 and as a teenager had travelled to Boston and acquired expertise in blacksmithing. He moved back to Millsville and lived in nearby Scotsburn, working for forty years as a blacksmith with his own shop.

After the death of his parents, he joined his brother J.W. in New Liskeard, Northern Ontario, working on his brother's farm. In 1912 he moved to Stalwart, Saskatchewan, and farmed there for twelve years. He then returned to New Liskeard at the age of seventy-four to live with J.W. and to supervise the clearing of a number of bush lots for Alfred's experiment in land settlement. J.W. died in 1928 and John moved to Edlund, one of the settlement sites. As Alfred's "homestead settlement" program flourished in the late 1920s, John took on labourer-teachers like Dr. Margaret Strang, H. Rokeby Thomas, and others to work the farm, teach, and live in the one-room school. As noted, by the early 1930s, the homestead settlement concept had lost government support, and John—farmer, blacksmith, and lumberman, now over eighty years old—had moved to Harty (now Val Rita-Harty), 350 kilometres northwest of New Liskeard, to run his own farm. Alfred often took the train north to Harty when he found the time, but the stresses and tumult of the 1929 to 1933 period at Frontier College kept him away.

In October 1932, with the degree-granting programs in abeyance, Alfred travelled to Harty more frequently, taking care of John who was in failing health. Alfred was afraid to leave him alone, so John came to Toronto for the winter and lived in a boarding house with Alfred.

After his resignation from the college board in May 1933, Alfred travelled north to farm and care for John. He later wrote that they were so tired in the evenings that they were unable to do more than read the newspapers. Nevertheless, by going back to his agricultural origins, Alfred seemed to be content. In 1934, he wrote to the college staff: "Dear Frontier, I dislike cooking and housekeeping but am not very lonely and have no fear night or day."

John died on May 1, 1934, and was buried next to his wife, Margaret, and brother J.W. in New Liskeard. Alfred was alone.

With the loss of his last surviving brother, Alfred decided to relocate to Toronto once more. He still maintained the farm and property in Harty, together with other property he owned in Northern Ontario, but would return to it infrequently, as travelling by train from Toronto to Harty exhausted him. It was clear to Bradwin and Jessie that he was in declining health and had not regained his "vigor" as Mrs. Craw had hoped. Nevertheless, he still had a voice to complain about the lack of social justice in Canada. His passionate fire for change had dimmed but not gone out.

Alfred never had a permanent home in Toronto, and now he continued his previous practice of renting a room or living in a series of boarding houses. The City of Toronto directories have no listing for a residential address for Fitzpatrick between 1932 and 1935. He had become much like the population he had served—itinerant.

In late 1933, Frontier College provided him with a small office in the same building as the college, which Alfred promptly filled with books. In addition, there was a typist who sorted his mail and typed his letters, articles, and a manuscript. In 1933, or perhaps earlier, Alfred had begun a new manuscript on topics that complemented his perspective as outlined in *The University in Overalls*, but it was somewhat less focused. Bradwin remarked in a letter to a donor that Alfred was busy writing on some themes that he had had in mind for years.

Although the surviving manuscript included a wide-ranging variety of political, historical, and educational references, it did have an overriding theme. The title of this work summarized how Alfred felt about a number of institutions in Canada. *Schools and Other Penitentiaries* was, not surprisingly perhaps, dedicated to George Monro Grant who, like Alfred, believed that equality of opportunity would solve most of Canada's social ills. This meant that the "hide-bound system of education" that the country was cursed with must be changed.

In this manuscript, despite references to Japanese politics, the Russian overthrow of its aristocracy, and Gandhi's support for the untouchables, Alfred still remained focused on his constant belief in the critical importance of "hand, head, and heart," that is, being capable of manual work, education for all, and altruistically helping others. Near the end of the manuscript Alfred wrote that his "religion" was to get privileges for all, that humankind was "entitled to food, clothing, and shelter, medical and surgical service, a home with running hot water and cold water and bath." Do this, he believed, and Canada would not have the violence that exists all over the world. Such a progressive change was very necessary in order to forestall a possible revolution in the country, he concluded.

Alfred would not be Alfred without a few swipes at institutions that he had considered obstacles to the positive changes he sought: "Run-of-the-mill College men are mostly selfish"; "Lawyers rarely rise above petty fogging mediocrity"; "The lecture room is largely a failure." He saved some of his most sarcastic criticism for the universities, which, with a few exceptions, had become his particular nemesis. He described them as not being with the working class or the destitute. They were instead "Off in a corner of a city…where white linen and praise of sports are of vastly greater interest than miserable workers."

In this, his last testament of matters that were important to him, some of his protestations have a contemporary ring. He deplored the "toothless League of Nations" and their lack of resolution in a dangerous world and recommended an international police force or "Peace Force," as he called it. He decried the small amount of money that was being spent on what he called the "untouchable." Sadly, it would instead be spent on monuments where "most individuals would rather give $100,000 to perpetuate the memory of some killer like the Duke of Wellington, Washington, Napoleon, Wolfe or

Montcalm...than $10,000 to assist the...privilege of reading and instruction of the working man." This was not a common sentiment in the 1930s about either monuments or working men.

Fitzpatrick dedicated one chapter of his manuscript to "Indian Education," a subject that he had rarely raised in his books, articles, or correspondence but one that he had obviously thought much about. Essentially, as with his conceptualization of the labourer-teacher pedagogy, Alfred opposed taking children out of the community to a school but wanted instead to have the teacher travel to them and "teach the whole Indian community." In exchange the teacher would learn from "the Indian" "his language and his work," thus becoming both a learner and a teacher. "The hand, head, and heart of the Indian, as of the white man, must all alike be educated." Alfred then briefly addressed the issue of land, criticizing the Province of Ontario for purchasing the tens of thousands of square kilometres on the east side of the Hudson Bay territory from the "Indian" for the "nominal" sum of $50,000. In his view "this is theft and retrogression," and he asked, "Are we to exploit this huge domain as we have robbed much of our other timber and mineral areas?"

Schools and Other Penitentiaries was never published, but fortunately a copy was preserved. Although a sprawling and scattered work, it does offer some insights into Alfred's life history and what he believed and still felt about the world he was now in. Despite his deep disappointment and shattered ego over the failure of what he believed Frontier College should be, he was still moved by a passion for change. With increasing physical fragility, this would be his last exploration of his thoughts on social justice and social reform. Within a year he would lose much of his mental acuity and cognition, in a different and much more difficult "Fight of My Life."

In late 1935, Alfred received word that in celebration of King George V's birthday, he had been recognized as an Officer of the British Empire (OBE) due to his lifetime of selfless service. He had been nominated by Prime Minister R. B. Bennett. By this time, Alfred's physical and mental decline had become precipitous. In early January 1936, he was barely capable of making the journey to Ottawa to receive the award. He had to be accompanied by an attendant. He "was far from well," according to Jessie Lucas. His condition was such that by mid-January he was admitted to "999" as it had been nicknamed by Torontonians—the psychiatric hospital at 999 Queen Street West. It had been founded in 1871 as the "Asylum for the Insane" and by 1919 was known as the Ontario Hospital Toronto, where, as Bradwin commented, there were so many men "in different states of mental dis-utility."

By early April of that year, Alfred was somewhat better and was moved to St. Michael's, a Catholic hospital also known as the "Urban Angel." News of his admission to St. Michael's was even reported on the radio. He was at times cogent about the present and frequently dwelt on his reminiscences, often sparked by the receipt of the *Pictou Advocate* newspaper, which Bradwin had arranged at Alfred's request. Bradwin remarked that Alfred often related stories about New Liskeard where he and J.W. had first settled and all the farm work that Thomas and Leander had done in Millsville. He mentioned Leander frequently as he was his favourite brother. Lee was tragically killed in California and was buried there in 1881. His death and Alfred's subsequent search for his grave and his brother Isaac in the 1890s marked the beginning of Alfred's long, unflagging journey to achieve social justice for the forgotten men of the camps. As is often the case, a family tragedy had far-reaching repercussions.

As his mental and physical health declined, Alfred spoke less and less. On June 16, 1936, Alfred Fitzpatrick died in hospital of a cerebral hemorrhage. He was seventy-four years old.

A lengthy obituary notice was prepared by the college and appeared soon after his death in several newspapers in Canada as well as in the United States, including in the *New York Times.*

Most noted Alfred's "long struggle for equality in elementary, secondary, and higher education." In addition, several editorials were published praising his work and that of the college. Given the important role that the media had played in his life, Alfred would have been pleased. For its part, the college raised a special fund, collecting from former labourer-teachers, the Willis family in Montreal, and financiers like J. P. Bickell and Joseph Flavelle to pay the hospital bills and burial costs and close the estate. Alfred was buried next to his brother Thomas in Mount Pleasant Cemetery, Toronto.

As executor of Alfred's will, Bradwin looked after what there was of Alfred's estate and corresponded extensively with the sole beneficiary and the youngest member of the Fitzpatrick family, Margaret Fitzpatrick Staples in New Hampshire. Not surprisingly, Alfred had not laid aside any savings, having spent much of his salary over the previous decades on college expenses, especially the homesteading program he had initiated. He had left $65 and his salary arrears amounting to $2,500 to the college.

His personal effects were of little value to anyone except as keepsakes that he had treasured. Despite his ceaseless writing, he had never written an autobiography except the occasional fictional, pseudo-autobiographical manuscripts that he submitted to publishers. These no longer exist. Often, however, even the scanty personal effects of an individual—the items they chose to keep—can indicate what they valued most in their lifetime. In spite of his constant nomadic existence, this was indeed the case for Alfred Fitzpatrick.

In Bradwin's correspondence with Alfred's sister Margaret, the last surviving member of the twelve Fitzpatrick children, he posted all the photos that Alfred had saved and a number of those objects which Alfred had kept through the years: the shoestring watch chain with a gold coin from his father that Alfred would use as collateral for small loans; the equity shares of his bankrupt companies, marking the early optimistic mining ventures of Alfred and brother J.W.; the Bible from an appreciative congregation in Wapella; his brother John's carpenter's bench, representing manual labour; a volume of his favourite author Thomas Carlyle; the OBE parchment recognizing his life's work; and two hooked rugs fashioned by his mother. These were the remnants of a life, talismans of times Alfred wished to remember. They were the physical remains of his reminiscences. Each item reflected his personality and his values: the interminable need to raise money and repay his debts; the love of literature, especially as it related to literacy; his duty to and respect for the labourers who worked with their hands; and the centrality of his family values with two once colourful, now faded rugs.

Alfred Fitzpatrick was born into the rural values of conformity in Millsville, namely family, farm, church, and school. The sectarian norms of the Presbyterian faith were deeply embedded in all four. Then, there were the secular values of Pictou Academy with its "Education for all" credo, as well as those of Queen's University that reflected and taught the changing societal values of the social gospel movement. Both sectarian and secular institutions were vital components of Alfred's intellectual growth.

Alfred's closeness to family led him to his "eureka moment" in the California redwoods. There he found his brother Isaac and a social cause that superseded his religious need to proselytize for Christianity. Instead he would strive to offer medical and educational assistance to tens of thousands of isolated workers. Other brothers were also supportive of his lifelong venture. Older brother J.W. assisted him financially with his entrepreneurial expertise in the early days of the Reading Camp Association. John, with his agricultural and lumbering skills, helped to sustain the Homestead Settlement program for the college until it was terminated in 1932. For his part, Alfred took care of John until his death in 1934 and also assumed responsibility for looking after his brother Thomas for a quarter of a century until his passing in 1924.

There is no doubt that Alfred was a practicing Christian—he attended churches regularly in Toronto and when he travelled across Canada. In the early days of the Reading Camp Association, after he had given up the ministry, churches would still invite Alfred to speak, and he would describe the work of the association. However, as Jessie remembered, he always said that he never wore his religion on his sleeve and disliked those who did. The same was true of his politics, which tended to be quite pragmatic. Political ideology was of concern to him only in as far as it would benefit the college. He was asked more than once to run for political office but declined. Perhaps the government that he worked most amicably with was the UFO under Premier Drury in the early 1920s; it most closely shared his values. As for federal politics, he took political support from both Liberals and Conservatives—wherever he could find it—as he desperately needed such support to push his Frontier College charter through the House of Commons. Although there was considerable resistance to his efforts by the Canadian institutions he criticized publicly, like churches, business, universities, and governments, there was always the thriving civic society in Canada that offered widespread financial and moral support for what he was trying to accomplish. But he worked frantically to earn this support with public presentations, incessant lobbying, articles, innovation, and constant travel. Consequently, the sacrifice for Alfred was very little home life and no social life. All was subsumed by the college and its mission. He was inextricably linked to the college, both wound round each other like a double helix.

As the college garnered wider and wider support and a national profile, Alfred took a personal interest in absolutely every aspect of its work. He was an energetic and restless man, and he did not know when, where, or how to stop. As one writer said, "he kept on going by taking on too much." With his frenetic travel, curious inventions, numerous and various books, articles, and editorials, and considerable lobbying skills, Alfred would always position the college foremost in his thinking, his finances, and his life.

Such single-mindedness would often lead to animosity and jealousy as well as a real or presumed rivalry with those closest to him, particularly Edmund Bradwin. For Alfred, the college must always be multi-tasking to the multitudes—with literacy work in camps, university education for all, homestead settlements for men and women, and a recognition of the importance of the environment. As far as Bradwin was concerned, there was a single focus—the isolated, semi-skilled worker in Canada's camps. All the many other things that Alfred worked for were seen by Bradwin as distractions from the college mission. He believed these distractions consumed time, energy, and financial support. However, despite the difficult, fractious years of the 1920s and 1930s for these two men, time, character, and circumstance facilitated the survival of the college beyond its possible demise and well into the twenty-first century.

Alfred Fitzpatrick was an educational innovator. He believed that education would bring about progressive change and social justice. Social justice to him was liberty with no class, privilege, or ethnic boundaries, and it revolved around the ideal of service. His philosophy included universal education—by taking education to where the people lived and worked and being focused on what they wanted to learn; the belief that a person's potential required an opportunity in order to be realized; the conviction that learning was a two-way exchange between teacher and student—essentially two learners; the understanding that language, literacy, and citizenship training was necessary for immigrants who chose to stay in Canada; and that education, as Alfred frequently mentioned in his writings, was for hand, head, and heart, that is, it should equally be vocational, academic, and altruistic.

In addition, Alfred was an outspoken activist. He was a social justice pioneer who opposed some of the religious, social, and political norms of his time. He continued to seek change through his public presentations and his writings well into his final years as evidenced by his unpublished manuscript *Schools and Other Penitentiaries*. For Alfred Fitzpatrick, it seems, the struggle was never over.

EPILOGUE

ALTHOUGH THE OFFICIAL HANDING-OVER HAD TAKEN PLACE IN
May 1933, Edmund Bradwin was already busy with a number of
Frontier College concerns and making every effort to balance continuity and change for the college. The year before, in a letter to
board member Edgar Patenaude in Montreal, Ed had stated that
although the degree-granting status was removed, the college could
still continue with its examining board to assist those who really
desired to study for a degree. Then, perhaps, a provincial university
would grant them recognition. However, the examining board was
effectively disbanded when Alfred resigned in 1933, and Bradwin's
idea was abandoned. Eventually, after four years of college lobbying,
the University of Toronto did recognize the three B.A.s of the
college in 1935, but the M.A. remained unrecognized.

There was also an attempt to affiliate with a university in some
fashion, and several discussions were undertaken with the administrative faculty and officials of the University of Toronto. McMaster
University was not considered a candidate as it had moved to
Hamilton in 1930. The new president of the University of Toronto,
H. J. Cody, was sympathetic but could not win the full support of
the faculty and staff. Interestingly, in 1936, the year of Alfred's death,
Cody made a national radio broadcast on the newly created CBC
touting the good work the college had done.

Dr. Edmund Bradwin in 1935. (LIBRARY AND ARCHIVES CANADA/
FRONTIER COLLEGE FONDS/ PA-139820)

The major task, as always, was to address the financial situation.
As early as 1932 Edmund was already planning a strategy to resolve
that issue. He wrote to Jessie Lucas that as soon as possible, "$2,000
a year must go into a Trust Fund or Foundation to help out when

pinches come. This should have been done long ago when times were good." He added, "Miss Lucas, F. C. will not sink." The times, however, were never all that good in the decades that followed, and it was not until 1997 that Frontier College was able to establish a foundation that allowed for a semblance of financial stability. Now, almost 125 years after its founding, Frontier College is still afloat.

With Alfred gone, the fundraising had fallen on Edmund's shoulders. By the last half of 1933, he was immersed in the careful choreography of raising cash. One of Bradwin's initial obstacles was that Alfred had maintained a large nationwide coterie of friends, many of whom donated due to a personal relationship with him rather than in consideration of the work of the college. Ed had only played a small part in this effort. He was much less persistent than Alfred, so he had to start from the beginning with the assistance of Jessie Lucas who was very familiar with Alfred's activities and colleagues. Ed lobbied government offices and funding organizations, including the Carnegie Foundation, about which Ed remarked, "I see a ray of hope for $2,000." He also began calling on businessmen as well as men's and women's clubs. Jessie herself wrote articles in *Echoes*, a publication of the Imperial Order Daughters of the Empire (IODE).

In November 1933, Bradwin, who often shared his fundraising "adventures" with Jessie, wrote to her about one such experience. He recounted a presentation he made at a tea organized by Dr. Helen R. Y. Reid, a prominent social reform activist in Montreal who was among the first group of women to attend McGill University in 1884 and was now an advocate for public health and women's education. The attendees at the tea included representatives of the Women's Canada Club, Social Council of Women, North End Women's Catholic Society, and Women's Imperial Club. Faced with such an audience, Bradwin wrote to Jessie that "I was ready to grab my hat and run" as "collecting takes every fibre aworking." The taciturn Bradwin, hopeful for financial support, came away with a mailing list of "casualties," as he put it sardonically and noted that he had received a verbal critique of his presentation by Dr. Helen Reid: "He talked too loud and didn't answer questions directly." Despite this criticism, Dr. Reid was a member of the college board a year later.

Ironically it was the economic depression itself that would provide for a monumental positive change in the financial stability and reputation of the college. This impetus for change involved the Ontario provincial government and the federal government in 1931. At the provincial level, George Henry, who had been Minister of Public Works and Highways (1923–30) became premier of Ontario in 1930. He was a staunch supporter of building highways in the province. With the federal relief grants the province was receiving, there was adequate funding to fulfill Henry's mandate of and passion for road-building. During his term in office, well over three thousand kilometres of roads were built, many of them with funding from the Federal Relief Act of 1930. Several of the road camps included a Frontier College labourer-teacher.

One such was A. Grant Bucknell who spent the winter of 1931–32 at a road construction camp in Deux Rivières, Ontario, managed by the federal Department of Northern Development. This was to be a section of the TransCanada Highway that was being constructed in each province across the country. Twenty million dollars had been allocated for unemployed workers to build the road. In 1931, Grant Bucknell was one of nine labourer-teachers who would be sent to this specific camp over the next five years. At times there was a road construction camp every four miles in Ontario, and these were in operation winter and summer. Bucknell, while a third-year arts student out of McMaster University, worked with the pick and shovel gang in Deux Rivières from November 1931 to April 1932. With axes and dynamite, some 125 men cleared the forest, earth, and rock for the new highway. The ethnic makeup of the camps varied. This one was 90 percent English Canadian, many of them previously unemployed.

Other camps like that of Campbell Murray, a labourer-teacher in 1932–33, were 80 to 90 percent immigrants. In Murray's camp, there were thirty workers coming to class nightly to a small wooden shack that served as a classroom and camp library. Working conditions were typical for the Canadian wilderness and not uncommon for the location. J. C. Willard, camp instructor, remembered in an interview decades later his highway building experience as follows: "most of those men were working long, long hours, and we were infested with black flies. I got to know the black fly up there pretty well and he was a real menace. We had to go around with citronel on us, and handkerchiefs soaked tied around our necks and covered right in. I used to wear breeks, and I would drop my breeks on the floor, and you would see two rings of dead black flies every night. They are a miserable little insect!" There were well over fifty labourer-teachers in camps like these in 1932.

R. B. Bennett had been elected prime minister in 1930 to lead a country in which 32 percent of the wage earners were no longer working. He had responded to the employment crisis with a number of measures, including the Unemployment Relief Act of 1930 and another Relief Act in 1932. These millions of dollars for infrastructure were intended to provide roadwork, rail repair, and new construction in all sectors of the Canadian economy, sectors in which Frontier College had been involved for over three decades.

The year 1932 was the nadir of the Depression with increased unemployment and a transient labour force. Added to this were the 116 strikes and lockouts that occurred in that year alone with many more to come. The federal government decided to assume a more aggressive role, and in October 1932, federal relief camps were created under the Department of National Defence and focused on assisting the unhoused, able-bodied, and unemployed young men of the country. A year later, in the spring of 1933, the federal government and Frontier College signed an agreement to provide

A wagonload of workers at the Petawawa Relief Camp, Petawawa, Ontario, in 1935. (LIBRARY AND ARCHIVES CANADA/FRONTIER COLLEGE FONDS/ A142914)

one labourer-teacher to every camp that consisted of 250 men or more. They would undertake "educational and recreational work" in each camp and also carry out the everyday labour with the men. Labourer-teachers were soon dispersed across Canada. That year there were eighty-seven labourer-teachers spread across the country at a variety of construction relief camps. Despite a national depression or because of it, the future of the college looked brighter.

Bradwin was overjoyed. The college was finally receiving sustained financial support from the Canadian government, something that Fitzpatrick had sought for decades. In addition, it had also achieved federal recognition for its programs that Bradwin wanted to build on. As he wrote in late 1933, "What an opportunity for us!

It must not fail. Here is a chance for Frontier College to take a Dominion place—but we must get bigger help, and get more effective supervision, must be up and doing."

At the AGM in 1934, according to Bradwin, the "amount of work is in excess of anytime previously." That year, eighty-five labourer-teachers were dispersed to camps across Canada, and petitions were being received from a number of camps asking that an instructor be placed with them. Where a college representative was not placed, large cartons of magazines and books were sent. Almost five thousand campmen had enrolled for actual study, double any previous year in the history of the college.

However, with protests, strikes, and a few riots due to the conditions in the relief camps, the unemployment program could not survive. In 1935, beginning in the relief camps of British Columbia, about one thousand unemployed men decided to take action to rectify their situation. They filled several train boxcars with the intention of conveying their grievances about work and wages to Bennett's doorstep in Ottawa. Their "On-to-Ottawa Trek" was halted in Regina on June 14. In their efforts to disperse the workers, the police precipitated the Regina Riot on July 1, 1935, in Market Square. In the wake of the trek and the riot, the new Liberal government of William Lyon Mackenzie King, which came to power three months later, established the R. A. Riggs Commission to fully investigate the conditions in some fifty camps across Canada. Edmund Bradwin was included as one of the three commissioners. Over the next year, the commission would depend greatly on the information that Frontier College collected through personal interviews and questionnaires that labourer-teachers carried out among the relief camp workers. Its conclusion was that many of the young men had "not acquired the habit of working or the sense of individual responsibility to society" due to the economic depression and therefore posed a serious threat "to the maintenance of our existing institutions." On this basis, by summer 1936, the final recommendation was that all relief camps be closed and that jobs with a decent wage be found in agriculture and railroad construction. This challenge would be undertaken by the Department of Labour, and Frontier College was chosen to play a prominent part in its work.

For Edmund Bradwin this was the culmination of a long sought goal. Frontier College was now recognized nationally, and in 1936 the college began to receive its first of many annual grants from the federal Department of Labour. This would stabilize and sustain the college's work for several years to come. At the annual general meeting of 1937, after a moment of silence for Alfred Fitzpatrick who had died the year before, Bradwin could report that there were 185 labourer-teachers in the field—the highest ever—and that for the first time in its history, "The Frontier College" had a clean financial slate. The books were balanced, no debts were owed, and the college had attained a national reputation. Bradwin had enabled Frontier College to survive and, by his efforts, lengthen "the shadow of one man," Alfred Fitzpatrick, its founder and one of Canada's early pioneers of social justice.

The Frontier College logo. (PRIVATE COLLECTION OF JAMES MORRISON)

ACKNOWLEDGEMENTS

FIRST MY APPRECIATION GOES OUT TO THE MANY ARCHIVES THAT safeguard our history and to the many archivists and their staff across Canada who assisted me in navigating these mountains of material in electronic and document form. I am grateful specifically to the following repositories: Canadian Pacific Railway, Montreal; City of Toronto; Maritime Conference Office of the United Church of Canada, Sackville, New Brunswick; McCulloch Heritage Centre, Pictou, Nova Scotia; McMaster University, Hamilton, Ontario; Archives of Ontario, Toronto; Presbyterian Church of Canada, Toronto; Public Archives of Nova Scotia, Halifax; Queen's University, Kingston, Ontario; United Church Archives, Don Mills, Toronto; University of Toronto; YMCA, West End, Toronto; and YMCA, Halifax, Nova Scotia.

I am especially grateful to Library and Archives Canada, which, since 1972, has continued to collect, sort, and preserve the Frontier College records.

The early research interest and subsequent publications about Frontier College by George Cook and Marjorie Zavitz were very valuable—especially the oral history interviews, which in turn were supplemented by former Frontier College President Ian Morrison's interviews. The genealogical work of the late James W. Fitzpatrick III contributed greatly to understanding the Fitzpatrick extended family and Alfred's role in it. And Dr. Gordon Young's expert knowledge of Millsville, Pictou County, was deeply appreciated.

The professional typing skills of Ghalia Mohamed and Jennifer MacDougall helped make this manuscript a reality. I am also grateful for the great competence and patience shown by Marianne Ward as she skilfully edited this weave of words into a coherent narrative. And a special shout-out to Sheree Fitch who believed Alfred Fitzpatrick's story must be told.

Finally my deepest gratitude to the staff at Frontier College, including Phil Fernandez, Michelle Fraser, and Erika Martin. I have had discussions with and interviewed most of the last six presidents of the college including Eric Robinson (1954–1971), Ian Morrison (1971–1975), Jack Pearpoint (1975–1990), John Daniel O'Leary (1990–2008), Sherry Campbell (2008–2016), and most recently, Stephen Faul (2016–2022). I have always been most impressed by the value and importance these individuals ascribe to the history of the college. For me the catalyst to write this book came from my long summers of learning, literacy, and labour in 1964 on the CPR Steel Gang as a teacher and spike hammer operator working our way across Canada.

As with so many other things in our half-century together, I am forever grateful to my wife, Sheila, for her patience, encouragement, and love when listening to my stories, finding my typos, and critiquing my prose. This will be the last one, I promise.

Responsibility for any errors or omissions in these chapters is mine and mine alone.

PUBLISHED WRITINGS BY ALFRED FITZPATRICK
(LISTED CHRONOLOGICALLY)

BOOKS

Handbook for New Canadians (Toronto: Ryerson Press, 1919)

The University in Overalls: A Plea for Part-Time Study (Toronto: Hunter-Rose, 1920)

A Primer For Adults: Elementary English For Foreign-Born Workers in Camps (Toronto: Frontier College, 1926)

JOURNAL ARTICLES

"Life in Lumbering and Mining Camps: A Plea for Reform," *The Canadian Magazine of Politics, Science, Art & Literature*, XXI:I (May 1901): 49–52.

"Social Amelioration in the Lumbering Camps," *The Canada Lumberman* (May 1904): 1–2.

"The Neglected Citizen in the Camps," *The Canadian Magazine of Politics, Science, Art & Literature*, XXV:I (May 1905): 43–48.

"Canadianizing the Immigrant," *Canadian Courier*, December 20, 1913: 6–7.

"Education on the Frontier," *Queen's Quarterly*, XXI:I (July, August, September 1913): 62–68.

"Swing-team boss," *World's Work*, April 27, 1914: 698–702.

"An American Graduate in a Canadian Construction Camp," *The Canadian Magazine of Politics, Science, Art & Literature*, XLVII:1 (May 1916): 34–37.

"Outnavvying the Navvies," *The Canadian Magazine of Politics, Science, Art & Literature*, XLVII:1 (May 1916): 21–28.

"Education in Canada," *Proceedings of the National Conference of Social Work (US)*, 1924: 578–81.

"Experiment in the Canadian Lumbering Industry," *Proceedings of the National Conference of Social Work (US)*, 1924: 349–52.

"The Frontier College and the Influence of Manual Labor on its Instructors," *Canadian Railroader*, IX:2 (1925): 26–29.

"The Frontier College," *The Queen's Review*, 4:4 (April 1930): 117–22.

BOOKLETS INCLUDED IN ANNUAL REPORTS OF THE READING CAMP ASSOCIATION

Library Extension in Ontario (1900)

Home Education Extension (1902)

Camp Education Extension (1903)

The Education of the Frontier Labourer (1904)

The Frontier Labourer (1905)

Camp Education (1907)

Canada's Frontiersmen (1908)

Education by Contact (1909)

A Corner in Education (1910)

The Diffusion of Education (1911)

The Immigrant (1912)

The Frontier College (1913)

Frontier Camp Schools (1914)

Settlement Camps (1915)

Canadianizing the Foreigner (1915)

University Settlement on the Frontier (1916)
The Diffusion of Education (1917)
The Instructor and the Red (1919)
The University and the Frontier (1920)
The Frontier College: Coming of Age (1921)

THE FRONTIER COLLEGE OF CANADA
ACADEMIC CALENDARS

1925–26

1927–29

1929–31

BIBLIOGRAPHY

DESPITE THE RICH DOCUMENTATION ABOUT FRONTIER COLLEGE at Library and Archives Canada, Alfred Fitzpatrick's life story has received very little scholarly attention. A number of articles and books mention him in passing, but there is no other biography of him. Fortunately there have been a number of publications focused on the work of Frontier College that have provided insights as to Fitzpatrick's contributions. This bibliography also includes references to a number of other publications I have drawn on to provide a context for his times.

PRIMARY SOURCE:

Frontier College Fonds: MG 28, I 124 Volumes 1–267 Finding Aid No. 736, Library and Archives Canada (LAC)

SECONDARY SOURCES:

Allen, Richard. *The Social Passion: Religion and Social Reform in Canada 1914–1928*. Toronto: University of Toronto Press, 1973.

Anderson, J. T. M. *The Education of the New-Canadian*. Toronto: J. M. Dent & Sons Ltd., 1918.

Avery, Donald. *"Dangerous Foreigners": European Immigrant Workers and Labour Radicalism in Canada, 1896–1932*. Toronto: McClelland & Stewart, 1979.

Baskerville, Peter A. *Sites of Power: A Concise History of Ontario.* Toronto: Oxford University Press, 2005.

Berger, Carl. *The Sense of Power: Studies in the Ideas of Canadian Imperialism, 1886–1914.* Toronto: University of Toronto Press, 1970.

Bland, Salem. *The New Christianity: The Theology of the Social Gospel.* Toronto: McClelland & Stewart, c. 1920.

Bradwin, Edmund. *The Bunkhouse Man: A Study of the Work and Pay in the Camps of Canada, 1903–1914.* Toronto: University of Toronto Press, 1972. First published 1928.

Bruce, Lorne. "Reading Camps and Travelling Libraries in New Ontario, 1900–1905," *Historical Studies in Education/Revue d'histoire de l'éducation* 26:2 (2014): 71–97.

Cameron, James. *Pictou County's History.* Kentville, NS: Pictou County Historical Society, 1972.

Clark, C. S. *Of Toronto the Good: The Queen City of Canada as It Is.* Montreal: Toronto Publishing Company, 1898.

Connor, Ralph. *Black Rock: A Tale of the Selkirks.* Toronto: Westminister Company, 1898.

————. *The Foreigner: A Tale of Saskatchewan.* Toronto: Westminister Company, 1909.

Cook, George L. "Alfred Fitzpatrick and the Foundation of Frontier College (1899–1922)," *Canada: An Historical Magazine* 3:4 (June 1976): 15–39.

————. "Educational Justice for the Campmen: Alfred Fitzpatrick and the Foundation of Frontier College, 1899–1922" in Michael Welton, *Knowledge for the People: The Struggle for Adult Learning in English-Speaking Canada.* Toronto: University of Toronto Press, 1987.

Cook, George L. with Marjorie Robinson. "The Fight of My Life: Alfred Fitzpatrick's Struggle for the Frontier Charter, 1902–1933," *Histoire sociale/Social History* XXIII:45 (May 1990): 81–112.

Gibson, Frederick W. *Queens University Volume II 1917–1961: To Serve And Yet Be Free.* Kingston and Montreal: McGill-Queen's University Press, 1983.

Grant, William Lawson and Frederick Hamilton. *George Monro Grant*. Toronto: Morang and Company, 1905.

Greenlee, James G. *Sir Robert Falconer: A Biography*. Toronto: University of Toronto Press, 1988.

Leacock, Stephen. *Sunshine Sketches of a Little Town*. New York: J. Lane Publishers, 1912.

Levine, Allan. *Toronto: Biography of a City*. Toronto: Douglas & McIntyre, 2014.

Martin, Erika. "Action and Advocacy: Alfred Fitzpatrick and the Early History of Frontier College." Master's thesis, University of Toronto, 2000.

McLean, Lorna R. "The Good Citizen: Masculinity and Citizenship at Frontier College 1899–1933" in R. Adamoski, Dorothy E. Chunn, and Robert Menzies, *Contesting Canadian Citizenship: Historical Readings*. Peterborough, Ontario: Broadview Press, 2002.

Mack, D. B. "George Monro Grant" in *Dictionary of Canadian Biography, Volume XIII (1901–1910)*. Toronto/Montreal: University of Toronto/L'Universite Laval, 1994.

————. "George Monro Grant: Evangelical Prophet." Dissertation, Queen's University, Kingston, 1992.

MacPhie, John P. *Pictonians at Home and Abroad*. Boston: Pinkham Press, 1914.

Mason, Jody. *Home Feelings: Liberal Citizenship and the Canadian Reading Camp Movement*. Kingston and Montreal: McGill-Queen's University Press, 2019.

Moir, John. *Handbook for Canadian Presbyterianism*. Toronto: Presbyterian Church of Canada Press, c. 1994.

Morrison, James H. *Camps and Classrooms: A Pictorial History of Frontier College*. Toronto: Frontier College Press, 1989.

————. "The Man, the Mission, and the Book: An Introduction" in Alfred Fitzpatrick, *The University in Overalls*. Toronto: Thompson Educational Publishing, Inc., 1999. First published in 1920.

Mutchmor, James R. *Mutchmor: The Memoirs of James Ralph Mutchmor.* Toronto: University of Toronto Press, 1965.

Palmer, Howard. "Reluctant Hosts: Anglo-Canadian Views of Multiculturalism in the Twentieth Century" in Gerald Tulchinsky, *Immigration in Canada: Historical Perspectives.* Toronto: Copp Clark Longman, 1994.

Parker, Rev. Stuart C. *The Book of St. Andrew's: A Short History of St. Andrew's Church, Toronto 1830–1930.* Toronto: St. Andrew's Church, 1930.

Patterson, George. *History of the County of Pictou.* Pictou: Pictou Advocate Press, 1877.

The People's School: Its Purpose, Its History, What the Professors, the Students and the Public Say About It. Halifax: Nova Scotia Department of Agriculture, 1922.

Prebble, John. *The Lion in the North: A Personal View of Scotland's History.* Hammersmith, England: Penguin, 1973.

Robinson, Eric. "The History of the Frontier College." Master's thesis, McGill University, 1961.

Ross, Murray G. *The YMCA in Canada: The Chronicle of a Century.* Toronto: Ryerson Press, 1951.

Stewart, Roderick and Sharon Stewart. *Phoenix: The Life of Norman Bethune.* Kingston and Montreal: McGill-Queen's University Press, 2011.

Sutherland, D. R. "Alfred Fitzpatrick and the Frontier College." Paper for Bachelor of Divinity, Atlantic School of Theology, 1968.

Wood, B. Anne. *Pictou Academy in the Nineteenth Century.* Pictou, NS: Advocate Printing and Publishing Company, 1997.

———. "Pictou Academy: Promoting 'Schooled Subjectivities' in Nineteenth Century Nova Scotia," *Acadiensis* 28:2 (1999): 41–57.

Woodsworth, J. S. *Strangers Within Our Gates: Coming Canadians.* Toronto: University of Toronto Press, 1972. First published 1909.

Zavitz, Marjorie E. *Frontier College and Bolshevism in the Camps of Canada 1919–1925*. Master's thesis, University of Windsor, 1974.

————. "Isabel Kelly: Pioneer Literacy Worker," *Canadian Women's Studies* 9:3–4 (1988): 24–25.

Zavitz Robinson, Marjorie. "Norman Bethune and Frontier College 1911–1912" in D. A. E. Shepard and A. Levesque, *Norman Bethune: His Times and His Legacy*. Ottawa: Canadian Public Health Association, 1982.

————. "Reading Camp Association in Alberta," *Alberta History* 29:1 (1981): 36–40.

INDEX

A
Acadia University 27, 173, 191
Algoma, Ontario 53
Anishinaabe (Ojibwe) 110
Antigonish Movement 170, 230
Anti-Loafing Act of 1918 181
Armstrong, George 232
Ashford, H. E. D. 212

B
Bear River, Nova Scotia 173
Beatty, Sir Edward 216
Bell, W. J. 85
Bennett, Prime Minister R. B. 252, 262
Bethune, Norman 109, 111, 113
Bickell, John P. 115, 229, 233, 253
Bill 68 199, 203
Black's Harbour, New Brunswick 174
Bland, Reverend Salem 47
Blue Nose in the Redwoods 204
Bolshevism 140, 172, 178, 182, 193, 197, 214
Borden, Sir Robert 123, 181
Bradwin, Edmund 71, 89, 99, 123, 124, 126, 142, 152, 161, 170, 173, 180, 183, 198, 202, 208, 210, 215, 222, 227, 229, 231, 235, 237, 239, 245, 258
Brandon, Manitoba 216
British Immigration and Colonization Association 220
Bucknell, A. Grant 261
Buntin, A. 42
Burke, John 157

C
Calgary Herald 222
Camp Borden, Ontario 153
Canadian Courier 154

Canadianization 142, 148, 172, 175, 180, 182, 199, 215
Canadian Magazine of Politics, Science, Art, and Literature 77, 155
Canadian National Railway 119, 198, 212, 215, 216
Canadian Northern Railway strike 178
Canadian Pacific Railway 48, 55, 56, 68, 119, 154, 211, 216
Carnegie, Andrew 80, 139
Carnegie Foundation 175, 232, 260
Charlton, William A. 61, 85
Chew, Manley 112
Chisholm, Miriam 173
Coady, Dr. Moses 170
Cobalt Mines 98
Cobalt, Ontario 92, 119, 218
Cochrane, Ontario 218
Cody, H. J. 258
Coleman, Vince 159
Collins, R. W. 172, 239
Colquhoun, A. H. U. 201, 202
Columbia University 104, 128, 162, 170, 212, 217, 226
Corbett, E. A. 102
Craw, Mrs. 247
Cree 110

D
Dalhousie University 24, 27, 29, 226
Dauphin, Manitoba 212
Dawson's Point, Ontario 97
Dawson, William 205
Dearle, Ray 148
Department of Immigration and Colonization 214
deportation 143, 182
Deux Rivières, Ontario 261
Diamond, William 151

Dominion Atlantic Railway 160

Dominion Bureau of Statistics 213

Dominion Coal Company 157 .

Dominion Lands Act of 1872 219

Doolittle, P. E. 229

Drake, John 216

Dr. Barnardo's Home Children 165, 220

Drury, Premier Ernest 195, 210, 221, 232

Dunlap, D. A. 198

E

Edlund, Ontario 222, 223, 248

Edwards, W. C. 123

Emmanuel College 201

English for New Canadians 164

Evening Mail 226

F

Falconer, Robert 137, 196, 200, 227, 232

Fasken, Sergeant S. A. 146

Ferguson, Premier Howard 195, 210, 216, 232, 235, 241

Fessant, Minnie 245

First World War 123, 125, 128, 133, 140, 142, 164, 167, 168, 178, 182

Fitzpatrick, Alexander 18, 24, 42, 54, 206

Fitzpatrick, Isaac 24, 49, 51, 54

Fitzpatrick, James 6, 16

Fitzpatrick, James William (J.W.) 24, 73, 76, 91, 92, 122, 188, 203, 206, 248

Fitzpatrick, Jane 25, 203, 206

Fitzpatrick, Jennie 25, 206

Fitzpatrick, John 24, 173, 222, 225, 247

Fitzpatrick, Leander 24, 49, 252

Fitzpatrick, Margaret 25, 42, 206, 253

Fitzpatrick, Mary 19, 54, 73, 206

Fitzpatrick, Mary Annie 25, 206

Fitzpatrick Mountain 6, 16, 17

Fitzpatrick, Thomas 24, 54, 73, 96, 206, 208

Fitzpatrick, Walter 24, 73

Flavelle, Sir Joseph 120, 144, 246, 253

Fleming, Sir Sandford 36, 38, 88, 119

Fort Qu'Appelle, Saskatchewan 52

Frontier College charter (section 10) 241, 244, 245

Frontier College film (1920) 177

Frontier College film (1954) 178

Fruit Cereal Company Ottawa 176

G

Garratt, Thomas 152

George, Prime Minister David Lloyd 190

Givens, W. E. 155

Globe 62, 84, 160, 231

Gordon, Daniel 205

Gordon, George 200

Gordon, Reverend Charles W. 64, 81, 156, 157, 189, 229

Graham, George 160

Grand Trunk Pacific Railway 119, 154

Grant, Reverend George Monro 32, 35, 50, 67, 83, 155, 205, 249

Grant, William Lawson 198

Gray, Angus 70

Gray, J. E. 146

Grey, Lord Albert 79, 119

Guest, W. J. 119

H

Halifax Explosion 157

Hamilton, Colonel Charles F. 214

Hamilton Spectator 222

Handbook for New Canadians 164, 167, 173, 180, 183, 190

Hanna, D. B. 119, 198

Harcourt, Richard 62, 65, 77

Hart House 139

Harty, Ontario 247

Hays, Charles 119

Henry, Premier George 235, 241, 244, 261

Hollinger, Benny 96

homesteading 147, 218, 247

Hooper, J. H. 153

Howe, Joseph 23, 83

I

immigration 105, 129, 135, 155, 175, 197, 220, 226

Imperial Order Daughters of the Empire 229, 260

Intercolonial Railway 29

International Workers of the World 178, 214

J

Johnston, Reverend Dr. Robert 234, 240, 241, 245

K

Kapuskasing, Ontario 218

Keeley, A.J. 88

Khaki University 133, 145

Kincardine, New Brunswick 49, 52

King, Prime Minister William Lyon Mackenzie 130, 190, 198, 223, 264

King's College 27

L

labourer-teacher 71, 89, 109, 162, 170, 173, 177, 180, 182, 211, 215, 230

Lanctôt, Gustave 228

La Presse 84

Laurier, Prime Minister Wilfred 105

Lausch, Roudolph 117

Laval University 191, 226

Laverie, B. M. 65, 173

Leacock, Stephen 94, 193

Lefebvre, Father P. E. 61

literacy 60, 91, 132, 134, 175, 180, 182, 203

Little River, California 50, 122

Longmore, Charles 246

Lord's Day Act 47

Lovering, H. L. 118, 164, 167

Lovitt, R. L. 150

Lucas, Jessie 51, 135, 166, 172, 197, 208, 235, 237, 239, 245, 260

M

MacDonald, E. M. 200, 229

MacDonald, J. E. H. 190

MacGregor, Reverend James 13

MacKay, A. H. 29, 206

Mackay, Ira 200, 202

Mackenzie, Arthur Stanley 205

MacKenzie, John W. 152

Mackey, Isabel 173

MacLean, A. 133

MacLeod, Dr. Norman 67

MacPhie, Reverend J. P. 205

Mail and Empire 75, 148, 199, 225

Martin's Camp, Ontario 110, 111

Mastukuk, John 213

McCrimmon, Abraham L. 192

McCulloch, Reverend Thomas 14, 30

McDonald, J. F. 65

McDougall, Donald 151

McGill University 152, 201, 226

McIntyre-Porcupine Mines Ltd. 115

McMartin, Duncan 119

McMaster University 120, 168, 191, 205

McMechan, Frances 120, 123, 156

medicine 58, 79

Melberg, Birger 213

Mendocino City, California 122

Mi'kmaq 9, 16

Millar, Reverend John 90

Miller, J. B. 119

Millsville, Nova Scotia 9, 16, 18, 20, 25, 73, 203, 205, 207

Millsville school 22

Miner, Jack 225, 233

Mohawk 16

Moody, Reverend Thomas B. 235

Moore, Tom 181, 229

Mount Allison University 212

Munro, Henry 226

Murray, Campbell 262

Murray, Dr. Walter 169

Murray, Janet 6, 17

Mutchmor, James Ralph 115

N

Nairn Centre, Ontario 53, 54, 56, 65, 72
National Conference of Canadian
  Universities 227
New Liskeard, Ontario 86, 92, 97
Niagara Falls, Ontario 177
Nipissing Central Railway 95
North Bay Times 84
Noseworthy, Joseph 115
Nova Scotia Free School Act 25

O

One Big Union 172, 210, 214
Ontario Companies Act 194
On-to-Ottawa Trek 264
Orillia Packet 80
Osler, J. B. 120
Ottawa Citizen 199

P

Patenaude, Edgar 258
Patterson, A. O. 65
People's School 169, 229
Petawawa, Ontario 263
Pictou Academy 15, 27, 137, 206
Pictou Branch Railroad 28
Pictou Grammar School 15
Pictou Literary and Scientific Society 13
Pictou, Nova Scotia 8, 12, 14, 27, 205
Pictou Philharmonic Society 13
Pinage Lake, Ontario 109, 111
Playfair, James 119, 167
Porcupine, Ontario 122
Presbyterian Church 11, 25, 36, 46, 90,
  132, 134, 205

Q

Queen's Quarterly 155
Queen's University 32, 34, 40, 45, 72,
  102, 128, 168, 191, 192, 201, 214
Queen's University Missionary
  Association 48

R

R. A. Riggs Commission 264
reading rooms 63, 65, 70, 86
Red Deer, Alberta 121
Regina Riot 264
Reid, Dr. Helen R. Y. 260
relief camps 221, 262
Renfrew Mercury 84
Renfrew, Ontario 123
Revelstoke, British Columbia 48
Roberts, Charles G. D. 228
Robertson, Lieutenant-Colonel D. M.
  118, 136
Rogers, Anderson 22
Rogers, Robert 129

S

Saint Mary's University 27
Schools and Other Penitentiaries 249
Scott, Mrs. Alex 65, 173
Searchlight Larder Lake Mines Ltd. 98
section 10 of the charter 241, 244, 245
Select Committee on Agriculture and
  Colonization 223
Shaganash, John 117
Shandong College 201
Shaughnessy, Thomas 68, 144
Shearer, Reverend J. G. 47
Shelley, Manitoba 211
Shortt, Adam 155
Sifton, Clifford 105
Sir John Middlemore's Children's
  Emigration Homes 220
Skelton, O. D. 155, 192, 200
Smith, Pauline 151
Soldier Settlement Act 147
Spirit Lake, Ontario 153
Spock, Benjamin 211
Stalwart, Saskatchewan 173
St. Andrew's Presbyterian Church 130,
  134, 135, 163
Star Weekly 193, 220

Stewart, Charles 199
Stewart, Dr. H. L. 226
St. Francis Xavier University 27, 169, 229
Strang, Dr. Margaret 223, 248
Swanson, Aaron 117

T

Tanner, Charles 200
Taschereau, Louis-Alexandre 233
Temiskaming and Northern Ontario Railway 92, 95
Bunkhouse Man, The 101, 104, 171, 217
Halifax Disaster, The 160
University in Overalls, The 23, 117, 139, 147, 156, 173, 185, 204, 206, 209, 218, 221, 249
Thomas, H. Rokeby 248
Thornton, Sir Henry 216, 238
Timmins, Ontario 95
Tompkins, Father Jimmy (J. J.) 169, 186
Toronto Daily Star 199
Toronto, Ontario 97, 124, 130, 133, 135, 249
Tory, Henry Marshall 146, 200, 227, 229
Treaty 9 110
Trinity Medical School 58
Turner, A. P. 85
Tuskegee Institute 63

U

Unemployment Relief Act 262
United Church of Canada 116, 205
United Farmers of Ontario 177, 195, 210, 232
United States 60, 143, 175
University of Alberta 229
University of British Columbia 229
University of Chicago 226

University of Manitoba 201, 226
University of Montreal 201
University of Toronto 100, 109, 133, 137, 168, 173, 201, 226, 242, 258
University of Western Ontario 223

V

Victoria Harbour Lumber Company 110

W

Waldie, John 110, 111
Waldie, Robert (Bob) 112
Wapella, Saskatchewan 52, 121
Ward, the 130, 134, 137
Watson, John 43, 155
Wearing, Joseph 88, 118, 122, 242
Webbwood, Ontario 55
Western Canada Colonization Association 220
Whitney, J. P. 77, 89
Whyte, William 119
Wickwire, Marjorie 173
Willard, J. C. 262
Willis, A. P. 76, 122, 231
Wingham, Ontario 99, 164
Winnipeg labour strike of 1919 197
Wishart, Frank 215
Woodsworth, J. S. 107
Workers' Educational Association 168, 186, 196, 229
World's Work 154

Y

YMCA 132
Young, Annie 42, 206
Young, Reverend Luther 90
Young, Thomas and Robert 21, 203